A
Short History of
English
Drama

SIR IFOR EVANS

UNIVERSITY COLLEGE, LONDON

Houghton Mifflin Company

BOSTON

To the memory of
SIR BARRY JACKSON
who devoted himself
so unselfishly to the drama
in England

CONTENTS

A Short History of

English Drama

CHAPTER ONE

Introductory

THE HISTORY of the drama in England is more than an account of authors and plays, for it concerns the whole continuing tradition of the theatre. To the creation of a play the author is only one contributor. For success co-partnership is essential, and in it actors, producer, designers and technicians must also be constituents. Conditions leading to the happy union of all these elements have occurred only infrequently in the history of the English theatre. When they have prevailed, as in Elizabethan times, the gain has been immediately apparent. Whatever may be unknown about Shakespeare's life it can at least be affirmed with certainty that he was an actor, interested in theatrical enterprises, so that during his years in London he spent a considerable portion of his time in the theatre. He was associated with the Lord Chamberlain's Men, later under James I, the King's Men, which was the leading Company of the age. Not only was he their main playwright but as a member of the Fellowship he shared in the profits and in the business of the theatre. The Company owned their own theatre, the open Globe, but later they had a second closed-in theatre at Blackfriars. Throughout all his years in London he was working in association with the same group, with an intimate knowledge of what each actor could achieve; tragic roles for Richard Burbage, comedy for William Kemp, and later more subtle comic roles for Robert Armin. It is true that a Company such as this had to contest with the antagonism of the Puritans and the civic authorities, but they had behind them the knowledge that the Court and the Queen herself enjoyed their work. Not only did they have the patronage of noblemen but among their number were those who had the closest friendships with some of the greatest national figures, as Shakespeare had with the Earl of Southampton. Such conditions of the sixteen-nineties of the close and continuous association of a group of artists never fully returned, and the drama has consequently suffered. During the Restoration period the cultivated public considered visiting the theatre as a regular and almost necessary part of their existence. When Pepys records his London years in his Diary he goes to a playhouse several times a week although he is a highly placed Government official. A century later this would not have happened, and by the nineteenth century whole sections of the cultivated classes did not visit the theatre except on special occasions. Nor has the situation changed markedly in the contemporary period.

The excessive and inevitable attachment of criticism to the author has had a number of unhappy consequences. In the first place an illusion, utterly false, has been created that drama can be appreciated in independence of the theatre. Unfortunately two of the noblest names in English literature have helped to perpetuate this heresy: Milton in *Samson Agonistes* and Thomas Hardy in *The Dynasts*. Milton's early interest in the drama was modified by his growing antagonism and natural hatred of the type of comedy popular in the Restoration theatre. When he wrote *Samson Agonistes* Milton was old, blind, had suffered arrest, and lived in poverty and in discontent with the times. How remote he was from the stage of that period can be appreciated on recalling that Wycherley's licentious comedy *Love in a Wood* was produced in the same year, 1671, as *Samson Agonistes* was published. Yet that Milton had an interest in the earlier and more reputable theatre is shown in his knowledge of Shakespeare and Ben Jonson, and in his own composition of the beautiful masque, *Comus*, which was performed at Ludlow Castle in 1634: its dramatic qualities have been confirmed by recent revivals. Thomas Hardy, whose experience of the attempts to adapt his novels for the stage had been unfortunate, went as far in his preface to *The Dynasts* as to speculate 'whether mental performance alone may not eventually be the fate of all drama other than that of contemporary or frivolous life'. Yet *The Dynasts* shows a distinct talent for the drama, and many novelists, including Jane Austen and George Meredith, could have succeeded in the theatre had conditions been more welcoming. Jane Austen's early novel *Pride and Prejudice* is mainly dialogue and its adaptation for the stage has been successfully achieved. The same detachment of the author from the living world of the theatre has been responsible for the fact that English literature is strewn with wholly unactable plays written by some of our major poets. For instance, most of the romantic poets wrote tragedies. Byron was probably nearest to the theatre, for he was at one time associated with Drury Lane, but when later he came to write his ponderous historical dramas it was with little thought of the stage in mind, and when in 1821 *Marino Faliero* was performed at Drury Lane it was against his wishes. Wordsworth and Coleridge both wrote dramas but they were remote from the theatre. Keats, despite his deep understanding of Shakespeare, failed when he attempted drama. Shelley, had he lived in England and had the conditions of his life been more normal, might have succeeded. His play *The Cenci* approaches actable drama, but its theme of incest rendered difficult its performance in the theatre.

The extremes to which this practice of writing 'closet' plays extended can be seen in the work of A. C. Swinburne. He was a great admirer of Elizabethan and Jacobean drama and wrote a number of valuable critical studies, but in addition he composed gargantuan tragedies on the life of Mary Queen of Scots, all written in blank verse that is both intelligible and interesting, but in plays that obviously could never reach the theatre. This tradition of 'dead' drama is puzzling. It may be admitted that at certain periods in the eighteenth and nineteenth centuries conditions in the theatre were such that men of cultivation and genius did not wish to be involved. This would be an adequate explanation of why they should not write plays, but it is no explanation of why many of them wrote these unactable verse tragedies. It would seem that Shakespeare and some of the Jacobean dramatists left the impression in the minds of later poets that all a play required was one fine rhetorical blank verse speech after another. Swinburne would certainly seem to be under some delusion that a verse tragedy was some such collection of rhetorical speeches in verse. The degree of dramatic design in the Elizabethan plays was underestimated as was the way that the poets had rendered their verse dramatically effective.

The actor himself has not been without his share of responsibility in this detachment of the stage from society. His art makes him inevitably a man apart. He goes to work when other men go to dine, and his hours of labour are inevitably other men's periods of leisure. In Elizabethan times, despite the friendship that Shakespeare and some others had with the nobility, the law set the actor apart from his fellow man, and in some ways he has insisted on some form of isolation even to the present day. He has maintained, all too often, that his art is some secret which the layman cannot understand. At certain periods he has shown himself devoid of general culture, and as a consequence has failed to make adequate contact with whatever was best and most distinguished in the society of his time. His art has often seemed to affect his personality, as if the task of filling one role after another, and so exposing himself to the public, had left his own character rather nebulous, in some instances almost a vacuum. A certain pathos surrounds the actor, for his art can live only as long as his own person is there to reveal it. With the coming of the film the actor's art can, of course, be recorded and retained, but the preparation of films has probably removed the actor and his way of life even further from that of ordinary men.

The path of the dramatic writer in England has usually not been an easy one. The economic requirements of the author of books are minimal compared with those of a dramatist. All the non-dramatic writer needs is leisure and the tools of his trade and an interval of modest economic freedom. But the dramatist must have financial backing if his work is to appear in the theatre. Again, the self-maintaining yet profitable conditions of Shakespeare's Company have not been possible at later periods. All too often the dramatist has had to sell his work for the exploitation of commercial managements, with deleterious effects on his art. Throughout the modern period independent theatre movements have risen to contend with the tyranny of commercial managements. Again as distinct from the author who writes books for sale to the public, the dramatist has had to face the incredible vagaries of the law of censorship. In Tudor times plays were censored as part of the general law by which all activities within the State were controlled. The authority came from the Sovereign in Council and was delegated normally to the Master of the Revels. So conditions continued until Cromwell ordered the closing of all public theatres from 1642, though drama survived until the Restoration of 1660 by an underground movement of private performances. Cromwell's action fastened on the theatre the stigma of Puritan disapproval to which it had already been subjected in Elizabethan times, and this has remained as an atmosphere, though in a very modified form, until the present day.

constructed between 1843 and the end of the sixties. Unfortunately it was a period in which there was little that was exhilarating either in the tradition of architecture or in the theatre itself. Almost one feels that the puritan tradition must in some cryptic way have revenged itself on audiences through the architecture of the theatre.

The theatre as built from the Restoration period onwards had a proscenium arch stage, or a picture stage as it is sometimes called. The audience sits facing a room in which one wall is missing. Some contemporary producers have grown weary of this conventional stage; they would like to see an open end stage with a platform in front of the proscenium arch; or an arena stage with the audience around half the stage, as Tyrone Guthrie achieved in the Canadian Stratford Theatre; and as has been developed by Sir Laurence Olivier at Chichester. He has responded to the more revolutionary desire to see a theatre in the round with the audience seated around the central acting area. In discussing these proposals it is well to remember that much English drama was written for the proscenium arch stage and would look very odd performed in any other way. What is distressing is the lack of a tradition of theatre architecture in England. One young critic, Richard Pilbrow, goes as far as to say[1] that the theatres built since 1920 are worse than those built before: 'Even', he adds, 'one of our most notable playhouses, the Shakespeare Memorial Theatre at Stratford, has—despite all its good qualities—at least one glaring defect. It was designed for a wagon stage—that is to say, a stage in which the scenery is carried on and off by wagons—but the architect omitted to provide any wing space into which the wagons might trundle, and so they have had to be run up the wall (by an ingenious makeshift), if they are to be used at all'. The architect lost touch with the theatre, because there was no demand for new theatres to be built. Some recent developments are discussed later, but it must be recorded that many English theatres were built in the eighteen-sixties and, apart from the discomfort of the spectators, they yield themselves only uneasily to all the developments in lighting and production that have been made in recent decades.

Drama in England has had to struggle against prejudice from large sections of the public. It has seldom been a natural and necessary part of the national life. Probably it must be conceded that all

[1] *Twentieth Century*, February, 1961

art is the activity of a minority, though this volume closes with a period when television drama may lead to a modification of this view. The plays considered in this history are those which once had a success on the stage. Some effort has been made to indicate the small number amongst these which have conquered the vagaries of public taste so as to become part of the permanent repertory of the English theatre.

CHAPTER TWO

The Origins - Miracles - Moralities Interludes

THE HISTORY of the drama can be made to look too simple, as if it were a regular succession from miracle play to morality, from morality play to interlude, and from interlude to a regular comedy and tragedy, and so on until modern times. The historian is in danger of treating literary forms as if they were organic growths. In point of fact there are many overlappings, and different types of entertainment; the new and the old flourish at the same time. Men had not forgotten the miracle plays when Shakespeare was writing, and while listening to the astounding power of his new language they still retained the capacity to enjoy those simpler dramatic forms. The records from which the history of the drama in the earlier periods can be constructed are very incomplete. Very few plays, for instance, are extant in the period immediately preceding Marlowe and his contemporaries, that is, in the 'sixties and the 'seventies of the sixteenth century. The history of acting, of the stage, of costumes and décor, is even more inadequate. The historian who tries to tell a complete story is relying to a considerable extent on theory and speculation.

It is usual to begin with medieval drama. In the early Christian period there had been a reaction among the Christians against Roman plays, and this for two reasons. The Christians objected on principle to acting, basing themselves on certain biblical texts, such as Deuteronomy xxii. 5: 'The woman shall not wear that which pertaineth unto a man, neither shall a man put on a woman's garment: for all that do so are abomination unto the Lord thy God'. That argument was sufficiently alive when Milton wrote his *Areopagitica* for him to oppose it with texts from St Paul.

More forcible was the rational and practical Christian objection to the excesses of the late Roman stage. At that period the stage had little room for literary drama. The theatre which at times was vast enough to hold 20,000 people, was a place of spectacle, and the actor often a slave or freedman. The productions, when they were not spectacles, were farce of a gross character. It is true that in Seneca the Elizabethans remembered one dramatist who wrote in the days of Nero, but his plays were composed not to be performed but for contemplation in the study. By the sixth century the incursions of the barbarians and the growing strength of the Christians had undermined the stage, and with few exceptions it ceased to exist as it had been known in Roman days.

In the Dark Ages, from the sixth to the tenth century, the theatre largely disappears as far as any record in documents is concerned, though probably it remained in a submerged way. If the stage disappears, the actor survives, and survives without a stage and without a drama. The poetry of Chaucer and Langland has frequent references to travelling players, 'Jonglers' and 'Joculators', and Langland condemned them as a social pest. These travelling players were of a number of different types. The German tribes before their settlement in Britain, and for some time afterwards, had their professional tale tellers or *Scops*. A mention of them is made in *Beowulf*, and that poem is told as a *Scop's* tale. One of the most beautiful of Old English poems is *Widsith* ('The Far Traveller'), which tells of the life of a *Scop*. The Christian attitude to the *Scop* was one of opposition for he was a part of a pagan civilization. Sometimes a Christian bias seems to have been given to his function and his tales modified and given a Christian emphasis.

A less dignified performer was the 'Mime'. He probably came into Britain through a Latin influence and with him were tumblers, dancers, and jokers of varying degrees of disrepute. The activities of such players were sufficient to cause the Church by the thirteenth century to pass a number of decrees restricting their activities. From the twelfth century to the fourteenth the 'minstrels' occupied an important part in the social life. Some of them were resident at Court and in the great houses, and some were strollers. They made songs for war and they praised and abused personalities. Even the Church, which formerly condemned such performers, came to recognize them and sometimes made use of them. It is difficult to know whether their activities ever approached a theatrical production. Apart from these individual players there grew up in the villages a number of activities of a folk nature. They had sufficient prominence for attacks to be made on them by the thirteenth century. Such celebrations were usually seasonal and of a communal nature. They were a method of indulging a natural desire for miming and were an expression of a normal urge to commemorate the spring or harvest time.

Not all the seasonal activities were confined to the villages. A similar desire for dramatic expression showed itself among the lower orders of the clergy, particularly in masking and dancing and in the burlesque of the offices of the Church. Sir E. K. Chambers, the foremost English historian of this period, sums up the psychology behind these burlesques by saying that 'it was largely an ebullition of the natural lout beneath the cassock'.[1] One of the most popular of these mock ceremonies was that of the Boy Bishop, in which the choir boys took on themselves the main functions performed normally by the clerical dignitaries.

All these and similar entertainments showed the survival of a play instinct though they were removed from drama even of a rudimentary type. Yet in the Middle Ages out of these conditions and activities drama re-established itself. It is a complex story of which the most important fact remains that while at the beginning of the Dark Ages the Church attempted to suppress the drama, at the beginning of the Middle Ages something very much like the drama was instituted in the Church itself.

The Mass, which had early developed as the central element in the service of the Church, had a dramatic element, particularly when on certain days special features were added which increased the dramatic significance. Out of this there came the presentation by voices chanting in Latin of certain crucial scenes in the Christian story, such as those of the Birth and Resurrection of Christ. For instance, two groups of voices would sing, the first asking

Whom do you seek in the sepulchre, you followers of Christ?

and the second group would reply

Jesus of Nazareth, who was crucified, O you who are of heaven.

Such presentations may have begun simply, but they became elaborate, and attached to the words was a ritual and a dumb show.

[1] *The Medieval Stage*, 2 vols. (Oxford University Press), 1903.

It is easy to imagine that these liturgical plays were more realistic than they probably were, but some step towards a dramatic presentation had obviously taken place, particularly at the festivals of Christmas, and of the celebration of the Resurrection.

Once established, they had an important effect on the history of the drama. They were, in all likelihood, fully established by the middle of the fourteenth century and by the middle of the fifteenth they had become secularized. Again it is difficult not to make the process seem simpler than it probably was. The liturgical plays at Christmas and the Resurrection were extended to include other incidents, until a fairly complete cycle of the biblical story had been made. For instance, the story of the Creation was easily presented in this manner, and with each addition the liturgical play grew closer to legitimate drama. The element of devotion decreased as the element of dramatic presentation increased. It was thus that out of the liturgical play there developed the miracle play.

With these extensions in the plays there came changes in the place of presentation. Again it is difficult to say exactly when these occurred. Nor is it necessary to assume that they were simultaneous in all places. In general it would seem that the plays began in the choir, and from the choir went to the nave, and from the nave to the outside of the Church. When the crowds outside the church became too unseemly for the holy precincts the play moved to the market-place, or joined a succession of plays which were shifted from one position to another in procession around the city. The change illustrates the desire of the clerical authorities to be less intimately associated with the drama, and it is obvious that once the play was in the market-place, and in competition with other forms of entertainment, its character would increase in secularity. The civic corporations organized the plays, and exercised some censorship over the choice and the method of presentation, while the craft guilds produced them and bore the cost. Each member of a craft guild paid a contribution towards the cost of production.

Of the many cycles that once existed a few have survived, most notably those of Chester, York, 'Towneley' (or Wakefield) and Coventry. Of these, the cycle of plays produced at York is interesting because it is complete, and it is known to have been performed as late as 1580 and as early as the beginning of the fourteenth century. The plays have not the outstanding features of the 'Towneley' cycle, but their verse, which is written in a combination of stanza and alliteration, is vivid and competent. Many of the plays in the York cycle are an elaboration of the biblical narratives without obvious dramatic features, but the anonymous writers are able to deal well with scenes of pathos such as Abraham's sacrifice of Isaac. Sincerity and tender simplicity of sentiment are again shown in the play of the flight into Egypt. The Wakefield or 'Towneley' cycle has some plays in common with those of York, but, in addition, it has five plays of a striking originality. These are the plays of Noah with his children, the First Shepherds' Play, the Second Shepherds' Play, the Play of King Herod, and the Play of Christ before Cayphus. In these plays there is close vivid description of a realistic nature. Such can be found in the description of the ship in the Noah play. Further, there is dialogue of a most natural, human and contemporary kind. It can be seen in the vivid characterization of Noah's wife.as a shrew. At the same time the dramatist can deal solemnly with such passages as God's discussion with Noah, and throughout he can manipulate a difficult stanza.

The outstanding success of this dramatist is the Second Shepherds' Play. This stands apart in dramatic and imaginative achievement from all other English miracle plays. It opens with a realistic account of the woes of shepherds and with a virulent attack on women. There is no attempt in this early movement to remember the sacred aspect of the theme, which is after all the celebration of the Virgin Mother. After a song by the shepherds, Mak the sheep stealer enters and complains of the noise that the children make. He says that his wife bears too many children. After a time the shepherds sleep and Mak steals a sheep. The scene shifts to Mak's home where his wife is made to pretend that the sheep is a child in a bed. Mak returns to the shepherds and after waking them says that his wife has given birth to a boy. The shepherds wish to give this child a present and when they arrive in Mak's home, after a comic interlude, they discover the stolen sheep. Then they hear the angel and in song they try to imitate him, and so they come to Bethlehem to honour the Infant Christ. It is difficult to know precisely what went through the mind of either the dramatist or the audience, for the whole of the early comic part seems to repeat in grotesque form the incidents which the religious element is celebrating, yet the whole is strangely moving.

Apart from the miracle plays, and developing after they were established, were a series of morality plays, in which the characters represent abstract qualities. At first sight this seems a dull method for drama, but the abstract qualities are given lively human features. One of the earliest of these moralities is *The Castle of Perseverance* (of the early fifteenth century) and the play is so finished that it suggests that there must have been others in the same tradition not now extant. The dialogue is written in an elaborate rhyming stanza, and the play gives an account of man's life from birth to his appearance at the Seat of Judgment. The most famous of the English moralities is *Everyman* which, it has been established, is the same as the Dutch play *Elckerlijk*. The English play was composed about 1500 and its popularity is shown by the frequency with which it was reprinted in the sixteenth century. Though its theme is not unlike that of *The Castle of Perseverance* it is much less prolix, with a fine quality of directness and pathos in its verse. Its theme is given the same human quality as is found in *The Pilgrim's Progress*, which is a very similar story. The audience of both these works knows that they are allegories, and yet they affect the mind in the same way as a piece of human adventure. Though the characters in *Everyman* are abstract, they have more variety than many of the individual figures derived from biblical narrative. They are far more contemporary than the biblical figures, and the morality method gives more opportunity for independent treatment by the dramatist.

Everyman is a man of his time, close to the audience, and in this strange way the morality play gains a realism of its own. The strength of *Everyman* lies also in the skill with which the scenes are developed. There is not the stale obviousness which marks some of the other less competent morality plays. Although the theme is allegorical it seems to be the story of an ordinary journey. God sends Death to Everyman and tells him to prepare for a journey, and there is a simple poignancy in the language of Death's first talk with Everyman. After Death's visit, Everyman appeals to his friends, to Fellowship, Kinsmen, and Goods, but they all desert him; Good Deeds alone will go with him, and there is again a definite, dramatic quality in the lines recording Everyman's encounter with Good Deeds. So at each stage of Everyman's journey the abstract is made concrete by lively figures and human situations.

Some of the moralities had comic elements. Of this type the play of *Mankynd* of the late fifteenth century is one of the best known. Its whole tone differs from that of *Everyman*. Mankynd is attacked by three rascals, Nowte, Newgyse and Nowadays, and he is befriended by Mercy. The three villains are real and contemporary figures. They have comedy and coarseness, and though the play may have little construction, it has a vivid quality in its language. The morality play was employed in many ways, as is shown in John Skelton's *Magnyfycence*, where the theme is political and not didactic or religious. Skelton shows how Fancy, armed with a false letter of introduction, comes to Magnificence, who later is led to destruction, though finally rescued by the teaching of the virtues. The figure of Magnificence is Skelton's satire against Wolsey.

Apart from the elements of secularism, which appear in the miracle and morality plays, there develops an 'Interlude', which is frequently made and produced solely for its dramatic interest. One of the earliest is *Hyckescorner* of the beginning of the sixteenth century. The title is the name of one of the characters. The play has little dramatic strength, and follows the lines of a morality play, though its theme is humanistic rather than didactic. The main plot is the conversion of Freewill and Imagination through the agency of Pity, Perseverance, and Contemplation. The household of Sir Thomas More had a taste for such dramatic entertainments and around More there were those who could make interludes and who had the means of circulating them. John Rastell, a printer and a writer of interludes, married Sir Thomas More's sister. John Heywood, the writer of interludes, was Rastell's son-in-law. William Rastell, who was John Rastell's son, was the printer of Heywood's plays. In such a community where drama and wit were both understood the interlude had an opportunity of development.

One of the plays whose authorship has been claimed for John Rastell is *Calisto and Melebea*. The writer based his play on an English version of the Spanish rogue story of *Celestina*. The Spanish tale tells of the love, inevitable and romantic, of Calisto for Melebea, and the outstanding character is Celestina, a bawd who is portrayed as firmly as Pandarus, and who brings the two lovers together. The intrigues multiply and lead to a tragic conclusion. The English writer fails to employ the Spanish story to the full, for while he opens with the two lovers he has such a firm eye on his 'moral conclusion' that he achieves little by way of plot. *The Four Elements* and *Gentleness and Nobility* are other interludes which have been assigned to John Rastell's authorship. *The Four Elements* is in the form of a dialogue, or discussion. Its purpose is to instruct 'Humanity' in the nature of the four elements (earth, water, air, and fire). 'Humanity' receives the information from 'Nature' whose points are further explained by 'Studious Desire', who calls in the help of 'Experience', while 'Sensual Appetite' disturbs the instruction of 'Studious Desire'.

John Heywood, whose plays were written soon after 1520, is the most considerable figure in the history of the interlude. Married to Rastell's daughter, he was in the centre of More's circle and it has been surmised that some of his plays were revised by More himself. Most of them are arguments and disputations between a number of characters with the addition of a comic element. Of these the neatest in its movement is *The Play of the Wether*. Jupiter appoints Merry Report to summon the people before him so that he may listen to the complaints of mortals on the weather. Merry Report ('a vyce'), is a comic rascal who addresses his master in witty and impertinent conversation such as Shakespeare's fools employ. Jupiter discovering that all the suitors require different types of weather decides to continue giving them an assortment, and the play ends with a sort of 'Magnificat' by all the suppliants.

Another of Heywood's plays, *The Four P.P.*, which is described as a 'new and very merry interlude of a palmer, a pardoner, a pothycary and a pedlar', is a discussion, and like *The Play of the Wether* has a monotonous movement. Its strength, as in all of Heywood's pieces, lies in the vigour of the dialogue. The discussion centres on a competition between the four men as to which can tell the biggest lie. The climax comes in the story of the pardoner, who tells of a visit to Hell, and of the rescue of a shrew. The palmer breaks in with the question 'Are there shrews in Hell?' He is surprised, for in all his travels he has never met a woman out of patience. His lie wins. Lest too much weight be attached to all this, the play has a tail-piece:

> *To pass the time in this without offence*
> *Was the cause why the maker did make it*
> *And so we humbly beseech you take it!*

The purpose of the play is comedy and not didacticism.

There remain two interludes by Heywood which have a more ample dramatic interest: these are *Johan Johan the Husband, Tyb his Wife and Sir John the Priest* and *A Merry Play Between the Pardoner and the Friar, the Curate and Neighbour Pratte*. The first of these is lively though crude. The plot turns on the love-making of Tyb and the priest, and the timid uneasiness of the husband. Whatever its limitations, the play has moved from mere discussion to dramatic action. The *Merry Play* is of a pardoner and a friar who come to the same church and try to preach at the same time. This leads to a fight with the parish priest and neighbour Pratte. Comedy has arrived at something of a separate existence in Heywood, though as yet there are few indications of its employment in anything but the crudest forms. Another memorable interlude which showed dramatic development within the form was *Thersytes* (of about 1530), a play probably designed for children. The theme, which is derived, is a comic study of cowardice and follows in some simple ways the mood which Ibsen was later to exploit so magnificently in *Peer Gynt*.

If one had to judge the interlude solely by these plays one would be unable to place its dramatic achievement very high. Fortunately there was discovered within living memory the play of *Fulgens and Lucrece* by Henry Medwall, Chaplain to Cardinal Morton. Of a date as early as 1497, this play shows by the cunning of its form and the adroitness of its dialogue how far the secular dramatist had progressed. The plot is based on a Renaissance Latin discourse by Bonaccorso entitled *De Vera Nobilitate*. A Roman Senator has a daughter Lucrece, who has two suitors, one of humble birth and the other a noble. She asks her father what to do and her father asks the Senate. The two suitors plead before the Senate and nothing is decided. This unpromising plot is handled in the play with great skill. Medwall introduces the play with the dialogue of two spectators, who are present to see the entertainment at a banquet, and their talk suggests that there were already present in England companies of players so well dressed that the gallants emulated their fashions. The two spectators prepare the audience for the argument. The plot is then developed dramatically for the suitors plead not to the Senate but in turn to the lady, who herself decides for the poor and virtuous suitor. There is a comic sub-plot, and the two spectators take sides, and finally enter the main theme as farcical suitors for Lucrece's maid. This play is an indication of what could be done already in the fifteenth century, independently of Italian models. It is a warning how incomplete are the records on which the history of drama is based, for the text of this play was unknown until a copy of it appeared in the Mostyn sale in 1919.

On the evidence which exists it is impossible to trace a regular development from the interludes to the more elaborate drama which follows. New influences came in, the plays of Plautus and Terence, the comedy of Italy, and, in tragedy, the influence of Seneca. All this disturbed any regular native development from the interlude to Elizabethan drama. The new forms were far more ambitious than the old, but they did not entirely replace them. As has been already recorded the York miracle plays were performed late in the sixteenth century, while some of the cycles continue to the seventeenth century. It is to the newer interests that the great dramatists largely attach themselves, though the more they are studied the more the ghosts of the older drama can be seen in the themes and values employed—however magnificent may be the new achievement. In comedy the break is much less definite than in tragedy, for the native tradition in comedy had been strong and vital. In tragedy there had been no native models.

CHAPTER THREE

The Beginnings of Tragedy, of the History Play, and of Comedy; The Development of the Theatre

THE SPECIMENS of plays extant from the sixteenth century are very incomplete. The conclusion which results from reading them is that drama made a sudden and spectacular step forward somewhere between 1530 and 1580. For 1530 is the probable date of *Calisto and Melebea* and *The Play of the Wether*, while by 1588 audiences were already familiar with *Tamburlaine*. Some influence had incited dramatists to far more ambitious achievements, and fortunately their genius was adequate to answer their needs.

In tragedy, the outstanding new influence was that of Seneca. He was known to the men of the Renaissance period as the author of ten tragedies. A Latin writer of the time of Nero, and the author of 'closet' dramas, Seneca had studied Greek drama, particularly the tragedies of Euripides. In his own tragedies he retained the chorus of Greek drama, though he placed it at the end of his acts, and did not allow it to interfere in the play. He retained something of the pattern of Greek drama, though its spirit no longer remained. Greek drama was religious in origin and the speeches were governed and disciplined by that consideration. In Seneca that religious element had disappeared, and the long, declamatory speeches remained shorn of their original purpose. He retained the 'messenger', who was employed in Greek drama to reveal action that had taken place 'off' stage, but he gave his long speeches usually a narrative rather than a dramatic quality. Mingled with the long speeches, and in violent contrast with them, were passages of stichomythia (dialogue in alternate lines of verse employed in argument). The themes Seneca employed were nominally the themes of Greek drama. But for the awe and terror which these possess he substituted an element of mere horror. In Greek drama the sense of Fate or Will behind the individuals represented in the action elevated the conception of the tragedy. For this Seneca substituted personal revenge as the main motive of action, and, following his example, this was employed in Elizabethan drama. Delighting in horrors Seneca introduced the Ghost almost as a definite member of the 'dramatis personae'. In language he was rhetorical and bombastic and his delight in horrors was paralleled by his equal affection for moral discourses in the manner of Polonius.

It seems strange at first sight that this unacted dramatist of the time of Nero should become the major influence on English tragedy in the sixteenth century. But he was, in the first place, far more easily accessible than any Greek dramatist, for few of the Elizabethan dramatists could have read a play in Greek. To the medieval tradition, still strong in the sixteenth-century mind, there was an obvious appeal in his long moral discourses, while to the Renaissance elements, Seneca had the advantage of seeming to give all the form of Greek drama, the unities, the chorus, and the values behind the themes. Above all, Seneca's indulgence in horror delighted men who knew a world where death was familiar and violence a part of the scene both domestic and political. Thus the main classical influence on English tragedy is Latin and not Greek.

In Italy, among the Renaissance writers most influenced by the Greeks, were Trissino and his followers, but in the forties of the sixteenth century a more popular dramatist on the Senecan model ousts Trissino and replaces him in popular favour. In England something similar happens. At first, a number of writers seem anxious to keep to the rules of classical drama as far as they know them, and then there emerge the popular Senecan writers who capture the stage. The influence in England appears mainly after 1560. Before that date classical names appear in a few of the interludes, of which *Thersytes* is the main example, and one of Seneca's plays, *Troades*, is performed in Latin at Cambridge. In the sixties the influence is considerable. Seneca's plays were translated, and in 1561–2 *Gorboduc* by Thomas Norton and Thomas Sackville, the first English Senecan tragedy, was acted before the Queen at Whitehall. Some learned Senecan plays were performed at the Inns of Court and a group of interludes (*Appius and Virginia*, 1567;

Damon and Pythias, 1564; *Horestes*, 1566–7; *Cambyses*, 1569), made a link between the academic and the popular tradition. The period 1570–80 is difficult to define because the records are so scanty, but from 1580 onwards there is evidence of an increased Senecan influence. By 1581 all the 'ten tragedies' had been translated, and Thomas Newton issued his collection of *Seneca, His Ten Tragedies Translated into English*. There was a revival of influence by the performance of some of his plays at the Universities, while learned imitations were also produced, *Ricardus Tertius* at Cambridge, and *The Misfortunes of Arthur* at the Inns of Court. By the end of the decade competent dramatists had captured a popular Senecan tradition for the ordinary stage. The outstanding example was Thomas Kyd's *The Spanish Tragedy* (1587–9). Senecan influence was present in Marlowe and Shakespeare and was revived later by Ben Jonson in *Sejanus* and in *Catiline*.

Meanwhile the English chronicle play had shown a parallel development with Senecan tragedy, though largely independent of it. Senecan tragedy was European while the chronicle play was English. Some of the elements which went to its making were the medieval pageants and the plays of the Lives of Saints, such as are known to have existed on the Life of St George. Further, there is evidence that there were some local traditions for the dramatic rendering of historical events.

The chronicle play relied for its sources on the English chronicles and dealt with some period of English history. It gained in the hands of Shakespeare an identity with tragedy, for to contemporary audiences *Lear* and *Macbeth* were chronicle plays. John Bale's *Kyng Johan* (1536) though the title promises an historical play, is a morality full of Protestant propaganda. Bale began life as a Catholic but was converted to Protestantism. After his conversion he wrote this play in defence of King John whom he presents as a Protestant hero. *Gorboduc* (1562) is important in that it links the Senecan tradition of tragedy with the native chronicle play: it takes an English story from Geoffrey of Monmouth and develops it on the Senecan pattern. Thomas Legge in *Ricardus Tertius* (1579) attempted to use the learned Latin Senecan tradition for an English theme. Richard III's career, as Shakespeare was later to discover, developed very easily from history into the pattern of tragedy. *The Misfortunes of Arthur* (1588), to which reference has already been made, was another attempt to apply Senecan form to national themes. *Locrine*, sometimes ascribed to Kyd, introduced more popular elements while keeping to the Senecan pattern.

The chronicle play answered one element of the demand for a popular presentation of history. That the demand was real and persistent is proved by the popularity of such a collection of historical poems as *The Mirror for Magistrates*, or later in the success of the chronicle poems of Daniel and Drayton. It can be seen also in the continued popularity of the chroniclers themselves, of Grafton and John Stow, and of Ralphael Holinshed on whose work Shakespeare relied in such an impressive way.

The earliest of the extant chronicles is *The Famous Victories of Henry V* (1588): a formless piece but one that had considerable popularity. The author makes no attempt at tragedy, but history is dramatically presented by a number of incidents taken from the reigns of Henry IV and Henry V. Shakespeare, who knew this early piece, went over the same ground with a more ample inclusion of historical material in *I* and *II Henry IV* and in *Henry V*. The Prince and his low companions are already present in the early play, but there is no Falstaff. The Senecan model is not employed, but unfortunately no other model has replaced it. From the absence of dramatic shape in a piece such as this one realizes what the dramatists gained by the example of Seneca, whatever may have been the incidental liabilities of his influence. *The Troublesome Raigne of King John* (1588–90), which has Holinshed's chronicle as a source, was an advance on the formlessness of *The Famous Victories*. The presentation of material is still diffuse, and even Shakespeare, who knew this play, failed to give the same theme a full unity. The comic matter is not so clownish as in *The Famous Victories*, and the chronicle matter is handled with an eye to dramatic propriety. The spirit is Protestant and this Shakespeare later modified into a national atmosphere.

The years around the Armada mark a great period of popularity of the chronicle and history play. Peele's *Edward I* (printed 1593), apparently a hastily written piece, seems to mark no advance on the general type. *The True Chronicle of King Leir* (1594, printed 1605) has a rough effectiveness and holds a proud place as the predecessor of Shakespeare's most profound tragedy. Similarly *The True Tragedie of Richard III* (printed 1594) is a source for the development of the chronicle into tragedy in Shakespeare's *Richard III*. With Marlowe's *Edward II* (printed 1594) a writer of genius has disciplined the chronicle into tragedy, and the events of twenty years are reduced to what may be digested in a play. Nor is the tragedy diffuse, for it concentrates on an uncommon conception of a weak man as a central protagonist, a type found again, with ample modifications, in Shakespeare's *Richard II*. It must be confessed, however, that perhaps *Edward II* is a better play to talk about than to see on the stage. Probably one of Shakespeare's earliest tasks in the theatre was his share in the three parts of *Henry VI*, and how great that share was remains a disputed problem in Shakespearian criticism. A reasonable view is that the whole of the second and third parts are his and some scenes of the first. It was from his attachment to the chronicle play that he discovered such original forms as *Henry IV* and *Henry V*, and it was through the history play that he made his way into his major tragedy.[1]

While these developments in tragedy and chronicle plays occurred during the sixteenth century there were also changes in comedy. As has already been suggested, comedy had a strong native tradition and might well have developed successfully, though in a different way, without foreign influence. The study of two Latin authors, of Plautus and Terence, gave to English comedy a sense of pattern which it had not previously possessed. This Latin influence was partly due to a number of schoolmasters who read Latin plays with their pupils. The first comedy on classical models is *Ralph Roister Doister* (1553–4, printed 1566), and this is the work of a schoolmaster, Nicholas Udall, who was a master first at Eton and later at Westminster. The main plot is simple enough: Ralph Roister Doister is in love with Dame Christian Custance. He fails in his love owing to his own pride and stupidity. To further his suit he employs a comic rascal Matthew Merygreeke who is developed into one of the major characters. More effective was *Gammer Gurton's Needle* (about 1553, printed 1575) which is described as 'a right pithy, pleasant and merry comedy'. The authorship is ascribed to 'Mr S. Master of Art'. Whoever the author was he had learned something from Latin drama, but in character, scene and plot he is native and original. His plot is farcical. Gammer Gurton was mending the breeches of her man Hodge. They were 'foul

[1] See page 56.

betorn', and needed a patch as 'broad as thy cap'. As she was mending them she spied Gyb, the cat, in the milk pan. When she returned her needle was gone. Around the loss of the needle the
author develops a play of farcical comedy, which has at the same
time a rough, native realism. The play has a crudity which may
limit its attractiveness to modern audiences, but the pictures of
rural life are genuine enough, and Hodge has lived down the centuries as the type of village labourer. Meanwhile in *Supposes* (1566)
George Gascoigne, basing himself on Ariosto's comedy of intrigue
I Suppositi, wrote the first prose comedy in English, and so gained
a new liberty of form for comic drama.

Such were the beginnings of tragedy, the history play and
comedy. Meanwhile there had been important developments in the
way in which plays were produced. The early, medieval drama had
been performed by the guilds and was the work of amateurs,
though presumably they had someone as producer who approached
to a professional status. Such performances continued long after
the professional theatre had been established, and there must have
been several types of performer between the amateurs and the
regular theatre. In medieval times the choir boys were associated
with the burlesque ceremony of the boy-bishop, and possibly they
were also used seriously in the liturgical plays. By the sixteenth century the choir boys under their master were engaged in the performance of regular plays. Very early in the sixteenth century the
Children of the Chapel Royal were engaged in performing plays.
Gradually the children of St Paul's and of the Chapel Royal were
organized into what amounted to regular professional companies.
The children in certain schools also gave plays. Later the regular
companies of children acted at times in competition with the male
professional companies of adult players. There are echoes of rivalry
between the boy companies and the adult actors in Elizabethan
drama, notably in *Hamlet* (II.2): 'Nay their endeavour keeps in the
wonted pace, but there is, sir, an eyrie of children, little eyases, that
cry out on the top of question and are most tyranically clapp'd for
it'. The child companies were involved in the great quarrel of the
actors in the early seventeenth century. They acted a number of
Ben Jonson's plays, and in 1601 they performed *The Poetaster*, Ben
Jonson's satire on the contemporary stage. This called forth
Dekker's reply, *Satiromastix*.

Throughout the Elizabethan period the professional theatre was affected by the attacks of the Puritans. If its complex history is to be briefly summarized it can best be described as an existence in which the open hostility of the city authorities with a Puritan bias was met by the support, genuine though never vigorously expressed, of the aristocracy and the Court. With drama at the Universities and the Inns of Court, or with performances at the Court itself, the Puritans were not much concerned. But they met with persistent hostility the growth of a professional theatre, basing their attack, first on the fact that plays were performed on the Sabbath, and secondly that the theatre was a centre of immorality.

When Elizabeth came to the throne there was an act against vagabonds, that is against any man without a craft. An actor was legally a vagabond unless he was attached as a retainer to a man of quality. Each of the Elizabethan companies therefore carried the name of some nobleman, such as 'the Earl of Leicester's Men', in order to give themselves a legal existence. This to some extent protected the actor, but it did not protect the theatre and the play. In the country the main control lay with the Justices of the Peace, and in London with the Municipalities. Under Henry VIII, the central authority intervened mainly to suppress sedition and ecclesiastical heresy. Elizabeth, on the whole, was prepared to leave things to the Municipalities, and these were goaded by the Puritans and by preachers not so much to license plays as to suppress them. The main excuse was the fear of plague. Efforts were made to make performances in London impossible, to which the players replied by moving to the suburbs, so that London's first theatres were built outside the city walls. In this way the corporations were out-manœuvred, but the Puritans persisted in their attack. They wished still stricter regulations in the city, and further they wished the city to enforce the suburban magistrates to stop plays. At length the Court, possibly through the influence of the great noblemen, made itself felt and in 1581 the Master of the Revels was given a general censorship of plays. The corporations and the Puritans continued their attack, but not so violently. As Sir Edmund Chambers has written: 'the palace was the point of vantage from which the stage won its way against the linked opposition of an alienated pulpit and an alienated municipality to an ultimate entrenchment of economic independence'.

Under such conditions the drama of Shakespeare and his predecessors developed. It is indeed amazing to see how a company such as that of the Lord Chamberlain's Men, to which Shakespeare was attached, contrived to expand in technical and creative effectiveness under such conditions. In their early years the Elizabethan companies had no theatre: they played in inn-yards, or hired a bear-garden. James Burbage, later Shakespeare's associate, built the Theatre, as it was simply called, in 1576, and it was the first of its kind in England, and there some of Shakespeare's early plays were presented. In 1597 the Theatre was abandoned and two years later the Chamberlain's Men opened the Globe. James Burbage had died but his sons, Cuthbert, and Richard, the distinguished actor of Shakespearian roles, continued his enterprise, using timbers from the Theatre in the larger and better equipped Globe. The pattern of the old inn-yard remained. As M. M. Reese has written[1]: 'Here, when they were building anew, was their opportunity, if they wished, to make drastic innovations to enable them to alter their style of playing. But they did not so wish: they retained the familiar design and all the essential features of the older theatres. A tier of galleries still encircled an unroofed yard and the platform still thrusts out into the middle of the yard, where the groundlings stood near enough to touch the actors'. Here was the wooden 'O' with the circle of spectators, the groundlings crowded into a very small space, galleries for the more distinguished, and a minute stage, where manœuvre must have needed great skill. Yet it is estimated that the Globe could hold audiences far larger than those in modern theatres. Later there came the indoor theatre, such as Shakespeare's Company acquired at Blackfriars. Still very small, it permitted of much more elaborate scenery and spectacle. It can be surmised that Shakespeare was never as happy here as on the open stage of the Globe.

When Elizabeth began her reign she was only twenty-five. She enjoyed plays and pageantry and the courtly chivalry of the tilt-yard, all, if possible, at other people's expense. There would be special performances in the banqueting-room of one of the palaces, usually between November and February, and especially at the Twelfth Night revels. Under Charles I's reign conditions had

[1] *Shakespeare, his world and his work*, 1953.

so developed that in 1634 his Queen could attend a play at Black-friars. This was a great change from the day when the players, scarce owning a legal status, and with no centre of their own, were struggling against the Puritans.

CHAPTER FOUR

Early Elizabethan Tragedy - Thomas Kyd and Christopher Marlowe

THOMAS KYD (1557–95), one of the shadowy figures of the pre-Shakespearian period, was the author of *The Spanish Tragedy*, among the most popular and effective of the early tragedies. It may indeed be the earliest tragedy in England in which the Senecan motives had been made theatrically effective in a play intelligible to a general audience. Written possibly as early as 1587, it went through a number of editions. Its plot depends on a revenge theme, with a number of the motives used in *Hamlet*, including a ghost and a play within a play. The central motive is the revenge of Hieronimo, marshal of Spain, for the murder of his son Horatio. The problem for the dramatist, as in *Hamlet*, is how the interval between the murder and its discovery can be filled. This Kyd achieves by showing the moods and frenzy of Hieronimo, and by arranging theatrically effective devices for exposing the murderers. The play is melodramatic but it has a successful wildness, a romantic daring and a certainty in stage effect that made its popularity deserved.

It is probable that Kyd handled the theme of Hamlet before Shakespeare came to employ the well-known traditional story. In 1589 Thomas Nashe in a prefatory Epistle to Greene's *Menaphon* in a passage which obviously refers to Kyd, wrote: 'English *Seneca* read by candle-light yields many good sentences as "blood is a beggar" and so forth: and if you intreat him fair in a frosty morning he will afford you whole *Hamlets*, I should say handfuls of tragical speeches'. The parallels between *The Spanish Tragedy* and the Hamlet story make Kyd's authorship of a play on the theme highly probable. Some editors even maintain that the first Quarto of *Hamlet* is Shakespeare's re-working of Kyd's version. Kyd's versatility is shown by his authorship of *Cornelia* (1594), a play which is a rough translation of an academic Senecan play by the French writer Charles Garnier.

While Kyd was a skilful man of the theatre he had no great gifts of vision and poetry. These were abundantly supplied by Christopher Marlowe (1564–1593), the most mysterious of all the figures of the Elizabethan theatre; next to Shakespeare the most brilliant, and in his death the most tragic. He was educated at King's School, Canterbury, and thence he proceeded to Cambridge and took a degree but did not proceed to holy orders. He appeared in London, and he seems to have engaged in some government work, as a spy, or an agent. In 1589 a bond demanded his appearance at the next Newgate Sessions. No one knows what was his offence. In 1593 Kyd, his fellow-dramatist, was arrested for the possession of 'aetheistical' documents which he said belonged to Marlowe. A warrant for Marlowe's arrest followed. On 30 May, 1593, Marlowe was at Eleanor Bull's tavern in Deptford with two suspicious characters named Frizer and Poley. After supper a quarrel arose between Frizer and Marlowe over who should pay, and according to the account before the Coroner, Marlowe wounded Frizer and Frizer in return killed Marlowe. The story told in the Coroner's Court was an improbable one, and some biographers have suggested that Marlowe was the victim of a political murder.

Out of this mysterious and rather sinister background emerged the great dramatist who in a few brief years wrote *Tamburlaine*, in ten acts (possibly as early as 1586); *Dr Faustus* (once dated about 1588, but possibly later, about 1592); *The Jew of Malta* (about 1589); *Edward II* (1592); *Dido, Queen of Carthage* (1593) and *The Massacre of Paris* (1593). *Tamburlaine*, played in 1587 or 1588 and printed in 1590, so contrasted in magnificence of conception and verse with all preceding drama that it had an immediate popularity that long endured. This genius, with his burning imagination and great power over language, made an outstanding contribution to English tragedy and left an influence on blank verse which has been permanent. The earlier blank verse of a play such as *Gorboduc* had little life. It was correct, but the meaning ended mechanically at the end of each line, so that to the ear it sometimes had the effect of rhyming verse without rhyme. Marlowe improved on this. He saw the necessity of running lines together until the blank verse was contained in verse paragraphs. Milton was describing the same effect when he spoke of the verse of *Paradise Lost* as 'the sense variously drawn out from one verse to another, not in the jingling sound of like endings'. Marlowe's innovation helped the young Shakespeare to discover himself in blank verse, though the later Shakespeare breaks up the verse much more and he gained a far greater variety of effects. In bringing blank verse to the service of popular tragedy Marlowe endowed it with an extraordinary beauty, which reached its height in Tamburlaine's praise of 'divine Zeno-crate', or in the speeches of Faustus. He employed some of the bombastic features of Senecan verse but he endowed them with an astounding sense of power. Drayton's praise of Marlowe has a recognition of this commanding strength:

> *Had in him those brave translunary things*
> *That the first poets had; his raptures were*
> *All air and fire which made his verses clear*
> *For that fine madness still he did retain*
> *Which rightly should possess a poet's brain.*

Marlowe had under his control an instrument of power eminently suitable for describing passion, pathos and the extremes of things. He lacked a verse suitable for all purposes, for lightness and wit, though there are signs in *Edward II* that before his death he was working out towards a more varied style.

While verse was his supreme attainment he added also to the conception of tragedy. Partly with Seneca's aid, he broke with the whole medieval conception in which tragedy was merely the fall of a great man. With Marlowe, as later with Shakespeare, tragedy is distress resulting from some over-weening feature of weakness or strength in the central character. In *Tamburlaine* it is a lust for power, and in *The Jew of Malta* a titanic version of avarice. In his early work Marlowe is able to bring out only one character in a play, as in Tamburlaine, or Faustus, but this he is remedying in *The Jew of Malta* and *Edward II*.

Tamburlaine is a play which modern audiences do not often have an opportunity of seeing in the theatre. Based on an historical figure, the Tartar, Timur Khan, of the fourteenth century, Marlowe built a great symbol of the quest for human power. He worked assiduously at this play and studied all the available sources. The tragedy has a certain monotony in action as one conquest follows another, but the ear is astounded by the imagery which searches out the farthest heavens to find words to describe the pleasures of earthly ambition. In *Faustus*, the problem of the plot development presented even more severe difficulties. The scene in which Faustus sells himself to Mephistopheles and the redemption scene are inevitable moments in the action, and Marlowe handled them magnificently, but the manipulation of the intermediate incidents proved very difficult. It has been urged that Marlowe may have left some of these scenes to other hands. The theme obviously moved him strongly, as if it belonged to his own spiritual autobiography. As has been noted he had himself held a scholarship which should have led to the Church, and instead he had turned aside to activities which were sinister and to views which gave him a reputation for 'atheism'. It is possible that *Faustus* was one of Marlowe's last plays, and shows how his mind, aggressive and passionate, still occupied itself with the problem of faith and anarchy.

The Jew of Malta has not the transcendent quality of the other plays. It has intrigue, rather than grandeur, and it is governed from the first by the sinister, Elizabethan conception of Machiavelli, while in some of its scenes melodrama is allowed a licence which at times is almost grotesque. T. S. Eliot feels that it may be described as a 'savage farce' rather than as tragedy. *Edward II* is a play on which the most varied opinions have been held. Marlowe has for the first time been diverted from foreign themes to an English story, and under the influence of the chronicle play he builds this tragedy out of English history. The material which he found in Holinshed's chronicle was not immediately promising, and, though Marlowe compressed a great deal, there are stretches of the play which do not avoid dullness. At the same time he clearly conceived that a play cannot be just a length of history cut off and put into the theatre. He has abandoned the Tamburlaine type of character, and shown the tragedy of weakness. Nor is the action restricted to one character, but is spread more evenly over the dramatis personae. The brevity of Marlowe's career has a keen poignancy and his early death was an incalculable loss to English drama.

CHAPTER FIVE

Early Elizabethan Comedy
and Shakespeare's other Predecessors

THERE IS nothing in early Elizabethan comedy to equal Marlowe's achievement in tragedy. The most considerable achievement is that of John Lyly (1554–1606), though his courtly comedies are so full of contemporary interests and fashions that they are little likely to appeal to a modern audience. All Lyly's dramatic work lay in comedy and his plays have a certain similarity of texture, notably in the euphuistic dialogue, and in a use of classical mythology, partly invented; but there is variety in design. They are all modelled for a courtly audience. They are all in prose, except *The Woman in the Moon*, and all of them make use of classical myth except *Mother Bombie*, a comedy with realistic features.

In one group of plays Lyly works an allegory connected with the court into a piece of classical myth. So *Sapho and Phao* (1584) is an allegory on the courtship of Elizabeth and the Duke of Alençon and *Endymion* (1588), the most elaborate of the courtly allegories, presents Elizabeth as Cynthia and the Earl of Leicester as Endymion. In *Midas* (1589–90) the myth is more obviously used to show Philip of Spain's grasping attempt to take England into his power. *Campaspe*, possibly as early as 1584, and certainly one of the earliest of the plays, and one of the most charming, is without allegory. Its plot deals with Campaspe, a captive of Alexander's with whom the painter Apelles fell in love, and the Emperor eventually resigns her to Apelles. Lyly strengthens this slight romantic plot with a number of episodes. *Gallathaea* (1588) shows Lyly's ingenuity, for he uses a tragic, classical myth and so redesigns it that it becomes a charming and ingenious device. *The Woman in the Moon* (1597), one of the most delightful of Lyly's plays, is in blank verse and free from the euphuistic elements which occupy such a large place in the prose plays. In contrast to these allegorical and classical plays Lyly wrote in *Mother Bombie* (1589–90) a Terentian comedy with a clever mixture of situations between parents and children.

Lyly pleased the courtly audience to which his comedies were addressed: it was the same audience that had welcomed his novel, *Euphues* (1578), with its elaborately balanced prose and its ingenious alliteration. So topical was Lyly, so neatly adjusted to his age, that much of the light and colour has now disappeared. Shakespeare obviously knew his work and benefited from his study, and, though he soon outgrew the clever euphuistic prose, he was in the early plays deeply under its influence. Shakespeare's comedies are at once more romantic and human but they retain much of Lyly's ingenuity. Further, in some more detailed ways Lyly's example was potent. Particularly do the witty servants of Lyly reappear in Shakespeare's comedies.

If Lyly has ingenuity and consistency, Robert Greene (1560–92), though more unequal, commands attention at times in an engaging way. As frequently with the Elizabethan dramatists, biographical material is scanty. Greene went to St John's College, Cambridge, where he met Nashe, and after taking a degree he travelled extensively on the Continent. He returned demoralized, though in a sentimental and self-pitying way he had a temporary and elaborate repentance. By 1580 he had begun a career as a writer, and the rest of his life was spent in the underworld of Elizabethan literature, which had its own strange contacts with the Court and where, however incredibly, great work was produced.

At first he wrote mainly pamphlets and novels. After Marlowe's *Tamburlaine* he tried, feebly it must be admitted, an imitation entitled *Alphonsus* (1588–91). His second play, and a very strange one, was written with Lodge and entitled *A Looking Glass for London and England* (about 1590): it is a mixture of elements from the moralities and the miracles and modern Elizabethan satire. *Orlando* (printed in 1594) was written after Greene had read Sir John Harington's translation of Ariosto. The play is ineffective. Then there followed *Friar Bacon and Friar Bungay* (possibly 1591) and *James IV* (earlier than 1594). Of these *Friar Bacon and Friar Bungay* is outstanding. The material seems a mixture of many traditions; of *Tamburlaine* and *Faustus* in the verse; of *Faustus* again in the pranks and devices of the action; with an odd, unhistorical history, as if in some acknowledgment to the growing tradition of the history play. But out and beyond these, not derived but created by Greene, is the drama of the English scene, with Margaret as its centre, the country girl, all English, despite the fact that she uses classical quotations. This is different from the native elements in the miracle plays and in *Gammer Gurton's Needle*. It is romanticized, idealized and yet made real with the milk pails, the fairings and the ale. Greene has devised ways of keeping the whole dramatic action together, the Court and the countryside and the world of necromancy. Out of much that was hurried and incongruous in his drama there had emerged something new, whose warm attractiveness is to be found again in Shakespeare's comedies. *James IV* also shows far more skill than Greene's earlier plays and again he achieves an original effect by combining several types of action within a single plot. The story is taken from Cinthio, from whom Shakespeare derived the plot of *Othello*, but it is softened, made romantic and transferred to Scotland where it is given a pseudo-historical setting. To this are added fairy interludes of Oberon, King of the Fairies, and of Bohan, a cynical, disillusioned figure, well enough contrived for Shakespeare to gather suggestions here for *A Midsummer Night's Dream*, and for Jaques in *As you Like It*.

Among the other predecessors of Shakespeare a definite place, both as poet and dramatist, must be assigned to George Peele (1558–97). In his *Arraignment of Paris* (printed 1584) he followed Lyly in employing classical myth freely for courtly purposes. Through the Paris and Oenone story he contrived to show that Elizabeth was fairer than all the goddesses. *Edward I* (printed 1593) was his ineffective experiment in history, from which he turned to the extravagant romantic tragedy, *The Battle of Alcazar* (performed about 1590). In *David and the Fair Bethsabe* (about 1593) Peele returned to the early tradition of the dramatic employment of a religious theme, but the play has little to commend it though the verse is well managed. By far the most original of Peele's plays was *The Old Wives Tale*, performed about 1592, in which Milton found some suggestions for *Comus*. The play opens with a realistic, contemporary, rustic scene in which Madge, the old wife, begins to tell a tale, making several false starts. She breaks off as the actors enter to perform the story she is narrating. In contrast to the homely realism of the opening, the tale is romantic and extravagant. Two brothers are seeking their sister, who is in the power of a magician. It is difficult to believe that Peele is wholly serious in this part of the play, yet the treatment is not designed in caricature. We are reminded that it is Madge's mind which is being dramatically presented.

Such is the achievement of pre-Shakespearian comedy. There is little here to compare with Marlowe. In the terms of acceptance by contemporary audiences Lyly is probably the master. Few, if any, of these plays can find their way back to the stage, and, though Shakespeare learned much from his predecessors, there is little here to announce his own achievement.

CHAPTER SIX

Shakespeare

IT IS difficult to say anything profitably of William Shakespeare (1564–1616) within the compass of one brief chapter. A library, rather too large, has already been written about his work. It can first be said that he was William Shakespeare, a Stratford man, an actor playwright and a member of the Managing Fellowship of a London Theatrical Company. He was not, as some misguided people have thought, either Francis Bacon, or the Earl of Oxford, or Marlowe, or any other candidate whose more absurd claims may have been put forward. Here, such space as is available, is devoted mainly to the plays, but a little must be recorded of the man and his background. Such was Shakespeare's knowledge of grammar and rhetoric that it is probable that he was educated at a Grammar School. There he discovered his interest and genius for language and it is the manipulation of language that dominates his whole creative life. His thought is on the whole unoriginal, but the language in which it is expressed is the greatest product of the imagination in English. At some moment in his life he came into a friendly, even intimate, relation with a great nobleman. This splendid life of the Court had á profound influence on his imagination. There has been dispute on the identity of the nobleman, but a solid claim can be made for the Earl of Southampton. It was to Southampton that he dedicated his poems *Venus and Adonis* (1593) and *The Rape of Lucrece* (1594); and, despite some respectable views to the contrary, he may well have been the friend in Shakespeare's *Sonnets*, which were known to be in private circulation as early as 1598, though not published until 1609, and then, presumably, without Shakespeare's authority. By some such route he came to London and to the theatre. He was an actor, a playwright, and by 1594 a full member of the Lord Chamberlain's Company. On James I's arrival in London the Company entered the King's service as the King's Men, the major company of the day, and with them Shakespeare remained, with frequent visits to Stratford, until he finally retired there after his last visit to London for the first performance of *Henry VIII* on June 29th 1613 when the theatre was burnt down. He obviously retained the friendship and esteem of the fellow members of his company, and in 1623, seven years after his death, two of his companions published the Folio edition of his plays. Had they not done so all record of nearly half of Shakespeare's work would probably have been lost.

His earliest extant work is in the Henry VI plays (Parts I, II, and III). Of these *I Henry VI* (Folio version only), has some scenes by Shakespeare, the Temple Garden scene and certain of the Talbot scenes, but much of the rest may be by other hands. Thus, as far as is known, he began as a practical dramatist in the native tradition of the English history play. It was to that form that he devoted a major part of his work as a dramatist, and from it there developed, by practice, rather than from theoretical preconception, his idea of tragedy. *II* and *III Henry VI*, which appear in the Folio, exist in Quarto versions as *The Contention betwixt the two famous houses of York and Lancaster;* the text in these versions differs widely from the Folio.[1] Since Malone's work on the text it has long been a tradition to consider that the Folio represented Shakespeare's revision of work by less competent contemporaries. The theory is improbable, for it is doubtful whether a very young dramatist, as yet untried, would be assigned such a task. It is more likely that the Quarto plays represent very corrupt versions of the same plays as are found in the Folio, and that Shakespeare can be considered as their sole author. *II* and *III Henry VI* had enough success to draw the envious attack of Robert Greene, the playwright, who, 'a Master of Arts of both Universities', suggested that Shakespeare was putting the scholarly wits out of business.

Thus he entered into the English history play and into the story of the quarrel of York and Lancaster, but he came to the story almost at its end. Later, and in more mature plays (*Richard II*, *Henry IV*, and *Henry V*), he was to go back to the beginning of that

---

[1] The reader is reminded that 'Quarto' refers to an edition of a single play, and that 'Folio' refers to a collection of the plays in one volume. Unless otherwise stated 'Folio', in this chapter, refers to the 'First Folio' published in 1623. The terms refer to the size of the page on which the book is printed.

history and make of the whole a dramatic epic of England. It was a great conception, but never formally planned, yet so consistent were his views of history and his vision that the plays possess a unity of design. Instead of going from the Henry VI theme to the beginning of the story Shakespeare continues to its end with *Richard III* (1592–3), a tragedy of the type which Marlowe had developed in *Tamburlaine*. Strong in purpose, firm in character, utterly unscrupulous and violent in action, Richard III became one of the most popular of Elizabethan dramatic figures. Six Quartos of the play were published before 1622 and there was a Folio version in 1623. Throughout these English history plays he had been dependent for material on Raphael Holinshed's *Chronicles*, with some help from Marlowe on how much history could be digested in a tragedy. What is miraculous is the degree to which he advances in his own art. The *Henry VI* plays followed largely the method of the native English chronicle plays. By *Richard III* and *Richard II* he had concentrated the theme on a single, major protagonist, and the advance between *Richard III* (1592–3) and *Richard II* (1595–6) is considerable. Complete independence from contemporary tradition comes with the two parts of *Henry IV* (1597–8). These are separated from the earlier history plays by *King John* (1596–7), which, though inconclusive in itself, shows Shakespeare working towards a new definition of historical tragedy, particularly through his interpretation of the Bastard, Faulconbridge.

During these same early years Shakespeare had begun to write comedies. The evidence for determining their order before *A Midsummer Night's Dream* is inadequate, and so conclusions about chronology must be a matter of taste rather than of fact. Here I employ the order *Love's Labour's Lost*, *The Two Gentlemen of Verona*, *The Comedy of Errors*, and *The Taming of the Shrew*.[1] All these plays contain elements which seem to find a unity in the *Dream*.

Love's Labour's Lost (no Quarto before 1598), even if it is not the first of the plays, must be one of the earliest and as such it is a miracle. The plot, unlike that in most of Shakespeare's plays, is

---

[1] Sir Edmund Chambers in his standard work on Shakespeare gives a different order and this is generally accepted: *The Comedy of Errors*, (1592–3); *The Taming of the Shrew* (1593–4); *Two Gentlemen of Verona*, *Love's Labour's Lost* (1594–5); *A Midsummer Night's Dream* (1595–6).

original. It is imaginary, but there are some references to almost contemporary French history, and much of the humour depends on topical allusions worked out in part through figures similar to those of the Italian *commedia dell' arte*. The play is one of the most astounding things that Shakespeare achieved. It is a sixteenth-century manners comedy, where the 'finer shades' of contemporary sentiment are subjected to the light of the comic spirit by one who is new to the stage, and almost a stranger to courtly life. One feels that the atmosphere of the play is achieved by the sudden entry into a nobleman's social life, such as might be found in Southampton's house, but by someone brought up in a different and more modest way. Nor is the world of this play previously discoverable in the drama. Shakespeare, apparently by invention, created a society sophisticated and elegant, like that in Molière or Congreve. The plot is dramatic. There is little in it that can be reduced to narrative, it has no story plot such as *The Two Gentlemen*, and so the central theme looks thin when it is retold as narrative. The King of Navarre and three courtiers swear that they will study for a fixed period and keep away from women. The Princess of France and her ladies come to them to negotiate affairs of state. Each man breaks his vow and falls in love with a lady. In addition there are complications, mistaken discoveries, incidental entertainments, foolery. But all is made dramatic to bring out the changes of mind in the main characters. The elegance is a little removed from reality, for wit and fantasy are its main qualities. Biron, who is a first sketch of Benedick, and Rosaline, an earlier Beatrice, move for a moment to reality before the close. As Walter Pater noted,[1] 'how many echoes seem awakened by those strange words, actually said in jest: 'The sweet war-man (Hector of Troy) is dead and rotten; sweet chucks, beat not the bones of the buried; when he breathed he was a man'. The central theme is the breaking of a vow, a fantastic vow it is true. Later as John Masefield has shown,[2] that theme of the breaking of a vow to oneself, to another, or to the state itself is the most frequently re-worked conception in Shakespeare's plays. Many features in the play are derived from Lyly and yet the total effect is altogether different. The comedy is more lively than courtly allegory, and the language more brilliant than euphuism. It is language

---

[1] *Love's Labour's Lost* in *Appreciations*.
[2] *William Shakespeare*, 1911.

that dominates the play. It is as if Shakespeare observed every device by which words could be the instruments of wit, or the play-things of sound and fancy. He exploits all that Walter Pater has described as 'the foppery of words' with gaiety and sophistication, realizing at the same time that words have other and stronger powers. He is engaged in that absorbing passion for words which leads from a game played for the pleasure of throwing coloured balls into the sunlight, to the compact, twisted, allusive verbal inventions of the tragedies and of the early part of *The Winter's Tale*. He shows already that language and its employment is to be the major and consistent occupation of his life:

> *Tafetta phrases, silken terms precise,*
> *Three piled hyperboles, spruce affectation,*
> *Figures pedantical.*

The Two Gentlemen of Verona (Folio 1623) was a romantic comedy with a story plot, perhaps Shakespeare's earliest attempt in this form. As he tells it, the story is of two friends, Proteus and Valentine; Proteus loves Julia and Valentine loves Silvia, but Proteus, separated from Julia, falls in love with Silvia—'the re-membrance of my former love, Is by a newer object quite forgot-ten'. The friends quarrel. After many adventures, some of them highly incredible, everything rights itself. This is a different type of play from *Love's Labour's Lost*, and, if one assumes that play to have come first, then Shakespeare has now rejected the method of fantasy and the elegance and good manners of a courtly world. Here one has to judge by normal standards. Yet two of the under-lying motives, as Masefield has suggested, remain the same, namely that passion is not guided or controlled by reason and that men in a state of passion are false to themselves and others. The whole is conducted in an atmosphere of exaggerated sentiment and improb-able adventure which belongs not to comedy but to the medieval romances. Instead of the exposures which comedy would bring to the excesses of Valentine and the uncertainty of Proteus, these characters are presented seriously and their actions brought to an unsteady conclusion. Genuine comedy, with an atmos-phere of common sense, exists only in the 'low-figures' such as Launce.

The Comedy of Errors (Folio text 1623) is another experiment.

As already suggested, the order of composition of these early plays cannot be precisely defined. *The Comedy of Errors* was performed at Gray's Inn in 1594: apart from that, there is no date by which its composition can be defined. Sir Edmund Chambers, as already noted, considered that it preceded *Love's Labour's Lost* and *The Two Gentlemen*. The precise order is not of much importance to the critic. Whatever the order it remains clear that Shakespeare is experimenting. The play is very short, and is a well-defined attempt to employ Plautine comedy in English. He borrowed from *The Menaechmi* of Plautus of which a translation was published in 1595, and from the *Amphitruo*. Shakespeare could probably read Plautus comfortably for himself in Latin. His scene is Ephesus, and in contrast to his romantic plays he preserves a unity of time and almost of place. He gives an initial sentimental argument to a comedy which depends on the confusions which arise from the existence of two sets of twins. The result is that he has rendered into a farce of situation what might in Terence or Plautus have been a comedy dependent on comment on society and the family. The Roman comedy cannot be transferred into English and retain its social purpose, for English society has such different values. The adroitness of the plot is such that the comedy has always been successful when it has been revived with adequate actors and producers.

In *The Taming of the Shrew* (Folio 1623) Shakespeare turns from the clever but mechanical farce of *The Comedy of Errors* to a vigorous and effective comedy dependent on character. The play has two plots, first the wooing of the shrew Katharine by Petruchio, and secondly the dull and dimly romantic plot of Bianca and her wooers. The *Induction* must be remembered, as it explains the values of the play, for the comedy is performed before Christopher Sly, a drunken tinker, dressed up as a lord, all of which seems to imply that it must not be taken too seriously. The mood is farcical with the wilful distortion and exaggeration of certain aspects of life and character for broadly humorous purposes. A strong-willed woman and a coarse, brutal man are shown in the rough and tumble of matrimony, with the final subduing of the woman. One must allow no sentimental values to intrude, for it is Sly's play, and even apart from that, Elizabethan views on these matters were different from our own.

There followed the wonderful creation of *A Midsummer Night's*

Dream (1st Quarto, 1600). The plot is apparently invented and most ingenious, and it is an incredible advance on anything that he had previously achieved. He retained all that he had learned from his earlier comedies and with this experience he moved into a new world. He is away from Italianate romance to Athens, a medieval and romantic Athens of Chaucer's *Knight's Tale*, made native by the folk ·lore of the English countryside. Like Greene, but with far greater skill, he combines a number of stories in a single plot. Theseus and Hippolyta are to marry and the ceremonies give a basis to the play, which may have been designed for a wedding. Amid the fantasy and romantic excesses these two characters preserve an element of normality. For the main plot Shakespeare retains pairs of lovers as he had already used them in the earlier plays. Lysander and Demetrius both love Hermia, and Helena loves Demetrius, but they are subjected to a genuinely comic treatment which was not achieved in *The Two Gentlemen*. The confusions of the love juice and the extravagance of their sentiments show how far they depart from reason, and this same irrationality of passion is emphasized by the Titania and Bottom plot. At the conclusion, the comic matter of Bottom and his friends is brought, by the performance of their play, into contact with the main action. All is made luminous by language reaching a quality of imagination he had not previously attained. Among many other passages there is Theseus's speech which probably defines Shakespeare's own definition of the creative process:

> *And as imagination bodies forth*
> *The forms of things unknown, the poet's pen*
> *Turns them to shapes, and gives to airy nothing*
> *A local habitation, and a name.*

The rustics and their play are one of Shakespeare's great achievements in comedy, apart, in a very different way, from the Falstaff scenes in Justice Shallow's house in *II Henry IV*. He brought the world of the theatre that he knew so well, with amateur and rustic variations, into the *Dream*. No passage in his whole work shows the degree of absorption in the world of the contemporary theatre as Bottom's instructions to his fellow players: 'All that I will tell you is, that the Duke hath dined. Get your apparel together, good strings to your beards, new ribbons to your pumps; meet presently at the palace; every man look o'er his part; for the short and the long is, our play is preferred'.

A Midsummer Night's Dream seems to mark a period in Shakespeare's work, for there he had captured a spirit of comedy, uniting the classical with the native, the Middle Ages with the Renaissance and gathering them into a plot which has an effortless coherence. In the period which followed he continued to write both comedy and history plays, while in *Romeo and Juliet*, and in the part-authorship at least of *Titus Andronicus*, he experimented in tragedy. *Romeo and Juliet* (completed by 1594-6, 1st Quarto, 1597) is tragedy conceived in the mood of the romantic comedies and explored in the sentiment of the *Sonnets*. It is unlike the later tragedies, for in language it is lyrical and its theme is love, while its crisis depends on accident instead of being an inescapable consequence of character as in the later tragedies. In them he would give more completely an impression that the action was not merely a story, but arose out of a world whose atmosphere and values were imagined in the verse. Despite the Italian atmosphere there is no world behind the play, as in *Hamlet*, to give reality to the whole action. The language is throughout brilliant, though its employment is at times self-conscious, yet here he moves beyond the artificiality of many of the earlier comic characters to the realism of the Nurse.

Of the comedies of this second period possibly the earliest is *The Merchant of Venice* (1st Quarto 1600). Justly one of the most popular, this combines the wooing of Portia at Belmont by the choice of the caskets, a faery-motived theme, with the sinister story of the Jew's bond, secured by the forfeit of a pound of flesh. These severely contrasting motives are resolved by the skill of Portia as a lady advocate, and a touch of lightness and comedy is added at the close by the incident of the exchange of rings. To enjoy the play one must not analyse the characters too closely, for Bassanio, considered with the precision of ordinary life, is little better than a rogue. The whole action is bathed in a wash of beautiful words which, while keeping the senses alert, dulls the intelligence into accepting the values presented. Yet not completely so, for Shylock seems to refuse to be bound by these artificialities and steps out of the pretty framework of the play, a figure of almost tragic dimensions.

Much Ado About Nothing (about 1599) continues in the same

tradition. The action is improbable and the romantic characters are unreal if brought out of the world of fine sentiment and witty language to which they belong. In Benedick and Beatrice, who are the critics of romantic sentiment, Shakespeare gives a depth and penetration of character stronger than anything in the comedy. Upon the general mood of light-heartedness Don John is permitted to intrude an episode of tragedy, but the audience need not be genuinely fearful that he, a villain who can be exposed by Dogberry, will be ultimately successful. Dogberry, one of the most amusing of the clowns, gives his comic misinterpretations of words in a way that only confirms Shakespeare's profound interest in language. Throughout the comedy the more gentle characters have a wit that is free and spontaneous:

> *Don Pedro :* I think this is your daughter.
> *Leonato :*   Her mother hath many times told me so.
> *Benedick :* Were you in doubt, sir, that you asked her?
> *Leonato :*   Signior Benedick, no, for then you were a child.

In *As You Like It* (1599–1600) Shakespeare seemed to gather all that he had learned in romantic comedy and to employ it in a play strong in native atmosphere, by exposing all the forms of melancholy and mood to which the mind is subject. Its gaiety, strongly contrasting with its reflective moments, the happy variety of scene, and the many firmly defined characters, Jaques, the Duke, Rosalind and Touchstone, have made it one of the most popular of all the comedies. Deliberately careless in detail, it has some confident strength of structure on which it moves buoyantly along. Though much of the play is in prose, it contains Jaques's speech, 'All the world's a stage', one of the most frequently quoted in Shakespeare, and such lyrics as 'Blow, blow, thou winter wind', and 'It was a lover and his lass'. Finally in *Twelfth Night* (about 1600) Shakespeare brought romantic comedy to a new perfection. To some modern spectators, and I am one of them, *A Midsummer Night's Dream* is the more delightful play; especially do I prefer Bottom and his men, unless their pranks are over-played, to Sir Toby Belch and his senseless crew. But even despite such personal prejudices, nothing can obscure the charm and unity of conception in *Twelfth Night*, where love in all its gentler moods of sentiment is explored and its kindliness and hypocrisy at once revealed. The characterization is firmer than that of the *Dream* and in Malvolio, a 'humorous' character that must have delighted Ben Jonson, Shakespeare exposed self-conceit with a satiric firmness, so that the conclusion seems almost excessive to the light delicacy of the treatment as a whole. He has returned to a comedy that is largely in verse with many passages of great distinction from the Duke's opening lines on 'If music be the food of love, play on' to his description of a lyric:

> *The spinsters and the knitters in the sun,*
> *And the free maids that weave their thread with bones,*
> *Do use to chant it; it is silly sooth,*
> *And dallies with the innocence of love,*
> *Like the old age.*

Within these years in which Shakespeare had matured his idea of romantic comedy, he had also moved forward in his development of history play and tragedy. By as early as 1596 he had completed the tragedy of *Romeo and Juliet*. As already noted, in this popular play he carried the theme of the comedies into a tragic setting, and exploited the imagery and language which he was employing, possibly at the same period, in the *Sonnets*.

By 1596 he had written *King John* (Folio, 1623), a play which, though it may have some unsatisfactory features, is vital in Shakespeare's development, as has already been suggested, and lies midway between the chronicle play and tragedy. The plot is derived from the earlier play of the *Troublesome Raigne*. In design it lacks unity, in attempting to bring together the widely separated themes of French and English antagonism, the murder of Arthur, the revolt in England and the papal plot. All this amorphous multiplicity of action seems to lead back to the diffuse methods of *Henry VI*, but the characters are now far more strongly presented and Shakespeare himself seems to be feeling his way through to some new conception. He has so developed the character of the Bastard, Faulconbridge, that he is a new creation, linking the perplexingly diverse movements of the plot, and at the same time, by his rough independence of mind, acting as a commentary, comic, satiric, and eloquent in turn, on all the values that the play suggests. Through Faulconbridge Shakespeare was seeing his way to Falstaff, even to Hamlet, and to the very original conception of the history play

which appeared with *I* and *II Henry IV* and *Henry V*. The Bastard
sees clearly through the pretence of chivalry in those around him.
Life he knows to be a deceit, for he was born by a deceit, so he will
judge not by accepted standards, but by life as he sees it, and he will
act for his own purpose, which is England:

> *Come the three corners of the world in arms,*
> *And we shall shock them. Naught shall make us rue,*
> *If England to itself do rest but true.*

Falstaff also saw through life, but his conclusion was self-indulg-
ence and a comic egoism. The Bastard sees through everything but
clings to a faith in England. He has a closely-worked intellectual
consistency which is not always recognized, and from its creation
Shakespeare learned much that he was later to use in the histories
and the tragedies.

King John led on the one hand to tragedy and on the other to the
supreme maturing of the history plays in *I* and *II Henry IV* (Quartos 1598 and 1600). The two parts unite into a single drama, which
is not tragedy but some separate mood, satiric or even comic in the
most profound sense of the term. The play is a solemn reflection on
civil commotion, of whose dangers Shakespeare was acutely aware,
and the comic sub-plot with its satire on the methods of warfare is
brought into close unity with the whole design. The characters are
depicted with a superb clarity, especially in the contrast of Hotspur
and the Prince. In this theme of English history Shakespeare has
placed Falstaff, who, next to Hamlet, is the most discussed character in the plays. At his simplest he is a buffoon, a laughter-creating
rascal, but he is more sinister, more profound, and in the second
part, capable even of poignancy, as some ageing wreck of great
abilities misspent. Laughter dominates, but through the laughter
there peeps almost everything else from philosophy to sentiment.
The comedy reaches in *II Henry IV* a subtle quality beyond anything that Shakespeare has previously achieved. There is Falstaff's
description of Justice Shallow: 'I do remember him at Clement's
Inn, like a man made after supper of a cheese-paring. When 'a was
naked, he was, for all the world, like a forked radish, with a head
fantastically carved upon it with a knife'. To this can be added the
poignancy of the ageing Falstaff remembering younger days: 'We
have heard the chimes at midnight, Master Shallow.'

This great play was followed by *Henry V* (Quarto 1600) which is an emblazoned and glorying exposition of national triumph in war, though with some human scenes as the King walks, disguised, among his men on the eve of battle. It is in *Henry V* that Shakespeare reflects on the inadequacy of the stage resources of his time:

> *And so our scene must to the battle fly;*
> *Where—O for pity—we shall much disgrace*
> *With four or five most vile and ragged foils,*
> *Right ill disposed, in brawl ridiculous,*
> *The name of Agincourt, Yet sit and see*
> *Minding true things by what their mockeries be.*

With *Henry V* Shakespeare's work in the English history plays ends, except for that elaborate piece of pageantry *Henry VIII* of which he was part author.

From English history he had moved with great success to a Roman theme in *Julius Caesar* (1599, Folio 1623). The plot avoids the episodical matter which the English history plays, even at their best, possess, and instead there is a concentration on the central theme marking a development of his conception of tragedy. From North's *Plutarch* he derived not only the theme but a richer model for language than Holinshed and his chronicles could offer. The single plot on which he concentrated, namely the struggle of the conspirators against a tyrant, offered technical difficulties, for the tyrant was killed half-way through the play. In part this finds compensation in the idea that the rebellion is not against Caesar but against Caesarism, and this the ghost helps to emphasize. The characters are as clearly defined as in *Henry IV* with the same use of contrast, as Cassius and Brutus and Antony are posed one against the other. It is on Brutus that Shakespeare concentrates, portraying there a philosophical type, treated elsewhere comically in Falstaff, and seriously in Henry VI, and in varying moods in Richard II and later in Hamlet; so it is to Brutus that he gives many of the most memorable lines in the play:

> *Between the acting of a dreadful thing,*
> *And the first motion, all the interim is*
> *Like a phantasma, or a hideous dream.*
> *The Genius, and the mortal instruments,*

Are then in council; and the state of man,
Like to a little kingdom, suffers then
The nature of an insurrection.

Julius Caesar is in many ways the prelude to the great tragedies,
but there occur in this same period three of the most puzzling and
yet interesting plays in his work. These are *All's Well That Ends*
Well (1601–2: Folio, 1623), *Troilus and Cressida* (1602, Quarto
1609; in the Folio, 1623, the play is called a 'tragedy'), and
Measure for Measure (1604: Folio, 1623). *All's Well* and *Measure*
for Measure are comedies developed in the mood of the tragedies.
The vessel of romantic comedy is being forced to hold a burden of
thought beyond its strength. The two plays have a similarity of
plot. In each a man is faithless and a woman faithful. In each a
woman is substituted or disguised as another in the performance of
the sexual act, and so regains the faithless man. All this is worked
out in a distress of spirit which penetrates beyond the story which
holds the theme. The mood in the main plot is fierce, and the
comic world of the sub-plot has a bawdiness and grossness not
often paralleled elsewhere in Shakespeare. The comedies have been
described as 'dark', and as the product of a cynical mood. Yet this
is not just, for a number of touches show a tenderness and a charity,
a faith in humanity even amid the faithlessness and obscenity of
individual men. *Troilus and Cressida* puzzled the early editors, and
has remained a puzzle ever since. Like *King John* it is a play in
which Shakespeare is breaking through to a new dramatic vision.
At times, as in Ulysses's speech on 'degree', it has some of the most
illuminating passages that he wrote, and its intellectual appeal
remains very strong. His imagination never worked in a more concentrated way than in Ulysses's lines:

> *Degree being vizarded,*
> *The unworthiest shows as fairly in the mask.*
> *The heavens themselves, the planets, and this centre,*
> *Observe degree, priority, and place,*
> *Insisture, course, proportion, season, form,*
> *Office, and custom, in all line of order.*

Yet one feels in seeing it that some part of the clue to its composition and intention is missing. Clearly Shakespeare began with the

medieval story of Troilus and Cressida as it was found in Chaucer, and gradually became absorbed with the fact that this theme was only a late accretion upon the great Homeric legend of the *Iliad*. Chapman's translation may have helped towards that change of emphasis, and indeed Shakespeare's dislike for the Greeks as compared with the Trojans may be linked with some motive of satirizing Chapman. As it is, Shakespeare begins with the Troilus and Cressida story and becomes involved, and indeed more interested, in the Achilles and Ajax theme. The Cressida story he found frustrating. If the lady is to be treated with any sympathy her career must be related in the values of honour as understood in the medieval courts of love. Once moral considerations dominate, and the seriousness of tragedy intrudes, Cressida becomes a wanton. Thus while the play never consolidates into a theme whose every motion is intelligible, it has a fascinating brilliance, as if it belonged to a world consistent with itself but all seen in a strange light.

There followed the great succession of tragedies which are Shakespeare's supreme achievement: *Hamlet* (1601: printed First Quarto 1603 and Second Quarto 1604); *Othello* (1604; Quarto 1622); *Macbeth* (before 1606; Folio, 1623), *King Lear* (1605; Quarto, 1608); *Antony and Cleopatra* (1606; Folio, 1623); *Coriolanus* (about 1606; Folio, 1623). He had also some share in *Titus Andronicus*, *Timon of Athens* and *Pericles*. The tragedies have a sufficient number of features in common to support the conclusion that Shakespeare from his long practice in the history plays had matured a conception of tragedy which, though never governed by any theoretical considerations, was gaining a certain precision in design. The protagonist was man, and one who as king, prince, or leader involved a whole people by his actions; so that at any moment his personal conduct might become part of the 'world's debate'. Each possessed a great nature and outstanding gifts and yet had some weakness or corruption which made him unequal to the situation with which he was faced. How deeply Shakespeare contemplated this conception of character can be seen from a complex and revealing passage in *Hamlet* (I, iv. 23–36):

> *So, oft it chances in particular men,*
> *That for some vicious mole of nature in them,*
> *As, in their birth—wherein they are not guilty,*

Since nature cannot choose his origin,
By the o'ergrowth of some complexion,
Oft breaking down the pales and forts of reason
Or by some habit that too much o'er-leavens
The form of plausive manners; that these men,
Carrying, I say, the stamp of one defect,
Being nature's livery, or fortune's star,
His virtues else—be they as pure as grace,
As infinite as man may undergo,
Shall in the general censure take corruption
From that particular fault.

The love interest, dominant in the comedies, becomes now of minor importance, and only in *Antony and Cleopatra* does it remain the main motive of the action. Comedy, though retained, is given a subsidiary place and is worked into subtle, even poignant, contrast with the main action as in *Hamlet* and *King Lear*. Language, particularly in the use of imagery, gains an enhanced power, so that each of these tragedies has its own world of symbols and of verbal associations that serve as an imaginative accompaniment to the action. Above all, each theme seems to take place within a world so consistent with itself and so familiar, that criticism has often been in danger of treating the characters as human figures with lives independent of the immediate action. Each play is able to appeal at a number of different levels. The theme is in one sense so obvious, and the characters so clear, and the incident so strong and active, that anyone interested in human life will be moved. But accompanying this there is a range of suggestion in the language and there is subtlety in the characters which endless exploration never seems finally to exhaust.

Despite these similarities, the tragedies are very different. *Hamlet*, on which criticism has already said too much, is the play with the greatest multiplicity of appeal. In this Renaissance world, art, literary criticism, the elegances of language and the speculations of philosophy, all have place along with the high tragic movement, so that satire, comedy, ironic comment, and moral reflection mingle with death, madness, suicide and revenge. The dramatic criticism to be found in the exchanges between Hamlet and Polonius when the players were at Elsinore shows how deeply

Shakespeare had contemplated his own art. Polonius is given in a few lines a summary of the contrast of the classical art with fixed rules and the free art which Shakespeare himself practised: 'Scene individable or poem unlimited. Seneca cannot be too heavy nor Plautus too light. For the law of writ and the liberty, these are the only men.' In contrast *Othello* has an atmosphere and theme more domestic than is usual in the tragedies, and a language of greater simplicity but of high and commanding imagination. Othello's final speech is one of the most intense and dramatically effective in Shakespeare. Othello is given passages of high rhetoric such as from Act III:

> *Like to the Pontic sea,*
> *Whose icy current and compulsive course*
> *Never retiring ebbs, but keeps due on*
> *To the Propontic, and the Hellespont;*
> *Even so my bloody thoughts, with violent pace,*
> *Shall ne'er look back.*

Much of his language is in direct statement but made in a state of intense passion:

> *I had been happy, if the general camp,*
> *Pioneers and all, had tasted her sweet body,*
> *So I had nothing known.*

The gain is in a supreme concentration, and, though the unities of the classical tragedy are not applied, by use of 'double-time', one for the incidents and another for the action, Shakespeare gives to the play an intense singleness of pattern.

In *Macbeth* he chose a character far more evil than he elsewhere employs as a major protagonist in tragedy. Yet he retains some sympathy for him, though it cannot be intellectually justified. The 'weird sisters' give to Macbeth's conduct a predestined inevitability, and to these supernatural promptings must be added the goadings of Lady Macbeth. The more evil he becomes the more does he evolve some strange pathos in his isolation; for the image of his own evil haunts him like a fever, and his poetic power, supreme among the tragic heroes, permits him to portray the symbols of self-torment with which he is afflicted. *Macbeth* is the tragedy of a brave mind diseased by ambition. *King Lear* shows the more normal decay of a proud, impassioned nature by the inroads of old age and senility. While *Othello* is the more compact, *King Lear* is the most extended of the tragedies, with an epic scale, and in the storm scenes a wild symbolical movement develops that seems to reach beyond any precise location of place and time. The fierce, tormented action, unremitting in its solution, makes this the most stark and harrowing of the tragedies and stretches the capacity of both actor and producer more than anywhere else in Shakespeare. Not here the intellectual background of *Hamlet*, but something primitive that permits the exposure of the ultimate and innate cruelty of man. It appears in the action and in lines such as those in which Gloucester explains to Regan why he has sent the King to Dover:

> *I would not see thy cruel nails*
> *Pluck out his poor old eyes; nor thy fierce sister*
> *In his anointed flesh stick boarish fangs.*

Antony and Cleopatra stands apart. Love has returned as a major theme and the woman is given a role equal at least to that of the male protagonist. So widespread are the scenes and so numerous that it would seem at first that Shakespeare was returning to the method of the history plays. But it is not so. For with the aid of Plutarch he has seized on this great theme of Antony's passion and of Cleopatra's 'infinite variety', and in language patterned with rich beauty, abundantly endowed with magnificence and power. It is to Enobarbus that he gives the romantic lines:

> *Age cannot wither her, nor custom stale*
> *Her infinite variety: other women cloy*
> *The appetites they feed, but she makes hungry*
> *Where most she satisfies, for vilest things*
> *Become themselves in her, that the holy priests*
> *Bless her, when she is riggish.*

But not all the language is in this romantic mood. Never did Shakespeare so extend himself from imaginative imagery and magnificence to simple and moving statement, as in Antony's lines to Eros:

> *Unarm, Eros, the long day's task is done,*
> *And we must sleep.*

Or in the beautiful and it would seem answering lines with which
Iras addressed Cleopatra at the end of the tragedy:

> *Finish good lady, the bright day is done,*
> *And we are for the dark.*

He has contrived an action moving and original, whose full force
must be discovered in the theatre and not from the printed pages
of a book.

Coriolanus, again a Roman theme from Plutarch, is in severe
contrast, though both deal with men of action rather than with
self-tortured figures such as Brutus, Othello, Macbeth and Lear.
Antony and Cleopatra is spacious and full of glamour, *Coriolanus*
confined as if the whole play were one continuous argument.
Antony's fault is human and close to ordinary human motives, but
Coriolanus endures a pride which is a specialized emotion. The
spectator can identify himself with Hamlet and Antony, but he has
to watch Coriolanus; even then his motives are discovered mainly
through the conduct and the speeches of others. The verse has a
severity which is deliberate, but seems restricted and colourless in
comparison with that of some of the earlier tragedies. The division
of the action over the play is novel and interesting, for it begins
with the bustle of a chronicle play and ends like a Greek tragedy.
The major theme finds, when competently performed, a strange
and unexpected relevance to modern political conditions.

The motive of reconciliation which struggles with tragic destiny
in *Lear* and *Coriolanus* becomes supreme in the last plays: *Cymbeline* (1609; Folio, 1623); *The Winter's Tale* (about 1610; Folio,
1623) and *The Tempest* (1611; Folio, 1623). These belong to the
period when his Company owned the 'closed-in' theatre at Blackfriars, where elaborate scenic effects were more possible. That
Shakespeare was uneasy in this new atmosphere can with some
certainty be affirmed. The plays have their own brilliance, but not
the advancing command of his earlier achievement, and the new
conditions at Blackfriars may have been one of his motives for
retiring to Stratford. In *Cymbeline* Shakespeare submitted to the
influence of Beaumont and Fletcher. The play has a large pattern of
incident but little depth of character portrayal. The main motive is
not unlike that in *King Lear*: a daughter, Imogen, offends her
father, Cymbeline, but now a reconciliation is permitted and only

the wicked elements are destroyed. Although the pattern of incident is elaborate, one is not conscious, as in the great tragedies, of a world behind the story. The skill lies rather in the control of the complex plot and particularly in its resolution in the fifth act. Throughout, the play seems full of echoes, especially in the motives for action: Cymbeline in his anger is reminiscent of Lear; the distrust of Imogen's virtue recalls *Othello*; the despair of Posthumus sends the spectator back to *Troilus and Cressida*, and the deceit of Iachimo to the so-called 'dark' comedies. It seems a transition play, full of charm and ingenuity, but lacking the uniqueness of vision and the strenuousness in its pursuit of the great tragedies. It contains one of the most beautiful lyrics in all the plays, the dirge over what seemed to be the death of Imogen:

> *Fear no more the heat o' the' sun,*
> *Nor the furious winter's rages;*
> *Thou thy worldly task hast done,*
> *Home art gone and ta'en thy wages.*
> *Golden lads and girls all must*
> *As chimney-sweepers come to dust.*

So with two comedies, very different in design but similar in motive, the plays come to an end. In the Folio of 1623 one of them, *The Tempest*, stood first and the other, *The Winter's Tale*, stood last among the Comedies. *The Winter's Tale* opens in the mood of the tragedies, and in the crowded and elliptical lines of Leontes explores again the Othello theme of jealousy. Then suddenly the mood relaxes. The change comes precipitously in a stage-direction: 'Exit Antigonus pursued by a Bear: Enter Shepherd'. With the Shepherd's entry romance and comedy and reconciliation return, and remain to the end. The rural and pastoral scenes with which the play closes are happily portrayed, and in Autolycus a new character is added to Shakespeare's comic figures. Critics have commented on the irregularity of the construction and the improbability of the theme. Of all this Shakespeare was aware as his Chorus of Time shows, but on the stage the whole finds unity in a strange delight, not realistic certainly, but with a soft mellow quality of its own. *The Tempest* is either the last of the plays or an early play revised later for some special occasion. It is known to have been performed in 1613 for the celebration of the wedding of the Elector Palatine and Princess Elizabeth. It differs from all the previous comedies. Like *A Midsummer Night's Dream* it is regular in form and has a close unity of theme. Many of the characters, unlike those elsewhere in Shakespeare, seem abstractions, and of these Caliban is a profound conception, based in part on his reading of Montaigne and of the voyages of discovery. The play uses the machinery and stage device which performance at Blackfriars, in a private theatre or at Court would permit, and ends with Prospero's speech which seems like Shakespeare's own farewell to the stage. It is a play never supremely successful on the modern stage, but infinitely full of suggestion and meaning as if the whole of life were somehow symbolized within it. Emile Montégut commenting on the fact that *The Tempest* appeared first in the 'Folio' wrote: 'Like the emblematic frontispieces of antique books it prepares the reader for the substance of all that follows. No other play will do this, none other is a synthesis of all'.

CHAPTER SEVEN

Shakespeare's Contemporaries Ben Jonson, Thomas Dekker Domestic Drama - John Heywood George Chapman

OUTSTANDING among Shakespeare's contemporaries was Ben Jonson (1572–1637), a writer of two learned tragedies, *Sejanus* and *Catiline*, and of many individual and original 'humours' comedies. The stepson of a bricklayer, he was taken before he had completed his time from Westminster School, and put into the family trade. Soon dissatisfied he became a soldier, and in the Flanders Wars killed his man in single combat. How he gained his learning has never been explained, but later it was recognized by both Universities, who gave him degrees by 'their favour not his study'. He married early ('a shrew yet honest') and had a number of children, and economic necessity probably drove him into a career as an actor. How he made his transition into dramatist is unknown, but by 1598 Francis Meres could describe him as 'among our best for tragedy' and in that same year he had succeeded in a new and original comedy, *Every Man in His Humour*. Though the precise biographical material is meagre, he stands out vividly as a character and we get a clearer conception of him than of many of his contemporaries. His conversations with Drummond of Hawthornden portray his downright comments. Thomas Fuller describes him, 'built far higher for learning [than Shakespeare], solid but slow in his performances.'

The contrasts between Shakespeare and Ben Jonson are marked and obvious. In *Hamlet*, Polonius, who, whatever his defects, was a learned critic of the drama, said that a play was composed either by 'the law of writ' or 'the liberty'. This shows that Shakespeare knew all the talk about the 'unities' and the classical rules. Shakespeare, however, was not bound by the 'rules' when he came to conceive what his own plays might achieve. He based his construction on 'the liberty' of his own imagination. To Ben Jonson the 'rules' were not merely practical precepts, to be used if convenient, but dictates founded on authority which every good man must follow. Though often forced by the necessities of the theatre and by concessions to his audiences to modify his ideal, he aimed at a pattern which would follow the ancients and preserve the 'unities'. As he writes in the prologue to *Volpone*:

> *The laws of time, place, persons, he observeth,*
> *From no needful rule he swerveth.*

Each play was to have one action, played in one scene, within the period of one day: such was the ideal. Jonson insisted that the audience should realize how clever he had been in his regular and original compositions, and in his prefaces and comments he hectored his readers into appreciating how cunningly he had constructed his plays. He is like some dowager insisting that all shall appreciate her ungainly daughters, though Jonson's dramatic daughters were far from ungainly.

Part of Jonson's originality is that he brings the scene of comedy from Italy, where Shakespeare had placed it, and normally sets his vigorous themes, with the notable exception of *Volpone*, in contemporary England. He did not at once achieve this increase in realism, for the first version of *Every Man in His Humour* has its scene in Italy, and only in the Folio version of 1616 do the characters appear with English names and on an English background. To this presentation of contemporary life he brought a definite theory of comedy based on the 'humours'. This conception was partly medieval, and in part an Elizabethan fashion. In Latin comedy each character belonged to a recognizable type, and maintained throughout certain well-defined attributes. This static conception of character Jonson maintained and re-affirmed by adapting the medieval belief that temperament was governed by an excess of one of the four 'humours', hot, cold, moist and dry. In Elizabethan times this medieval physiology was not treated with complete seriousness, but its vocabulary became a popular fashion in sophisticated conversation and this again Jonson exploited. In the comedies the result is that one quality was affixed to each character and this was exposed in the action. It gave to Jonson's figures a strong though static quality, with often a satiric mood dominant, and it remained a feature of comedy long after his death.

Chronologically Jonson's comedies are separated by his two tragedies. The earliest group precedes *Sejanus* (acted 1603, Quarto 1605). The middle group includes the great comedies, *Volpone* (1606); *The Silent Woman* (1609); and *The Alchemist* (1610). These lie between *Sejanus* and *Catiline* (1611). Then follow the last comedies beginning with *Bartholomew Fair* (1614).

The earliest of the 'humours' plays, *Every Man in His Humour* (acted 1598, Quarto 1601 and revised version in the Folio 1616), is a theatrically effective play. A simple and original plot permits the dramatic exposure of a number of characters: the elder Knowell, the stern father; Kitely, the jealous husband; and Bobadill the braggart soldier, who is the outstanding portrait. They are all broadly based and identifiable characters. There followed *Every Man Out of His Humour* (acted 1599, Quarto 1600), which is preluded by an open declaration of the aim of 'humours' comedy and of its intention of stripping 'the ragged follies of the time':

> *when some one peculiar quality*
> *Doth so possess a man that it doth draw*
> *All his affects, his spirits and his powers*
> *In their confluctions all to run one way,*
> *This may be truly said to be a humour.*

A deepening satiric mood leads to the presentation of a gallery of 'humours' figures conceived with some bitterness. The characters are not so natural as in *Everyman in His Humour*. The play has no central theme except that Macilente, having exposed the weaknesses of the characters, has in turn his own envy exposed. One of Jonson's most able critics, Miss Ellis-Fermor, suggested that he had in his temperament a 'non-dramatic' element, and that in some plays of this period he 'imposed dramatic form upon his own recalcitrant imagination'. He was attacking romantic comedy though it is difficult to see that he has found an adequate or entertaining substitute. His intentions are shown in the Induction in the speech of Asper, 'the presenter',

> *my language*
> *Was never ground into such oily colour*
> *To flatter vice and daub iniquity.*

This approach to drama would certainly seem to be true of *Cynthia's Revels* (acted 1600, Quarto 1601), in which masque and myth mingle with contemporary satire. In his prologue Jonson made a claim for originality:

> *In this alone his Muse her sweetness hath,*
> *She shuns the print of any beaten path;*
> *And proves new ways to come to learned ears.*

But the 'new ways' are full of incongruity. Of the same type, though more firmly constructed, was *The Poetaster* (acted 1601, Quarto 1602), where the Roman scene is applied to the exposure of the complicated rivalries of the Elizabethan dramatists, particularly in an attack on Dekker and Marston. The play was not popular with audiences in the theatre and so Jonson determined to leave comedy for tragedy:

> *Since the Comic Muse*
> *Hath prov'd so ominous, I will try*
> *If Tragedy hath a more kind aspect.*

In *Sejanus* (acted 1603, Quarto 1605), he designed a learned Roman tragedy on the factual record of history as found in the *Annals* of Tacitus and in Juvenal's satire. He passed from *The Poetaster*, and his satirical humour in the court of Augustus, to tragedy in the court of Tiberius. Hazlitt called it 'a mosaic of translated bits', and Jonson had already given a similar impression with all his apparatus of notes, but less than a quarter is actual translation. Though Jonson respects the unities he modifies them in order to keep closer to history, and from an attempt to compromise between the classical drama of Seneca and the known desires of his audiences. Shakespeare had by this time written *Julius Cæsar*, and possibly Jonson was attempting to compete in his own conscientious and factually accurate way with the Shakespearian picture of the Roman world, which ignored detail, but remained living and dynamic, and proved very popular. In essence it was tragedy on the old medieval theme of the fall of the proud man. Its characterization was static as in the comedies, and indeed seemed in a way a 'humours' conception elevated to a tragic scale. Had he maintained this central dramatic theme he could have attained success, but the action was complicated by some forty characters and these led to undramatic confusion. Yet in constructing the tragedy he must have felt that he was compromising with his audience, for he diverted from the unity of time, and he dispensed with the chorus; but this did not compensate for the lack of those qualities found in Shakespeare's *Julius Cæsar*, 'the presentation', as Dr Boas has written, 'in melodious and lucid dialogue of contrasted characters— a Brutus, a Cassius, an Antony—Roman in origin but embodying eternal and universal types. Here Shakespeare gloriously followed the lead of Plutarch in North's translation. Jonson turning to a mass of classical sources became entangled in intricate historical issues unfamiliar to Globe audiences'.

Sejanus it must be confessed belongs to the dead drama: it has its place in the history of the theatre, but it has no hope of revival on the living stage, as have the comedies.

There followed the three great comedies. Of these *Volpone* (acted 1606, Quarto 1607), is the comedy of the author of *Sejanus*. It has a grim outline, sometimes reminiscent of tragedy. This magnificent play has captured audiences whenever it has been competently revived. The theme is of Volpone, a man of seeming virtue who enjoys roguery, and by a consuming avarice has gathered riches which Tamburlaine might have envied. So he salutes his gold as if here were the supreme earthly felicity:

> *Open the shrine that I may see my saint,*
> *Hail the world's soul and mine.*

The follies of the other characters are shown in the various ways in which they seek legacies from Volpone. The main agent of the action is Mosca, the cunning servant of Roman comedy, developed almost beyond recognition. The plot structure has a masterly simplicity, and the transference of the scene from Rome to Venice gave it an actuality for contemporary audiences. The comic mood has darkened since the composition of the early plays, and their author now sees his characters as embittered children in a life which is pathological and diseased. To give a little relief to this dark comedy Jonson introduces three English visitors to Venice, all well endowed with 'humours'. In *Epicœne or The Silent Woman* (acted 1609), Jonson returned to something approaching comedy in the more gay sense of the word. The play has farcical elements, such as the marriage of a morose or recluse to a talkative person, in the belief that she is silent, and the later discovery that the marriage is a trick and the 'silent woman' a boy. The sudden dénouement seems to have displeased contemporary audiences, and this, the happiest and most farcical of Jonson's comedies, was not an immediate success. The secret of the silent woman is kept back not only from the spectators but from the other players until the final moment and this seems to have disconcerted the audience. Dryden and Samuel Pepys were later to enjoy the play, which indeed has something of the elegance of the 'manners' comedy cultivated in Restoration period.

Jonson considered deeply the comparative failure of *The Silent Woman* and, recalling the success of *Volpone*, he may have been led to *The Alchemist* (acted 1610, Quarto 1612), the neatest and possibly the best of all his comedies. The play shows three rogues, Subtle, Face and Doll, in possession of the house of Lovewit, who has left London on account of the plague. They pretend to powers of alchemy and magic, and so expose the greed and pretence of a number of clients. The play which opens vigorously with one of the finest rows in Elizabethan literature, works up to a crescendo which is brought to a more genial conclusion than is usual in Jonson's comedy. The unities are easily and naturally maintained, and for its earliest audiences the comedy must have been highly topical. A certain geniality accompanies the action, and Jonson is neither as astringently moral nor satiric here as in a number of the other plays.

From this period of mature comedy Jonson returned after eight years to Senecan tragedy in *Catiline* (performed in 1611, and published in Quarto in 1611; there were a number of later editions in Quarto and it appeared in the Folio of 1616). It was a more severe play than *Sejanus*, and one that by the end of the second act had lost the interest of contemporary audiences. Yet the tragedy attracted wide attention and Jonson himself regarded it as his best achievement in this kind. Its prospects of theatrical success were frustrated by Cicero's very long speech in the fourth act. Jonson was now making the minimum concession to popular taste and, as if he despaired of his audiences, he followed his own conception of Senecan tragedy more rigorously than in *Sejanus*. He introduced the play with a Ghost, and employed choruses between the acts. This rigidity in design, combined with his excessive loyalty to the details of Sallust's accounts and of Cicero's speeches, deprived the play of theatrical effectiveness. What is surprising and unexplained is the attention given to a tragedy, unpopular when first performed. The quarto editions are themselves an evidence of continuing interest and the play itself was revived in 1668, with Nell Gwynn speaking the Prologue.

The comedies of Jonson's last period have had a very varied critical reception, but it is generally agreed that the first of them, *Bartholomew Fair* (acted 1614, Quarto 1631), was one of his happiest and most popular achievements. Jonson, having failed in tragedy constructed on his own principles, seems to go on holiday. It is rather like a seventeenth-century gallery of pictures in a Dickensian manner, though Jonson, belonging to a less squeamish age, is able to indulge in a realism and frankness not permitted to Dickens. The Induction proclaims it as: 'a new sufficient play . . . merry, and as full of noise as sport; made to delight all and offend none'. There is little academic intrusion either in character study or in plot structures; the Puritans are vigorously condemned and the low figures of the Fair most vividly presented. Even to modern audiences the picture still remains crowded and lively, and for Jonson's contemporaries this portrait of Jacobean London must have appealed by its keen verisimilitude. The four comedies which follow have sometimes been described as 'dotages'. I would only affirm a personal opinion that I think they are far better than is usually believed, and that they should be tested on the stage, the only place where a play can be fairly judged. *The Devil is an Ass* (acted 1616) describes the visit of a minor devil to London, and contrives to combine some morality material with adroit and entertaining contemporary satire. *The Staple of News* (acted 1625, Quarto 1631) is a satire on newsmongering, and also on the technical slang and cant language of various groups. Such is its originality and strength that it is difficult to perceive any mental weakening in the author, though probably it will never reach the living stage again. *The New Inn* (acted 1629), is more unequal and was badly received on its first production. Jonson seems to have realized that his work was almost over, for in *The Magnetic Lady* (produced 1632), he brings his 'humours' comedy formally to an end.

Shakespeare and Jonson were obviously aware of each other's achievement, as the prologues to *Every Man in His Humour* and *Henry V* indicate. But apart from some rivalry and a steady determination not to be influenced by one another they seem to have held each other in affection. Jonson is recorded as criticizing Shakespeare's unlearned and rapid methods, but he paid a warm tribute on Shakespeare's death. This was a generous gesture for Shakespeare was obviously more popular with contemporary audiences, and Jonson had a learning which, however acquired, Shakespeare did not possess.

Apart from his plays Jonson showed his theatrical skill in the production of courtly masques. These entertainments, in which nobly-born amateurs, and sometimes royalty itself, played their graceful parts, developed in splendour under the lavishness which the Stuarts expended on the arts that pleased them. Jonson, who could fashion massive, even ponderous, tragedies, seems to have enjoyed these lighter exercises, and in their 'bodily part' he was fortunate in having the collaboration of Inigo Jones. Already in 1605 he had contrived the *Masque of Blackness* in which the Queen and her ladies had appeared. Throughout his career he brought classical learning, lyrical skill and great ingenuity to bear upon this artificial, courtly pleasure. In 1608 there followed the *Masque of Beauty*, prepared by royal command, and others followed, including in 1609 *The Masque of Queens*. The greatness of his achievement lies elsewhere, but the masques, like his odes and lyrics and his critical works, show the versatility of his mind and of his creative genius. His personality is difficult to assess, for it can pass from large and architectural design to light and graceful exercises. Out of the same mind came *Catiline*, *The Alchemist*, the masques; and how he obtained all his knowledge has never been fully explained.

Apart from Shakespeare no one can compare with Jonson in range and power of creative achievement. One of those who shared something of his satiric talent was John Marston (1576–1634). Of this strange personality little is known biographically, though recent years have added to the meagre amount of knowledge available. He was a Shropshire man, graduate of Brasenose College Oxford and a member of the Middle Temple, though from the first he seems to have devoted himself more to literature than to the law. He was a verse satirist before he was engaged in drama and his attack on Jonson prefixed to *The Scourge of Villany*, 1598, led to the feud between the two dramatists. His early work was as a satirist, but it would seem that about 1599 he began writing for the stage. Later he gave up the theatre and entered the Church. One feels that Marston's biography, if the material were available, would be a rewarding study. He brought to the drama some of the savage and satiric aggressiveness which had distinguished his verse in *The Scourge of Villany*. He entered into the quarrels of the players, and he is satirized in a number of Jonson's plays.

His main work in tragedy is *Antonio and Mellida* and *Antonio's Revenge*, a play and its sequel in ten parts, which was acted by 1600, published 1602. This tragedy is on a revenge theme, and it parallels at a number of points incidents and motives in the Hamlet story. Marston has the ghost of a father appearing to a son, a weak mother, a play within a play, and a melancholic view of the worthlessness of life. It has been surmised that Shakespeare was led to re-work an early Hamlet play by Kyd because a play with some elements of the theme by Marston had become popular. As a play Marston's piece will not compare with *Hamlet*, for it is undigested and theatrically unsure. But part of the conception is there and a great deal of the atmosphere. Incidentally it is of interest that Shakespeare went out of his way in *Hamlet* to discuss the controversy of the boy players and the adult actors, and this was a matter in which Marston was deeply involved. Both parts of his tragedy were acted by the Children of Paul's and he made use of the musical accomplishments of his child players. In verse and language Marston belongs to the earlier Elizabethan tradition, and seems ever in danger of straining the verse too far. It may be that Shakespeare had some such thoughts in mind in his comments on verse in *Hamlet* in the player's speech.

Marston has one memorable comedy, *The Malcontent* (published 1604). The play is comedy only in that it avoids a tragic conclusion. Its subject is elaborate intrigue, and its story has something in common with *Measure for Measure*. A banished duke returns to his Court under the name of Malevole. After watching the intrigues and immoral actions of his associates he finds an appropriate moment in which to reveal himself. He is largely a 'humours' character, and this is Marston's study of that malcontent figure found in *Othello* in Iago, and in *The Duchess of Malfi* in Bosola. His anger and contempt spread beyond Pietro who had dispossessed him and the adherents of the corrupt court, as he himself says: 'his highest delight is to procure others vexation, and therein he thinks he truly serves heaven'.

By 1604 Marston had composed his quarrel with Jonson and in 1605 together with Chapman these three contrasting personalities were jointly responsible for the comedy of *Eastward Hoe*. The tone of this piece is much lighter and more genial than that of the plays for which Marston was solely responsible. The play contained references to the Scottish courtiers who had streamed south with James I, and these satiric allusions led to the temporary imprisonment of the writers. *Eastward Hoe* is allied to plays of the citizen type. The characters are presented in Jonson's 'humours' manner and the values are moral. But the whole is conceived more lightheartedly than in Jonson's own work. There are some excellent realistic scenes of Thameside London.

A number of writers had shared with Jonson a desire to bring drama to the English scene. Among them one of the most interesting and successful was Thomas Dekker (1572–1632). Of his life little is known, except that he was born and bred in London, but he had a long career as a dramatist, and much of his work was done in collaboration. Two of his earliest plays, *The Shoemaker's Holiday* and *The Comedy of Old Fortunatus* were published in 1600 and acted before the Queen. *The Shoemaker's Holiday* is admirably contrived in a contemporary setting of citizen life, a little too kindly and romantic one might imagine, yet oddly authentic. Simon Eyre the 'true shoemaker' is one of the most lively figures in Elizabethan comedy: 'Prince am I none, yet am I nobly born, as being the sole son of a shoemaker'. Equally sympathetic are the portraits of Hodge, his foreman, and of Firk, his journeyman, and his concern and affection for them when he finds himself enriched and a Sheriff and well on the way to being Lord Mayor of London. When the King comes to dine he still remembers the members of his trade and as Lord Mayor procures Shrove Tuesday for them as the 'Shoemaker's Holiday'. There are underplots less strong but skilfully contrived in the romantic story of Rose and Lacy. The whole is given a naïve atmosphere and a good-humoured charm. In structure it has a certain rather obvious development, but the scenes are full of effective and amusing touches, and the characterization is strong; the fresh and open geniality of the comedy has won it a permanent place on the stage. All the knowledge which he was to show as a prose writer in his pamphlets, such as *The Seven Deadly Sins of London* (1606), and *The Gull's Horn Book* (1609), seem present in this play. Its romantic realism contrasts with the moral 'humours' comedy of Jonson. The Simon Eyre element Dekker derived from Thomas Deloney's *The Gentle Craft*.

Old Fortunatus (acted by 1600) was in a less realistic manner and here probably Dekker had a collaborator. The origin of the play was a German legend of how Fortunatus, visited by Fortune, was allowed to have a number of his wishes. In the later acts Fortune visits the sons of Fortunatus. Both father and sons fail to please the Goddess and they die. The play has a mixture of motives, at times it is reminiscent of the morality plays and sometimes of Marlowe's *Faustus*. To a modern audience it may seem dull and preposterous and the tragic ending oddly incongruous, but obviously Elizabethan audiences accepted with delight the mixture of mythology, the supernatural and allegory. Despite formlessness it has vigour and some poetry. It appears as an example of an older type of drama living on and competing with newer and more sophisticated forms. In 1602 in *Satiro Mastix* Dekker replied to Jonson's *Poetaster* and the tedious feud of the dramatists, though the main theme is a romance based on a most unhistorical picture of the England of William Rufus.

More ambitious was *The Honest Whore ;* in the first part, printed in 1604, Dekker seems to have had Middleton as a collaborator. The second part, not printed until 1630, would seem to be wholly Dekker's. The play is an example of domestic drama with comedy elements mingled. Heywood's *A Woman Killed with Kindness*, the chief example of the type, to which reference is made below, had been published in 1603. *The Honest Whore*, like all of Dekker's work, has little strength of structure. Its quality is derived from individually effective scenes and from well-defined characters. The Duke of Milan prevents his daughter, Infelice, from marrying the Count Hippolito. Bellafronte, a harlot, makes protestation of love to Hippolito who refuses her, and she repents of the life she has led. By a ruse, at the close, Hippolito marries Infelice. In an unrelated subsidiary plot Candido, an honest citizen, endures the attacks of his shrewish wife and the pranks of the young wits. In the second part Hippolito, now married, tries to seduce Bellafronte, but she repels him. In revenge he almost ruins her. The Candido comic plot is still maintained as an independent theme, nor does the author aim at unity, except that he brings all the characters to Bridewell at the close. Despite its apparent deficiencies the play has strength. Bellafronte is depicted with genuine pathos, for realism and sentimentality seem to strengthen one another in the portrayal of her character. The scenes in her house are some of the most graphic pictures of contemporary life in Elizabethan drama. This is helped in the second part by the very original conception of the character of Matheo, Bellafronte's worthless husband, and of Orlando Friscobaldo, her pathetically faithful father, who serves to solve the complications of the action: Hazlitt in his comment on the play described Friscobaldo as one of the characters who 'raise, revive and give a new zest to our being'. Nothing in Dekker's work equals *The Shoemaker's Holiday* and the best parts of *The Honest Whore*, yet he wrote a number of other plays either alone or in collaboration. They illustrate the variety of taste and achievement which Elizabethan and Jacobean audiences would tolerate in the drama. *The Whore of Babylon* (published 1607, and acted in the same year) was historical allegory with Elizabeth, as Titania, contrasted with the Papacy, as abusively described in the title.

In the survey of Jonson and Dekker the tradition of basing plays on contemporary and realistic scenes has already been noted. Shakespeare had chosen another way, and although his drama is thronged with contemporary figures the scene itself in the comedies is normally set outside England. In the seventeenth century both these methods had their adherents. Beaumont and Fletcher, as will appear later, were to construct a tragi-comedy and tragedy on scenes which were far removed from any contemporary reality. On the other hand a number of writers, both in comedy and in tragedy, showed the domestic scene not too far detached from the background of their audience's life.

The theme of infidelity committed in a circle where the responsibilities are solely domestic had not been a motive that interested Shakespeare, but its popularity is shown by the appearance of an early work, *Arden of Feversham* (published 1592), and attempts have been made to ascribe this piece to Shakespeare. A play of no exceptional merit, it yet contrives to tell clearly its story of the murder of Arden by his wife Alice because of her love for Mosbie. Much of the play is concerned with unsuccessful attempts at this murder, and the culmination lies in its execution. Up to the moment of her final, and rather unreal, repentance, Alice's character is well conceived. She is outlined as a strong personality, very certain of her hatred for her husband and of her love for Mosbie, very passionate and direct, and a welcome contrast to the indeterminate women who appear in some of the later tragedies. A similar play of later date was *A Yorkshire Tragedy* (about 1606, printed 1608), a short piece which dealt with the Calverley murder.

The main practitioner of domestic drama was Thomas Heywood (b. between 1573–5, died 1633). Of his biography little is known: his father seems to have been a Lincolnshire clergyman, and he was educated at Cambridge before he came to the world of the theatre in London, where he was an actor as well as a playwright. He was a prolific writer, as he himself affirmed in the address to the reader in *The English Traveller* (1633), where he wrote: 'one reserved amongst two hundred and twenty, in which I have had either an entire hand or at least a main finger'. Apart from drama he translated Sallust and wrote a vast poem in seventeen cantos, *Troia Britannica*. His career was typical of the dramatic journeyman working rapidly in a great variety of styles. In his preface to *The Fair Maid of The West* (1631), he spoke with contempt of the dramatists who took pains over the publication of their plays, and particularly he seemed contemptuous of Ben Jonson's elaborately prepared Folio of 1616. 'My plays', he wrote, 'have not been exposed to the public view of the world in numerous sheets and a large volume'.

Probably the earliest of his extant plays was *The Four Prentices* (1600, Quarto 1615), which is one of the extravagant citizen plays attacked later by Beaumont and Fletcher in *The Knight of the Burning Pestle*. In it the crusades are adapted to citizen heroics. There followed a great variety of plays of various types, history, adventure, comedy, farce, with themes both classical and modern. Of all these hybrid pieces one of the most vigorous is the two part play, *The Fair Maid of the West* (published 1631). Elizabethan adventuring has now replaced the Crusades, and the audience follows the fortunes of Captain Spencer, who is in love with Bess Bridges, the tavern maid. The wild and improbable action which follows was enjoyed in its own day by a royal audience, but is never likely to see the stage again. It shows the absence of design, and the readiness of the audience to accept very uneven material. When all seems to be over a new set of adventures, including a shipwreck, begins; all of which as A. W. Ward commented, 'must have gone near to surfeit even an Elizabethan audience.'[1]

Out of all this dramatic activity Heywood's most individual contribution remains in domestic tragedy and in the domestic problem play, with *A Woman Killed with Kindness* (1603, printed 1607) as his outstanding contribution; and a play of great popularity as shown by the reference in the third edition of 1617, 'as it hath been oftentimes acted by the Queen's Men'. Frankford permits an impecunious friend, Wendoll, to stay in his house. Wendoll seduces Frankford's wife and this Frankford discovers. In the usual heroic or tragic drama, as in *Othello*, Frankford would have killed both his wife and her lover. Here instead, pitying his wife, he sends her to live in seclusion on one of his estates and there she dies in his presence. Heywood is less interested in the motives which lead to the infidelity than in the results which arise from repentance. He is more occupied by Frankford's strange and morbid mercy than by the love of Wendoll and Alice. This leads to a naïve and elementary presentation of the character of Wendoll, who is made to expose himself in a series of declamatory and narrative speeches. There are fewer stranger speeches in Elizabethan drama than Frankford's response to his wife's repentance:

> *As freely, from the low depth of my soul,*
> *As my Redeemer hath forgiven his death,*
> *I pardon thee, I will shed tears for thee, pray with thee*
> *And in mere pity of thy weak estate*
> *I'll wish to die with thee.*

Such speeches leave the way wide open to the sentimental drama of the eighteenth century. In contrast to Wendoll, the character of Frankford is revealed with some psychological insight. Heywood from his prologue seems to be conscious that he is attempting something fresh in drama:

> *Look for no glorious state, our muse is bent*
> *Upon a barren subject, a bare scene.*

Heywood's other attempt in this domestic drama, *The English Traveller*, was printed as late as 1633, but was composed at a very

[1] *Cambridge History of English Literature*, Vol. VI.

much earlier date. A young traveller returning home falls in love with the wife of a friend, an old man, who has been good to him. He refuses, however, to compromise the lady. Meanwhile an unfaithful young gallant seduces the wife and some of the blame attaches to the young traveller. The wife repents and dies. Again one has the impression that Heywood is not interested in giving adequate motives to the action. For him the attraction lies in the moral dilemma of his characters and in the sentiment aroused by the contemplation of their suffering and their repentance. With all its inadequacies Heywood had established a drama nearer to the lives and interests of many of his audience than romantic tragedy and tragi-comedy could ever be. In the decades of the seventeenth century which precede the closing of the theatre other types of drama were on the whole to be more popular, but in the eighteenth century the bourgeois interests represented by domestic drama would again prevail. In its own age it seems to belong to a different world from that of Chapman, Webster, Beaumont and Fletcher, and Tourneur.

George Chapman (1559–1634) is one of the most individual and learned of the writers for the theatre. His life was a long one, for he had in his younger days completed Marlowe's *Hero and Leander* and he lived on to be a collaborator in the fourth decade of the seventeenth century with James Shirley. Though his major contribution lies in tragedy, he was a versatile composer of comedies and had gained success with *The Blind Beggar of Alexandria* as early as 1596. How varied is his talent can be seen by comparing *The Gentleman Usher* (printed 1606), a theme of romantic tragi- comedy, and *The Old Joiner of Aldgate* (acted 1602), which is based on a sordid contemporary scandal over a marriage lawsuit. Though the play is not extant Professor Charles Sisson has established its plot from the records of legal proceedings. In *The Gentleman Usher* he can ascend to elevated passages, as when the heroine Margaret, to escape an enforced marriage, proposes a platonic relationship with Vicentio her official lover's son:

> *Are not the laws of God and Nature more*
> *Than formal laws of men? are outward rites*
> *More virtuous than the very substance is*
> *Of holy nuptials solemnized within?*

This may be preposterous but it is so in an elevated way. In *The Old Joiner of Aldgate*, he seems prepared to sell his talent to a disappointed suitor, as if he were a hack journalist.

Of Chapman's life little is known, but active though he was in the theatre, his whole energies were not thus absorbed. He had early conceived the highest admiration for Homer: 'Of all books extant in all kinds, Homer is the first and best'. He began the publication of his translation of the *Iliad* in 1598 and concluded it in 1611. The *Odyssey* followed and in 1616 the two poems were published together in Folio. Unlike Homer though Chapman's translation may be, it is in itself a great poem, as Keats discovered, while Chapman had himself confessed that it was 'an absurd affectation in the interpretation of any author to turn him word for word'.

Some have seen in Chapman the 'rival' poet of Shakespeare's sonnets, and it is possible that in the disputes of the players Shakespeare and Chapman found themselves on different sides. Jonson thought well of Chapman's work, particularly his masques. Indeed, he considered the masques of Chapman and Fletcher as comparable with his own. Chapman was, with Jonson, the most learned of the dramatists and his mood was far from Shakespeare's ever improvising genius. He is an uneven writer, but one of great energy and power. He came to the drama late in his career, for he was forty when he began writing comedies in 1596, and these are his main dramatic output for a decade. Earlier criticism has inclined to ignore these plays, but recently ample justice has been done to this side of his genius. He seemed capable of a wide range, from theatrical reportage to an anticipation of Jonson's 'humours' comedy in *A Humorous Day's Mirth* (1597: printed 1599) or the comedy and romance of such a play as *Monsieur D'Olive* (published 1606). It is indeed difficult to discover in these plays the rugged powers of Chapman the translator and tragic poet.

Some reputation as a writer of tragedies he had as early as 1598, but his main achievement lies in the years from 1603 to 1613. Here he produced tragedies, which were original in conception and method, and unlike anything else in his age. The most notable were: *Bussy D'Ambois* (acted 1604); *The Revenge of Bussy D'Ambois* (acted about 1611); and *The Tragedy of Byron* (acted 1608). He employed themes derived and elaborated from nearly contemporary French history, mingling characters of his own invention with historical figures. Though he is to some extent indebted to Seneca in his employment of ghosts and messengers, the general design of the tragedy is neither Senecan nor Shakespearian. If he owed any debt it is rather to the arrogant protagonist developed in Marlowe's tragedies. In *Bussy D'Ambois*, basing his scene on the court of Henry III, he portrays the love of the adventurer, Bussy, for Tamyra, wife of the Count of Montsurry, and the death of Bussy which follows when Montsurry takes his revenge. The play had some success on the stage, mainly for the bold way in which Bussy's character is struck forth, for he has the same gesture of magnificence and ambition as is to be found in Marlowe's figures. Chapman combines violence and melodrama with rhetoric and passages of finely composed reflective poetry.

In *The Revenge of Bussy D'Ambois* there is a less conclusive plot based on a variation of the revenge theme. Clermont D'Ambois, a brother of the dead Bussy and a character of Chapman's invention, achieves the death of Montsurry and his own suicide. The ghost of Bussy stalks the stage, aggressively, as if he has as much right to be there as any of the living characters; and it is he, like Hamlet's father, who stirs up the call to revenge; the play, in fact, shows a number of influences from *Hamlet*. *The Conspiracy and Tragedy of Byron* is a continuous piece in ten acts. The theme again follows French history. The plot, like that of *Coriolanus*, is the story of a proud and ambitious man. It is as if Chapman had looked back at the figure of Tamburlaine and contemplated the whole theme of power again, but more philosophically. The verse has great eloquence and the thought is profound, unfortunately the dramatic skill is not adequate to the mind that lies behind the play. It has been said that here is an epic in ten acts, rather than a drama. Yet this is probably Chapman's greatest achievement; and a considerable one.

The plays of Chapman do not seem good stage plays, but as they are never seen in the modern theatre it is impossible to judge them in the only way that ultimately matters. Shakespeare was able to give poetry and a good stage play, for his poetry, even when most exuberant, was at the service of his drama. Chapman at his worst approaches some nineteenth-century dramatists who feel that a play can live by its poetry alone. His language, though magnificent, is often obscure and possesses a certain 'monotonous eloquence'.

Swinburne, who wrote one of his best essays on Chapman, contrasts his obscurity with that of Browning. In Browning the obscurity often arises because the poet is thinking too quickly, but Chapman's obscurity depends upon a certain confusion in his massive and original thought, 'the treasure hidden beneath the dark gulfs and crossing currents of his rocky and weedy waters'. It is difficult to believe that any audience in the theatre was able to understand the complexities of the involved and elliptical sentences in which his rhetoric is contained. Dryden, who belonged to an age that sought strenuously for clarity, condemned Chapman's language, but this is unjust, for there is a nobility in both the language and thought, a fury in the eloquence, and each idea as it arises in the author's mind seems decked and expanded by almost unending comparisons. It is as if one who possessed all the ingenuity of a metaphysical poet had determined to write verse for the theatre. Of particular injustice is Dryden's attack on *Bussy D'Ambois*: 'I have sometimes wondered in the reading what has become of those glaring colours which amazed me in *Bussy D'Ambois* upon the theatre; but when I had taken up what I supposed a fallen star, I found I had been cozened with jelly; nothing but a cold dull mass, which glittered no longer than it was shooting; a dwarfish thought, dressed up in gigantic words, repetition in abundance, looseness of expression, and gross hyperboles; the sense of one line expanded prodigiously into ten; and to sum up all, incorrect English, and a hideous mingle of false poetry and true nonsense, or at best, a scantling of wit, which lay gasping for life and groaning beneath a heap of rubbish'. Some of this is fair if harsh comment on Chapman but much more is it illustrative of the great barrier that divided the imagination of Dryden and the eighteenth century from that of their predecessors.

The personality revealed in the tragedies is a noble one. Chapman had a high ideal for the human mind, and this he attempted to express in tragedy. It can be found in the dedication to *The Revenge*: 'material instruction, elegant and sententious excitation to virtue and deflection from her contrary, being the soul, limbs and limits of authentical tragedy'. Chapman's view that man is capable of nobility and high-mindedness is comparable to that found in Wordsworth's *The Happy Warrior*. Against that conception of nobility his mind dwelt with the conception of power and the quest for human greatness. Though these are developed dramatically much of their treatment comes in passages which read like essays in verse. Shakespeare used that method, as in Ulysses' speech on 'degree' in *Troilus and Cressida*, but he was sparing in its employment and he attempted to relate it to the action. Chapman, guided often by memories of Seneca, Epictetus, and Horace, is apt to allow philosophical reflection to take an excessive place. This style he followed in the series of tragedies, and in the non-dramatic poems. In the comedies, the style has a greater directness and clarity.

Among the early seventeenth-century dramatists one of the strangest and most individual is Cyril Tourneur. Of his life little is known. He was probably born between 1570 and 1580. The earliest record of him is the publication of his poem in 1600, the *Transformed Metamorphosis*. His plays belong to his middle period and then in the later part of his career he was involved in a number of duties which touched affairs of State at a subordinate level. He was entrusted to carry Government papers. For some unknown reason he was imprisoned and released on Sir Edward Cecil's guarantee. He was at Cadiz on Sir Edward Cecil's unhappy expedition of 1625 and died in the next year. His reputation rests on two plays, *The Atheist's Tragedy: or the Honest Man's Revenge*, 'as in diverse places it hath often been acted' (c. 1608, published 1611), and *The Revenger's Tragedy* (acted 1607, and published in the same year though without Tourneur's name, but assigned to him in a list of plays made in 1656). There has been much dispute about the authorship of this play but its general spirit conforms so closely to *The Atheist's Tragedy* that it would seem reasonable to assign it to Tourneur. In date Tourneur is a little earlier than Webster, and he is before Fletcher, Ford and Shirley who are considered in the next chapter. Yet he seems by his spirit to belong to the latest mood in Stuart drama. He has something of that strange atmosphere which is to appear later in Middleton's *The Changeling*. Tourneur's mind seems pitiless, and his cruel world is one into which normality is never permitted to intrude. Unlike Webster, he never relents towards his tormented characters. Dramatically and poetically *The Revenger's Tragedy* is much more able than *The Atheist's Tragedy*. A number of theories have been constructed to place *The Revenger's Tragedy* second, but there is no satisfactory evidence.

The Atheist's Tragedy opens with a brilliant first scene in which D'Amville expounds his philosophy to his instrument Borachio. His aim is to help his nephew Charlemont to the wars so that in his absence he may kill Charlemont's father and help his own sons to wealth. The plot becomes involved after this direct start, and scenes which are filled with violence and horror move in rapid succession. D'Amville finally loses his sons and is himself killed by the axe which was meant to bring Charlemont to his death. Amid all the melodrama and the terror the audience are made to feel the presence of a contemplative mind which surveys this evil world, believes in its existence, and seeks out its meaning.

The Revenger's Tragedy is a more powerful play. Professor Allardyce Nicoll, who has prepared the most satisfactory edition of Tourneur, draws attention to the excellence of the opening. Vindice, holding in his hand the skull of the woman he loved, whom the ancient Duke had violated, swears to be revenged, not only on the Duke, but on his son Lussurio, his bastard Spurio, and the Duchess. From that opening there follows a succession of scenes of horror and death that involves all the characters. Yet Tourneur contrives to give the impression that this is no melodramatic holocaust, but a poetic view of the world, of a cruel, diseased, lecherous, revengeful world, from which there is no escape, and in the midst of which there is no pity. It is this originality of vision that dominates all the absurd details of plot and the violence of the melodrama. As C. E. Vaughan wrote:[1] 'it is as a poet that Tourneur claims our attention: a poet whose imagination is poisoned by the sense of universal vanity and corruption, but who lights up this festering material with flashes of high genius, and who is capable, at rare moments, of rising to visions of true beauty and even of grace'.

[1] *Cambridge History of English Literature*, vol. vi, chapter vii.

CHAPTER EIGHT

John Webster - Beaumont and Fletcher - Philip Massinger Thomas Middleton - William Rowley John Ford - James Shirley

IT IS difficult to mark precisely the division between the drama of Shakespeare and his contemporaries and that of the following age. In the early work of Shakespeare and Jonson there is an awareness of a moral world, and an acceptance that normal standards exist, even though individual characters may depart far from them; all of this becomes less apparent in the later Jacobean drama. Yet technically, and in other ways, some of Shakespeare's later plays, such as *Cymbeline*, differ profoundly from the comedies and histories of his early period, and belong more to the later tradition. There is a continuous development throughout the first four decades of the seventeenth century, with, as its most marked feature, an increase in sophistication, and in theatrical as opposed to natural emphasis. The stage is a private one, closed-in, and the action is devised for audiences where complexity of intrigue is of far greater importance than any moral issue. In its later phases this theatre explores situations and passions that are removed from normality.

Some of the dramatists here discussed differ little in values and methods from those explored in the previous chapter, and to that degree all divisions are unsatisfactory. Yet the reader or the audience in the theatre, familiar only with Shakespeare's work, would certainly be aware of a marked change of atmosphere on coming to the plays of John Webster and those of Beaumont and Fletcher. It is with the appearance of their plays, and those of their successors, therefore, that a new phase in the drama can be definitely defined, though it could be urged that there is little to divide Webster from

Tourneur. John Webster (1575–1625), was a marked contrast to Chapman, for instead of a verbal and reflective complexity, which appeared in Chapman's most distinctive tragedies, and often seemed untheatrical, Webster showed himself in two of his tragedies such a master of the stage that his plays, whenever adequately presented, gain the interest of modern audiences. The whole of Webster's dramatic achievement is difficult to define. He began as a collaborator, but about the year 1612 he produced two tragedies of outstanding individuality and power: *The White Devil* (about 1610–12, published 1612, and later known as *Vittoria Corombona*) and *The Duchess of Malfi* (acted before 1614 and published 1623 'as acted privately at Blackfriars and publicly at the Globe'). His other plays nowhere attain the compelling poetic and dramatic quality of these tragedies. The nearest approach is his *The Devil's Law Case* (written c. 1620, published in 1623), but despite its dramatic adroitness it is negligible in comparison with the two main works. These two tragedies have some similarities: they are both based on Italian themes and the plots are loosely connected with events which happened in sixteenth-century Italy. Love and revenge are the motives in both plays, and behind them, governing the action and illuminated by the verse, is a world, cruel, passionate, irrational, fierce; a view of life which is never far removed from magnificence or corruption. The strange thing is that while Webster worked in the theatre for some twenty years he should have had this singular rise from mediocrity only in two plays.

The White Devil is based on a series of incidents connected with the life of Paolo Giordano, Duke of Brachiano, and is related to events that took place in the early fifteen-eighties, in Webster's lifetime. The story was well-known and widely circulated in a number of versions. Presumably Webster must have had one precise source, but it is unknown. In the tragedy, as he conceives it, Brachiano, the Duke, falls in love with Vittoria Corombona, wife of Camillo who is nephew of Cardinal Monticelso. The motives of the action lie largely with Vittoria. She has a 'dream' through which she is able to suggest to Brachiano that he shall kill his wife and her husband; and, once conceived, the intrigue is helped by her brother Flamineo, a Machiavellian character. The audience is not spared the horrors of these deaths, for Brachiano through a conjurer has an image of the intricate devices by which they are accomplished built up before him. There follows the trial of Vittoria, a scene to which Webster devotes his whole range of poetical and dramatic skill. She becomes the centre of the action, and so, despite a multiplicity of episodes, she remains to the end. She meets tempestuously, and with a grand gesture, the retribution of the crimes which she initiated. The scene is written with that stormy intensity which characterizes so much of Webster's poetry. The Cardinal who should have been her judge becomes her accuser, and she answers him with an undaunted courage. This movement in the play is resolved by Brachiano's rescue of Vittoria, whom he marries. Webster, having exhausted the motives with which his play began, now regroups his characters for a new crisis. Brachiano develops a jealousy of Vittoria, whom he taunts, and she in reply still shows a defiant anger and courage, though it contains elements of retrospective sadness. Thus the tragedy moves to its climax in which revenge and accident so overwhelm the characters that at the close all are killed. It could be urged that the plot is not skilfully presented: it has the ordering of a narrative rather than a drama, but all this becomes irrelevant as the tragedy is successful on the stage. Sometimes the characters seem inconsistent, motiveless, and yet this adds to the power and intensity of Webster's tragic world.

In *The Duchess of Malfi*, a more mature and less violent play, Webster was using a widely popular story which had been told by Bandello and Belleforest and in English by William Painter. The Duchess, a wealthy widow, secretly marries her steward, Antonio. Her brothers, Ferdinand and the Cardinal, are opposed to any remarriage. Their motives are confused, for they wish to retain her wealth, and they are fearful that she may marry beneath her, while Ferdinand has a feeling towards her that, at times, amounts to a sinister passion. The centre of the action lies in Bosola, an evil and melancholic figure, who, with a mind corrupt and disappointed, sees the whole of life as a thing diseased. He acts as Ferdinand's spy and gives the lovers away. The punishment of the Duchess is contrived with severity and horror. She is tortured and finally strangled and her children are killed. As in the earlier play the ultimate catastrophe overwhelms all the characters including Bosola, who is made to feel a bitter remorse before his death.

The summary of the plots gives no true impression of Webster's power. In bare narrative, they seem baldly melodramatic, and improbability competes with violence. But Webster's sombre spirit, aided by his poetic powers, raises them from melodrama to tragedy. Such is his genius that his characters do not move as in a story, but in this strange, cruel, irrational world which is peculiarly his own. Bosola is the clearest spokesman of that world, for he sees life to be diseased and men and women helpless puppets incapable of steady or reasonable action. This view of life is ultimately philosophical, though Webster supports it with scenes of mechanical horror, such as that of the conjurer in *The White Devil*, or of the dance of the madmen in *The Duchess of Malfi*. Rupert Brooke, in his essay on Webster, emphasized the force and consistency of this vision behind the tragedies: 'Maggots are what the inhabitants of this Universe most suggest and resemble. The sight of their power is only alleviated by the permanent, calm, unfriendly summits and darkness of the background of death and doom. For that is part of Webster's universe. Human beings are writhing grubs in an immense night. And the night is without stars or moon. But it has sometimes a certain quietude in its darkness: but not very much'. Webster's profoundly moving poetic power is more strongly operative in this tragedy than in *The White Devil*. Such are Bosola's lines to the Duchess, when he is tormenting her:

> *Hark, now everything is still—*
> *The screech-owl, and the whistler shrill,*
> *Call upon our Dame, aloud,*
> *And bid her quickly don her shroud.*
> *Much you had of land and rent,*
> *Your length in clay's now competent.*

There follows Webster's supreme line when Ferdinand sees the body of the dead Duchess:

> *Cover her face: Mine eyes dazel: she died young.*

There is in Webster little smooth development of action, little design. He is less interested in the plot as a whole than in the great dramatic scene, and he is less occupied by any subtle presentation of character than in exploiting some moment of great passion. His plays are apt to become a series of theatrically effective crises, bound together by action which at its worst is carelessly contrived. This apparently haphazard development lends a certain brutal force to the tragedies, as if life itself were governed by chance, not reason, and as if human beings acted from passion rather than from consistent conduct governed by consecutive thought. Yet this will not explain all, for some of the coincidences, improbabilities, and forced effects, are weaknesses and excesses of dramatic structure and are apparent as such in the theatre. Yet such defects gain abundant compensation in the overwhelming tragic effect to which Webster's vision as a poet makes a major contribution. Thus the moving lines given to the Duchess:

> *I'll tell thee a miracle;*
> *I am not mad yet, to my cause of sorrow;*
> *The heaven o'er my head seems made of molten brass,*
> *The earth of flaming sulphur, yet I am not mad.*
> *I am acquainted with sad misery*
> *As the tann'd galley-slave is with his oar;*
> *Necessity makes me suffer constantly,*
> *And custom makes it easy.*

The moral world of Webster is different from that of Shakespeare. Here love is the sole theme of tragedy, and evil, though it meets retribution, is present everywhere throughout the action. Webster's power lies in the sense of magnificence which accompanies the evil, gaining its supreme illustration in *The White Devil*. Brutal as her world may be, and corrupt as are her motives, Vittoria's audacity and dignity give to her life some great gesture even if it lacks virtue and nobility. In the lyrics, which act as it were as a symbol of the mood behind the tragedies, Webster seems to suggest the piteousness of life, though he never weakens into sentiment nor relaxes from his vision that violence, corruption and passion are inevitable.

In the later years of Shakespeare's dramatic career there appeared two writers, John Fletcher (1579–1625), and Francis Beaumont (1584–1616), both of great competence, and they are found frequently working together in happy collaboration. Their clever and sophisticated romantic tragedies and tragi-comedies captured popular taste, and Shakespeare in such a play as *Cymbeline* would seem to have imitated them. A contrary view has been advanced that, in fact, Shakespeare led the fashion and that Beaumont and Fletcher followed, but to this I find it difficult to subscribe. They came, rather, as brilliant purveyors for a narrow society that had elements of moral decadence along with its enjoyment of wit. Shakespeare, for all his bawdiness, may well have felt himself out of place in this world and he was sensitive enough to realize that a new fashion had arisen. Dryden summarizes the contemporary view in his comparison of Beaumont and Fletcher with Shakespeare: 'they understood and imitated the conversations of gentlemen much better, whose wild debaucheries and quickness of wit in repartees no poet can ever paint as they have done'.

Fletcher is the more prolific and the longer lived. His association with Beaumont seems to have begun about 1607 and to have continued to 1616. He also wrote independently, and with Massinger and others. Beaumont died when he was thirty-two, but he had already combined with Fletcher, in a dominating way, in a number of plays. Though in their own age held in high esteem, and much admired by such a sensitive critic as Dryden, and for a century compared with Jonson and Shakespeare, they have failed to make any impact on the theatre of our own time. The very bulk of their work is a little disconcerting for the Folio of 1679 contains fifty-two plays. That they met so exactly the taste of their time may explain to some extent their subsequent falling off.

They were both of good but not prosperous families; Fletcher's father was a bishop of London and Beaumont's one of the Queen's Justices of Common Pleas. They met in London as young bachelors, and began to exploit the private closed-in theatres which gave so many more opportunities for elaborate scenery and machines than the open theatre in which Shakespeare had begun his career. They had both attempted plays separately, though without success, before they collaborated in *Philaster*. Beaumont had composed between 1607–10 the clever but not very successful drama of *The Knight of the Burning Pestle* (published 1613), while Fletcher had produced a brilliant adventure in the poetic pastoral play, which contemporary audiences entirely rejected, *The Faithful Shepherdess* (acted 1608–9).

The Knight of the Burning Pestle owes its origin to the Don Quixote of Cervantes, and is a mock-heroic play, parodying many fashions in the theatre, particularly the 'citizen' plays of Dekker and Heywood. The prologue gives the temper of the acting. A citizen complains that citizens are not depicted respectfully on the stage, and that if Ralph, his apprentice, were given a suit of clothes he could do great deeds. So it is arranged that Ralph shall be a character in the play and the citizen and his wife spectators of the action. Ralph's adventures are in part a parody of the chivalrous romances, and Ralph himself satirizes all baseness dressed up in magnificent pseudo-heroic trappings. Apart from this the play is full of memories taken from many sources, including Kyd's *Spanish Tragedy*, while in the plot of Jasper, the apprentice who marries his master's daughter, the values of the romantic plays are effectively satirized.

The Faithful Shepherdess belongs to a very different world. Fletcher makes use of the idealized conventions of the pastoral for a graceful poetic play in which through a complicated intrigue all types of love are revealed. The main theme is the love of Amoret, the faithful shepherdess, for Perigot, while the opening motive in which Clorin, a Shepherdess, laments her dead love and is tempted by a satyr, is very similar to the theme used later by Milton in *Comus*. Against these are placed the sensual Amaryllis, and the lust of Amaryllis and the Sensual Shepherd. Fletcher's verse has very distinct qualities. He uses an eleven-syllable line with frequent feminine endings, that is, endings on an unaccented syllable. A typical example from *The Faithful Shepherdess* is:

> '*And wanton shepherds be to me delightful*'.

This effect is to produce a blank verse less regular than that of many of his predecessors, but very lively. It has a natural effect, and is nearer to conversation than declamation. He can be regular, and at times careless. His language is less compressed than that of Shakespeare, nor does it seem to bear the same pressure of thought. Charles Lamb has described the difference effectively: 'Fletcher lays line upon line, making up one after the other, adding image to image so deliberately that we see where they join. Shakespeare mingles everything: he runs line into line, embraces sentences and metaphors; before one idea has burst its shell another is hatched and clamorous for disclosure'. Though the play has few and only superficial relations to Guarini's *Il Pastor Fido* (1585), Fletcher, as his preface shows, is thinking of his pastoral in the terms of tragi-comedy: 'in respect it wants deaths, which is enough to make it no tragedy, yet brings some near it, which is enough to make it no comedy'. In a number of ways this charming, artificial, and unsuccessful play foreshadows the plays, the moods of tragi-comedy with which in collaboration the two authors were to gain their later successes. In *Cupid's Revenge* (1607–12), in which Beaumont may have had some share, Fletcher was to continue with a preoccupation with some of the themes of *The Faithful Shepherdess*, deriving his plot, in part, from Sidney's *Arcadia*.

One of the earliest and most successful of their tragi-comedies was *Philaster* (1609–10). The play has an ingenious plot, newly conceived by the authors, though some of the scenes are reminiscent of scenes in Shakespearian tragedy and comedy. Philaster, the rightful heir to the throne of Sicily, is allowed the freedom of the Court by the usurping king. He is loved by this king's daughter, Arethusa, and she is betrothed to Pharamond, a prince of Spain. There are well-contrived scenes, early in the play, in which Arethusa declares her love for Philaster. The lovers decide to use as a go-between a page, Bellario, who is in fact a girl, Euphrasia. She is in love with Philaster and employs this disguise so that she may be near him. From this basis an elaborate superstructure of misunderstandings and complexities is evolved, all of which are fully exploited. At the conclusion, which is unnatural and complicated, Philaster and Arethusa marry. The play had certain features which remain common to the whole type. For instance, the scene was removed from reality, and many of its motives were as in the sphere of romantic comedy, despite the fact that the situations themselves were presented with tragic seriousness. There was little characterization, but much ingenuity in incident, and many excellent individual scenes, well contrived theatrically. It is as if error and accident were competing to place the characters in complex and embarrassing situations, as if the world of *Cymbeline*, whose motives belong to romantic comedy, were dignified into tragedy. The characters have no individual strength, but exist for the scenes in which they occur, and when, at the conclusion, they fall outside the overcrowded pattern of the dénouement, they are ignored as if they had never existed. Something is owing to Fletcher's pastoral convention, worked out into more human terms, however remote, and there is much elegance in the verse and clever devising of the plot. One can see what Swinburne meant when he described this as 'the loveliest though not the loftiest of tragic plays which we owe to the comrades or successors of Shakespeare'.

A King and No King (performed 1611, published 1619) followed a similar pattern. The scene was set in Iberia, an unreal country with characters possessing equally unreal names, a gesture still to the pastoral convention. The theme again is ingenious, invented and unnatural. Arbaces, the King of Iberia, conquers Tigranes, King of Armenia, and offers him noble treatment and his sister for a wife. Tigranes' affections are already committed to Spaconia, one of his own fellow countrywomen. Arbaces, owing to his long campaigns, has not seen his sister Panthea for a long time, but when he catches sight of her he is seized with an incestuous passion. Tigranes too, forgetting his own lady, falls in love with Panthea. Arbaces, in anger for this, throws Tigranes into prison, where he repents and is visited by Spaconia, who forgives him. Later it is discovered that Arbaces is the son of the Lord Protector and Panthea is not his sister, so that the way of their love is open. The play has many features which distinguish it from Shakespeare's tragic world. The theme is a dangerous one and handled so as to emphasize its unnatural elements, while the tragedy is resolved not by death but by artifice. The characterization is indistinct, and indeed the interest depends rather on the ingenuity of incident than on the firmness of character portrayal.

In *The Maid's Tragedy* (1610–11), the authors face a tragic conclusion in a play which retains some of the atmosphere of *Philaster*. It is as if tragi-comedy had been adapted to the revenge play, and it must be admitted that the motives are stronger and more natural than in the other plays of this group. The king (of Rhodes this time, but all these are theatrical kingdoms), commands a gentleman, Amintor, to marry Evadne. After the marriage, Amintor discovers that Evadne has been mistress to the king. Complex and elaborate action follows, but, in the conclusion, Evadne kills the king and then takes her own life. Here the whole action is more consistent, at least in its main plot, and the marriage is not such a blatant device as the elements which start the action in the other plays.

Among the dramatists associated with Fletcher was Philip Massinger (1583–1639). He was educated at Oxford but left without a degree and then disappeared into the theatre world of London. His dramatic work suggests that he had a stubborn and independent spirit, and more than once he was in trouble with the authorities for the too-candid expression of political views in his plays. His early work was in collaboration, mainly with Fletcher and Dekker. With Fletcher he wrote 'humours' comedy, such as *The Little French Lawyer* (about 1619), with a more liberal movement of intrigue than in Jonson. He also wrote with Fletcher *The Spanish Curate* (about 1622), which has lively and ingenious scenes. He collaborated again with Fletcher in tragedy, and here the contrast of their natures becomes apparent, for Fletcher was easy, gracious and immoral, while Massinger had a religious and ultimately a moral outlook. From Fletcher he learned an adroitness in dramatic arrangement but throughout, while he carries a number of reminiscences from other writers, he maintains a great independence of spirit. Among the tragedies in which Massinger combined with Fletcher were *Thierry and Theodoret* (printed 1623), an elaborate but not very effective play on a sixth-century theme; and *The False One*, based on the love of Cæsar and Cleopatra. Massinger wrote other tragedies, some in collaboration and some independently. With Dekker he wrote *The Virgin Martyr* (before 1620), a play on the persecution of the Christians under Diocletian. It would seem most probable that the main conception came from Massinger, for he had a strong religious interest. Despite its popularity the tragedy lacks any effectiveness that could give it a permanent hold. It is a horror drama in a Roman setting, and possibly Dekker supplied only the rather poor comic relief.

Massinger emerged as an independent writer in *The Renegado* (about 1624). The play is one of complex and incredible adventure, set in Tunis and with a mixture of Catholics and infidels. The central character, who brings the various actions together, is the Jesuit, Francisco, and the strange thing is that Massinger is able, when anti-Catholic feeling ran so high, to make him a sympathetic figure. Apart from this fantastic tragi-comedy, Massinger wrote independently in tragedy and in comedy. In tragedy he contrived three plays which lie between the work of Shakespeare and Webster and the more decadent school of Tourneur, Ford and Shirley. In *The Unnatural Combat* (1623) he employs the themes of parricide and incest in a free treatment of the Cenci story, a theme which had an historical reality some twenty years before the composition of Massinger's tragedy. In *The Duke of Milan* (printed 1623) the death of one of the characters is contrived by the fact that the face of a dead woman had poison placed on it. The most impressive of these tragedies is *The Roman Actor* (1626). The play is set in the reign of Domitian, and the main character is the actor, Paris. Here, while there is horror and an atmosphere of decadence, one is aware also of elements not present in the other plays. The final movement depends on the murder of Paris by Domitian, jealous because of his wife's infidelity with the actor. Outstanding in this tragedy is Paris's plea for the art of the actor and of the theatre. One can imply that whatever scenes of horror he may display the moralist is never far from Massinger's mind. The stage must portray the world and the audience brings into the theatre from life itself the evil that it finds there displayed:

> *When we present*
> *An heir that does conspire against the life*
> *Of his dear parent, numbering every hour*
> *He lives, as tedious to him; if there be,*
> *Among the auditors, one whose conscience tells him*
> *He is of the same world, we cannot help it.*

On the other hand, Paris affirms that the actor displays virtue more effectively than the philosopher:

> *If there is*
> *Virtue and valour in the commonwealth*
> *Actors may put in for as large a share*
> *As all the sects of the philosophers:*
> *They with cold precepts (perhaps seldom read)*
> *Deliver what an honourable thing*
> *The active virtue is; but does that fire*
> *The blood, or swell the veins with emulation,*
> *To be both good and great, equal to that*
> *Which is presented in our theatres.*

Massinger thought *The Roman Actor* was the best of his plays, ('the most perfect birth of my Minerva'), and the directness and strength of the conception allied to the portrayal of Paris does much to justify his view. As sources he had used the chronicles of Suetonius and Dio Cassius but he had contrived to extract from them all that was necessary while maintaining his own unity of design.

The two comedies in which Massinger's genius is most distinctly revealed are serious in intent: *A New Way to Pay Old Debts*, written by 1626, is followed by *The City Madam*, by 1632. He employs 'humours' comedy for a moral purpose. Little is known of Massinger's relations with Jonson. It has been surmised that they were unfriendly, but whatever may have been their personal feelings Massinger obviously studied Jonson's comedy closely. *A New Way to Pay Old Debts* (published 1633) has had a very long and successful history on the stage, a tribute to its well-constructed plot and the strong but simple lines of its characterization. The main 'humours' figure is Sir Giles Overreach, and his cruelty and callousness are clearly etched out and emphasized. The plot is the 'untrussing' of Overreach, who is outmanœuvred in his project of effecting a wealthy but unromantic marriage for his daughter Margaret. She helps in the process and gains the young man whom she wants, Tom Allworth. Overreach is the strongest dramatic portraiture in the play, and he represents something which Massinger was often trying to reveal; for he has the unscrupulous and evil cruelty which parallels that of Domitian in *The Roman Actor*. He makes no attempt to disguise his character to his creature Marrall;

> *'tis enough I keep*
> *Greedy at my devotion : so he serve*
> *My purposes, let him hang or damn, I care not,*
> *Friendship is but a word.*

A little later he adds,

> *I would be worldly wise ; for the other wisdom,*
> *That does prescribe us a well governed life,*
> *And to do right to others as ourselves,*
> *I value not an atom.*

With such a character one cannot expect subtlety, but the play shows Massinger's own strong character, his serious and challenging thought.

The City Madam, licensed in 1632, and not published until 1658, has the same atmosphere of confident competence. On this occasion it is a woman whom Massinger satirizes in the person of Lady Frugal. In both the plays the characters are of a citizen type. The whole setting is removed from the courtly background of Fletcher's plays and the values are different. The citizens are not comically portrayed, but their loves and emotions are explored seriously and often in a mood of satire. *The City Madam* is, in some ways, a transition from the 'humours' play of Jonson to the 'manners' comedy of Congreve. Lady Frugal is a proud, extravagant female martinet, who rules her daughters and her husband's raffish brother. The moral is expressed in the conclusion by Sir John Frugal:

> *Make you good*
> *Your promised reformation, and instruct*
> *Our city dames, whom wealth makes proud, to move*
> *In their own spheres; and willingly to confess*
> *In their habits, manners, and their highest port*
> *A distance 'twixt the city and the court.*

One of the best scenes is that in which Lady Frugal tries to make an astrologer show the suitors for her daughters' hands how they should treat them. The scene is very like the courtship of Millamant and Mirabell in Congreve's *The Way of the World*. The extent of Massinger's achievement makes any comprehensive survey here impossible. The more his work is studied the more powerful seems his skill as a dramatist and the seriousness and distinction of his mind. Inconsistent he certainly is and open to influences, as in his collaboration with Fletcher. Further he fell upon a period in drama which emphasized his weaknesses and did nothing to cherish his strength.

The career of Thomas Middleton (1580–1627), stretches over a long period of the drama. His biography, like that of most dramatists of the period, remains obscure. Born in 1580, and not as was previously conjectured in 1570, he was educated at Queen's College Oxford, and by 1602 there are already payments entered for him in Henslowe's diary as part-author of plays. He attempted both comedy and tragedy, and he worked both alone and in collaboration. He was a prolific writer, producing pageants as well as plays, and in 1620 becoming City Chronologer and Inventor of its 'honourable entertainments'. Yet little is known of his life, and in his plays, too, he remains remote. T. S. Eliot wrote of him; 'A great observer of human nature, without fear, without sentiment, without prejudice, without personality'.[1] His very detachment has

[1] T. S. Eliot, *Elizabethan Essays*.

made it difficult to establish his work from that of a collaborator. As Una Ellis-Fermor writes: 'as he appears to have no rigid moral theory, so has he few theories, rigid or otherwise, of art. He appears to work by that instinctive process which is thrown instantly out of gear by self-criticism or awareness of itself . . . His ease of adapta-tion, resulting as it does in a Shakespearian breadth and liberality, in marked contrast to the specialized sympathies of Webster, Tour-neur and Ford, is enough in itself to make judgement difficult; we cannot even determine with any certainty the canon of the plays.'[1]

Much of Middleton's early work lay in comedy. Una Ellis-Fermor has noted in the early comedies an easy acceptance of life similar to that found in Chaucer, and Middleton himself referred to Chaucer as 'that broad, famous English poet'. Such is the atmo-sphere of *A Trick to Catch the Old One* (published 1608), where a setting in citizen life allows of many amusing devices and of an atmosphere which is good-humoured if moral values are not ques-tioned too closely. The play was popular at Court and with the public. It centres in Witgood, a spendthrift young country gentle-man, who has to mortgage his estate to a grasping uncle, but tem-porarily regains his favour by making his mistress pose as a rich widow. From this basis begin complications too elaborate to re-hearse, though Middleton contrives to control them within the action. A change comes with *A Chaste Maid of Cheapside* (about 1613), where a far more sardonic mood prevails and satire has replaced gaiety. The main plot reveals how the parents of a chaste girl, Moll, plot to force her into marriage with a dissolute Welsh knight, Sir Walter Whorehound. There is little laughter in the Whorehound scenes in this play, nor is the mood merely cynical. Middleton seems penetrating with deep satire into the vices of his characters. Whorehound has many children by Mistress Allwit while her husband is a complacent cuckold and one of Middleton's most brilliant scenes is the christening of yet another child of this unrestrained debauchery. Allwit describes the last arrival as 'a fine plump black-eyed slut' and congratulates himself that Whorehound will have to pay for the christening feast:

> *I'll go bid Gossips presently myself,*
> *That's all the work I'll do; nor need I stir,*

[1] *The Jacobean Drama.*

> *But that it is my pleasure to walk forth,*
> *And air myself a little; I am tied*
> *To nothing in this business; what I do*
> *Is merely recreation, not constraint.*

Here are scenes of satire and realism which in their various ways
Hogarth and Fielding would have appreciated. Middleton was also
the author of *The Witch*, a play not successful at the time and preserved in manuscript until 1778. It is not surprising that contemporary audiences did not accept the play. In contrast to his
comedies it has a gruesome and unrewarding plot, and apart from
all this the action is confusedly conducted. The figure of Hecate
and the witches' songs were transcribed from this into the corrupt
Folio text of *Macbeth*.

Of William Rowley little is known except that he was an actor
and that he collaborated with Middleton. After less successful
attempts as in *A Fair Quarrel* (published 1617) and *The Spanish
Gipsy* (performed before Prince Charles in Whitehall, 1623), the
two authors contrived together a memorable play in *The Changeling*
(1623, published 1653). The title is derived from a negligible comic
underplot which may be Rowley's work. The main plot is built up
with great dramatic skill and touches the emotions deeply, and this
is due to Middleton's skill. The audience is thrown, almost violently, into the midst of the action. Alsemero loves Beatrice, who is
betrothed to Piracquo. De Flores, the evil genius of the tragedy,
loves Beatrice, but she hates him:

> *I never see this fellow but I think*
> *Of some harm towards me, dangers in my mind still;*
> *I scarce leave trembling of an hour after.*

To save herself from her own dilemma Beatrice lays herself in De
Flores' power by consenting that he shall kill Piracquo. Gradually
Beatrice comes to realize that the price De Flores intends to exact
for his action is her love. The scenes between them are handled
with great power:

> *Why 'tis impossible thou canst be so wicked,*
> *Or shelter such a cunning cruelty,*
> *To make his death the murderer of my honour!*

> *Thy language is so bold and vicious*
> *I cannot see which way I can forgive it*
> *With any modesty.*

To which De Flores replies:

> *Pish! you forget yourself*
> *A woman dipped in blood, and talk of modesty.*

The conclusion is presented with sustained force. Beatrice's evil deed is discovered by Alsemero and she suffers death at the hands of De Flores who then kills himself. In some strange way the audience is made to realize that these figures are more than puppets. They have an individual strength despite their evil, for De Flores has consistency and Beatrice a romantic devotion which transcends all moral values. The verse has poignancy and the whole is so well contrived that the tragedy stands high amid those of the period.

It was probably before *The Changeling* that Middleton had written independently the tragedy of *Women Beware Women* (about 1620), a play of involved sexual intrigue. Isabella's father Fabricio tries to force her not only to marry but to love a rich dolt. Her aunt, Livia, intervenes on her behalf. Livia is one of Middleton's most brilliant and complex portrayals, and later she is involved in a number of intrigues. Her brother Hippolito tells of his incestuous love for his niece, Isabella, and to encourage this Livia persuades the girl that Fabricio is not her father. Apart from this action, she is involved with Bianca, who begins innocently enough as a fugitive from rich parents, and the wife of a poor but honest man. But when the Duke seduces her she succumbs, and it is while this is developing that Livia and Bianca's mother play chess in one of the most brilliantly contrived of Middleton's scenes. Ellis-Fermor has given the most effective summary of Livia: 'her astuteness and her impercipience, her bluff comradely affection for her brother and her accompanying coarse moral obliquity, her level-headed business sense and her equally business-like sensuality are just such a blend of qualities as make us exclaim at sight upon the truth of the portrait'.[1] To the theme of chess Middleton returned with great skill in a satiric play with a political theme, *A Game at Chess* (acted

[1] *The Jacobean Drama.*

1624). The play is based on the proposals of a Spanish marriage for
Prince Charles which was planned by Gondomar, the Spanish
Ambassador. The whole project was unpopular with the public,
and when the Prince returned from Madrid without the bride there
was great popular rejoicing. Middleton's play answered this feeling
and had great success until the Spanish Ambassador intervened.

Outstanding among the later Stuart dramatists was John Ford
(1586–1640). He had commenced a career as a writer as early as
1606 with an elegiac poem, but his work for the stage came later.
Much of his early work was in collaboration; the best of this is to
be found in *The Witch of Edmonton*, where he worked with Rowley
and Dekker, and made an impressive play out of the story of
Elizabeth Sawyer who was executed for witchcraft in 1621. Outstanding in his own work is *The Lover's Melancholy* (acted 1628,
published 1629), where he was influenced by Burton's *The Anatomy of Melancholy*. The play has the usual complexities of love
intrigue, but it also has some verse where Burton's influence can be
heard:

> *Minutes are numbered by the fall of sands*
> *As by an hourglass; the span of time*
> *Doth waste us to our graves.*

In 1633 he published *Love's Sacrifice* which was acted and well
received, and again has an influence from Burton's *The Anatomy of
Melancholy*. The play now seems inconsistent, complex and not
fully controlled and does not match his greater tragedies, *The
Broken Heart* (published 1633) and *'Tis Pity She's a Whore* (published 1633). *'Tis Pity* shows Ford's very individual power in
tragedy, and seems to mark the culmination of this tradition. The
background is horror with passion elevated and made inevitable,
even as if it were a substitute for a moral motive. There is a contrast
between the grave solemnity of much of the verse and the scenes of
horror curiously contrived. As ever, the plot is elaborate, and highly
improbable, though it has its own inner and weird consistency. The
theme is incest openly expressed, as when in the first scene Giovanni acclaims that no convention of morality shall stand between
him and Annabella:

> *Shall a peevish sound,*
> *A customary form, from man to man,*

> *Of brother and of sister, be a bar*
> *'Twixt my perpetual happiness and me?*

Annabella's father forces her to marry a suitor Soranzo, who, after some complexities, discovers that Annabella is already pregnant with Giovanni's child. To save her from Soranzo's revenge he kills her, and then in a riotous scene rushes into Soranzo's feast with her heart upon his sword. He kills Soranzo and is in turn himself killed. *The Broken Heart* has the same tragic quality, but worked out on what is nominally a Greek setting, and through a series of bewildering intrigues. There is the same clarity of thought, the grave, moving verse, with the exploration of strange territories of experience, from which all ordinary moral values have disappeared. The emphasis is on tragic suffering. Again the central action concerns a brother and a sister though here there is no incestuous motive. Ithocles, returning victorious from the wars, will not let his sister, Penthea, marry her lover Orgilus but forces on her Bassanes a rich nobleman. Even when Bassanes is killed, she will not, in that deeply moving way of Ford's characters, let Orgilus have her as it were at second-hand:

> *Org :* Penthea is the wife to Orgilus,
> And ever shall be.
> *Pen :* Never shall, or will.
> *Org :* How!
> *Pen :* Hear me; in a word I'll tell thee why,
> The virgin-dowry which my birth bestow'd,
> Is ravished by another; my true love
> Abhors to think that Orgilus deserv'd
> No better favours than a second bed.

The tragedy moves from one horrifying spectacle to another until they are overwhelmed by death. Ithocles who found love in Calantha is among the dead, and the final and moving scene encompasses the death of Calantha herself.

James Shirley (1596–1666), has claims to be considered the last of the dramatists of the Elizabethan and Stuart periods. His career as a dramatist extends from 1625 to the closing of the theatres in 1642. He was on the King's side in the Civil War, and after the Restoration he returned to London where his plays were still popular, though he did not add to their number. He lost his house in the Great Fire of 1666, and, soon after, both he and his wife died on the same day. A large number of his plays survive, for when the Puritans closed the theatres Shirley turned his attention from the production of plays to the printing of them. He ranges from comedy and tragi-comedy to tragedy. Shirley himself thought that his tragedy, *The Cardinal* (1641), was the best of his plays. It is an honest opinion, though some think he over-estimated the strength of this, the last of his tragedies. Already ten years previously, in *The Traitor* (1631, printed 1635), he had written a play of equal power. *The Traitor* is a free treatment of the career of Lorenzo de Medici. It is a brilliant and macabre picture of the ambitious and licentious duke, who worked his way through a mass of intrigue in order to gain his own passionate end. Finally he oversteps himself and is overwhelmed in a scene of massed horrors. F. S. Boas, in an excellent summary of this play, suggests that as 'the test of tragic art does not lie in the number of victims at the close', the play, 'hovering often between rhetoric and poetry', misses true greatness.

The Cardinal owes much to Webster, but to a Webster who has been fairly and purposefully studied. The cardinal himself is the central interest of the play, though he is held in the background until the fifth act. At first he seems merely a schemer anxious to help his nephew to marry Rosaura. Instead she marries D'Alvarez, and at the wedding festivities the nephew and other masquers enter and lead D'Alvarez away with them and then bring back his corpse and throw it at her feet. In all this the Cardinal has seemed but a subsidiary figure, but he now comes forward to a horrible and dominating prominence. Ultimately he kills Rosaura and meets his own death. The play is wholly involved in horror, and it is with horror that there ends the great series of plays which had begun in Elizabethan times over half a century earlier.

In 1642 the theatres were closed by an ordinance which affirmed that 'public sports do not well agree with public calamities, nor public stage-plays with the seasons of humiliation'. There were, however some private performances, and plays were still published even when they could not be performed. Leslie Hotson in his brilliant study of *The Commonwealth and Restoration Stage* has discovered a number of miscellaneous theatrical activities in the Commonwealth period. Many of the players joined the King's army, and one company played to the Royalist soldiers at Oxford. Some players contrived to play, fairly openly in London, in 1647. At the Red Bull plays seemed to continue whatever Ordinances were passed.

The main link between the pre-war period and the Restoration was Sir William Davenant (1606–68), son of a vintner of Oxford, and some would say Shakespeare's godson. His father was a man of substance and William himself chose the road to the Court and not to the University and became page to the Duchess of Richmond. Of his life in the years which follow more is known than of many of his contemporaries. He had a link with the older Elizabethan age by his service with Sir Fulke Greville, Sir Philip Sidney's friend, and his contact with King Charles was shown by his appointment in 1633 to the Laureateship in succession to Ben Jonson. In between he had killed his man in a duel and had gained pardon for the homicide after a threat of transportation. He was later involved in Royalist plots and in 1642 he was on the Continent with the King's Court. One of his later adventures led him back to England and to imprisonment but, with luck, of which he seems to have had a generous share, he gained a pardon from Cromwell. Throughout the whole of this strange and varied career he retained a strong ambition to succeed as a dramatist. From 1656 he was already organizing entertainments in 'private places' with the help of a few highly-placed Puritan sympathizers. In 1656 he contrived to produce *The Siege of Rhodes*, an entertainment in verse with music, and thus, through a form of opera, drama came back to the stage. In 1658 he also produced two similar pieces, *The Cruelty of the Spaniards in Peru*, and *The History of Francis Drake*. Neither has any notable dramatic merit, but they are evidence of Davenant's determination to keep the drama alive despite all difficulties. In May 1660 Charles II was recalled, and the necessity for all subterfuge as far as the performance of drama was concerned had passed.

CHAPTER NINE

The Restoration Period

THE ENGLISH theatre of the years 1660–1700 differed profoundly from that of the age of Elizabeth and of the early seventeenth century. Particularly in the days of Elizabeth the theatre seemed to be at the centre of the community. It served the Court, and it had as its main patrons the noblemen who gave the cloak of legality to the actors, but it had a wider awareness, not only of the major issues of the age, but of the lives of those to whom courts and great houses were remote dreams. The dramatist served society at all levels, with his eye firmly on the tastes of the Court, his heart and sensibilities extending out to many sections of the people. In the Restoration period all was more restricted, for the Court dominated: there was no *A Midsummer Night's Dream* in the Restoration period. Something died out of the theatre and out of England too with the seventeenth century. There was a decadence in the drama, elements of corruption and materialism, and all this seemed to culminate in the Civil Wars with a sense of loss, profound, though most often intangible, as if the whole shape of the national landscape had changed. In the Restoration period the dramatist wrote for the Court, the audience consisted largely of courtiers, and their entourage. That the court was corrupt there can be no doubt; morality, particularly sexual morality, was ignored, and any form of licence, as long as it was entertaining, was permitted. If it could also be elegant, this was an advantage, but not essential.

The mind of England was never fully portrayed in those last forty years of the seventeenth century in the drama. The characters on the stage do not, for instance, reflect such a personality as Samuel Pepys. He was a zealous play-goer, and no very strict moralist in sexual matters, and to that degree he was close to the atmosphere of the Restoration theatre. But he was also a public servant of great skill and assiduity, and by his administrative ability the founder of the British navy, and of such activities the theatre of the age has no reflection. Charles II, as corrupt a monarch as could well be imagined, had been made a cynic by his period of exile. His Court had a laxity in morals which seemed limitless and he was determined, whatever happened, never to go on his travels again. Though naturally indolent, he was yet a man of great intelligence. Those who condemn the morals of the monarch and his Court are apt to forget that these were the years of the founding of the Royal Society, which was to become the basis of the systematic study of science in England, and also the acquisition of both New York and Bombay. In England itself there were at work many powerful minds to whom the Restoration drama meant nothing, and who served to show that many sections of society had still a strong and independent life. Of these John Bunyan (1628–88) was a man of outstanding genius. It is true that for the early part of Charles's reign, from 1661 to 1672, he was in Bedford gaol because he would not give up his right to preach freely. It was an easy imprisonment and permitted him to write *Grace Abounding* in 1666: he was in gaol again, when, in 1678, he published the first part of *The Pilgrim's Progress*. A working class puritan of genius he had no awareness of the court and its immoral and elegant drama, but there was an audience in that England to give him acceptance and to render his works popular in his own life-time. England also sustained intellectual learning of a high order in these decades as can be seen in the life of John Locke (1632–1704), one of the greatest and certainly the most representative of English philosophers of the modern period. Locke's involvement in politics did lead to years of exile, but he was also able, in this Restoration age, to pursue his philosophical studies without hindrance until public affairs enmeshed him. In the theatre itself the taste of the age was not confined to contemporary plays: Samuel Pepys' diary records one playgoer's enjoyment of much of Shakespeare and of Ben Jonson, and indeed of earlier writers.

That the Court was licentious needs no emphasis. Anthony Hamilton, an Irishman, who had followed the court into exile, and in the Restoration period wrote the memoirs of his brother-in-law the Chevalier de Gramont as the *Mémoires du Comte de Gramont*, reveals all the incredible intrigue and debauchery. There are other sources to confirm that he was not exaggerating. Court ladies disguised themselves to visit their lovers, and courtiers shared in a similar masquerade. The king and his immediate favourites indulged in every amorous exercise that the mind could invent, and at the background there was a harsh and sullen element of violence. The nature of the phenomenon has never been fully explored. There was a king who had lost any desire for prestige, and regarded safety and pleasure as sufficient motives in life. There was a mood of inquiry that undermined a number of loyalties, and there were ample opportunities for indulgence which the wealthy and the idle have seldom found it possible to resist. There was little national pride, and everywhere, uncertainty. Samuel Pepys, who was a libertine with a sense of responsibility, reflected on the days when Cromwell was at Whitehall and England was feared by her neighbours. Now, no one knew from day to day what might happen, and the Dutch might be at Sheerness, or the king might once again have to go on his travels. Pleasure without thought for the morrow was the rule. Even in the personal life there was a mood of uncertainty, and experiment, and certainly an absence of romance. Sex and intrigue and wit were in the ascendant and sentiment was at a discount.

Charles Lamb in one of his engaging *Essays of Elia* praised this 'artificial comedy' of the Restoration period because it had no relation to life: 'I could never connect these sports of a witty fancy in any shape with any result to be drawn from them to imitation in real life. They are a world of themselves almost as much as fairy-land', and of the characters he writes that they 'in their own sphere do not offend my moral sense; in fact they do not appeal to it at all. They seem engaged in their own proper element. They break through no laws, or conscientious restraints. They know of none. They have got out of Christendom into the land—what shall I call it?—of cuckoldry—the Utopia of gallantry, where pleasure is duty, and the manners perfect freedom. It is altogether a speculative scene of things, which has no reference whatever to the world that is'. This is charming reverie but it has no relation to fact. The intrigue which the ladies and gentlemen of the Restoration audience saw played on the stage was the exact parallel of that in which they indulged in their own life. Lord Macaulay came much nearer the truth in his review in 1841 of Leigh Hunt's edition of *The Dramatic Works of Wycherley, Congreve, Vanbrugh and Farquhar*. 'The case,' he wrote, 'is widely different with what

Mr Charles Lamb calls the conventional world of Wycherley and Congreve. Here the garb, the manners, the topics of conversation are those of the real town and of the passing day. The hero is in all superficial accomplishments exactly the fine gentleman whom every youth in the pit would gladly resemble. The heroine is the fine lady whom every youth in the pit would gladly marry. The scene is laid in some place which is as well known to the audience as their own houses, in St James's Park, or Hyde Park, or Westminster Hall.'

'Restoration comedy,' it has been noted,[1] 'is the product and reflection of sophisticated youth. Its most successful writers were young men, most of whom outlived their careers as dramatists because they also outlived the spirit of youth. Etherege, Wycherley, and Congreve finished writing for the stage by their thirtieth year, and Farquhar died very young.'

The earliest of these writers to practise the comedy of manners was Sir George Etherege (1635–91), who in 1664 produced *The Comical Revenge or Love in a Tub*. Etherege was the young town Gallant, the friend of Buckingham and Rochester, one who without effort or much learning gathered the moods of fashion and dissipation into a not very shapely farce with a romantic and sentimental plot added. But it served, for it was of the mood of the age. His next comedy, *She Would if She Could* (1668), showed how quickly he was learning. As far as the main plot is concerned he reduced the incongruous groups and actions of the early play into four characters, Courtall and Freeman, fashionable gentlemen in search of ladies, young and endowed with fortunes as well as beauty, and Ariana and Gatty, who are sprightly, adventurous and fully capable of looking after themselves. When Freeman first saw the heroines in Mulberry Garden, he commented: ''Sdeath, how fleet they are! Whatsoever faults they have they cannot be broken-winded.' Courtall, the bolder of the two, encourages Freeman on one occasion with the comment; 'Never fear it; whatsoever women say, I am sure they seldom think worse of a man, for running at all, 'tis a sign of youth and high metal, and makes them rather pique who shall tame him.' Unfortunately he did not maintain the whole comedy in this mood. Relying on Jonsonian 'humours' he created two heavy types in Sir Joslin Jolley and Sir Oliver Cockwood,

[1] *William Congreve* by D. Crane Taylor, 1931.

country characters, ever ready for ale and lechery. There is a massive incongruity between them and the elegant light-hearted-ness of the young people. More effective is the naturalistic portrait of Lady Cockwood, with her pretensions of conventional morality and of faithfulness to her husband, all denied by her over-eager sexual desires. Etherege is not a social moralist: it is her vanity, her hypocrisy that are condemned not her behaviour, except where that leads to dullness instead of wit. So successful was Etherege's second play that when Pepys went to see it he could find no room in the pit and had, grudgingly, to pay for a box. It may have been this that led him to say that the play was badly acted, that Etherege had to find 'fault with the actors, that they were out of humour, and had not their parts perfect'. Eight years were to intervene before Etherege produced *The Man of Mode* in 1676. Here he has freed himself largely of the Jonsonian incongruities and conceived his most original work, whose philosophy is that of his own poem 'The Libertine':

> *Since death on all lays his impartial hand,*
> *And all resign at his command,*
> *The Stoic too, as well as I,*
> *With all his gravity must die:*
> *Let's wisely manage the last span,*
> *The momentary life of man,*
> *And still in pleasure's circle move,*
> *Giving t'our friends the days and all our nights to love.*

Dorimant, the most complete of his creations, is a cynical young gallant who tells his former mistress Mrs Loveit, that, as he has fallen in love with Harriet, she must look elsewhere. In Dorimant it was thought that Etherege might be portraying Rochester,[1] for he had 'his Wit, his Spirit, his amorous Temper, the Charms that he had for the fair Sex, his Falsehood, and his Inconstancy'. There are elements of cruelty in him, though one may doubt if contemporary audiences would have so considered them. Much of his promiscuous outlook is kept within the range of a buoyant and witty light-heartedness: 'Constancy at my years! You might as well expect the fruit the autumn ripens i' the spring.' Harriet

[1] John Dennis *A Defence of Sir 'Fopling Flutter'*, London 1712.

has the wit to match him, and never did Etherege devise dialogue exchanges better than between these two.

Har : I did not think to have heard of Love from you.

Dor : I never knew what 'twas to have a settled Ague yet, but now and then have had irregular fits.

Har : Take heed, sickness after long health is commonly more violent and dangerous.

Dor : (*Aside*) I have took the infection from her and feel the disease spreading in me.

In *The Man of Mode*, as indeed in all of Etherege, the triumph is not of virtue over vice but of wit over dullness. Dorimant has wit and the elegancies of fashion; he can turn the temper of a woman with an epigram, and excuse his own conduct with a paradox. In his love intrigues, he exploits the foolishness of Sir Fopling Flutter, a pseudo-courtier, full of French fashions, who has all the ineptness of manners that Etherege, and the courtly society to which he belonged, would condemn. Etherege, who in dialogue and description gives a vivid picture of his age, pictures Sir Fopling: 'He was yesterday at the play, with a pair of gloves up to his elbow and a periwig more exactly curled than a lady's head newly dressed for a ball.' Early criticism of Restoration comedy neglected Etherege: he did not appear in Leigh Hunt's edition, and he would have been trounced by Macaulay for the wildness of his life, and its darker incidents of violence. Had he not been indulgent and indolent he would have achieved more than three plays, and it is sad that he did not, for his art was gaining in precision and mastery. He had great gifts of dialogue and he gave the pattern by which the irresponsible, witty, profligate but elegant life of his time could be portrayed in comedy.

Etherege's success led naturally to a number of imitations such as Sir Charles Sedley's *The Mulberry Garden* (1668), which followed the general pattern of Etherege's *The Comical Revenge* while borrowing certain details from Molière. A far more powerful mind entered into the comedy of manners in William Wycherley (1640–1716). His reputation is based upon four plays: *Love in a Wood*; *or St James's Park* (1671, written possibly as early as 1659); *The Gentleman Dancing-Master* (1672, written possibly by 1662); *The Country Wife* (1675); *The Plain Dealer* (1676, written in part possibly as early as 1666 and revised before production). In many ways the most powerful personality among these dramatists, Wycherley at fifteen had gone to France, and mixed in groups interested in wit, gallantry, and good conversation, and this left a permanent impression on him. On his return he tried the Law but gave up these studies to be a courtier. As a contemporary said; 'he soon left the *Dry Studies* of the Law, and gave in to *Pursuits* more *Agreeable* to *His own Genius*, as well as to the Taste of the Age'. His earliest play soon brought him the patronage of those who could establish his reputation, including the Duchess of Cleveland. He seems to have had a larger physical virility than some of his contemporaries; it has indeed been thought that he was at sea in the wars against the Dutch. Charming, everyone seems to have found him, but outspoken, and with a depth and fierceness in his plays that have led some to mistake him for a social moralist; yet that he had some interest in ideas beyond some of his contemporaries can be seen by the fact that born a Protestant he was converted to Catholicism in France, reverted to Protestantism in England, and then died a Catholic. Beyond religion, he sought reason, and the spirit of scepticism was strong in him, which he may have attempted to employ reason to assuage. According to Pope he would read himself to sleep with Montaigne, Rochefoucault, Seneca, or Gracian. Their maxims were slyly introduced into his plays and their rationalism mixed with the tenor of his own thought. Yet, no less than Etherege or Congreve, he was a libertine, an enemy of restraint, a satirist at times, but not a moralist, above all a wit with sex, scepticism and the foibles of humanity as his themes. His earliest play *Love in a Wood* deals with contemporary fashionable life and, following Sedley's *The Mulberry Garden*, has its setting in St James's Park, a scene which would be recognized by all the audience. The plot consists of love intrigues, which are sufficiently complicated and numerous to rob the play of its unity and design. It has passages of satire, giving Wycherley's work a depth unusual in his contemporaries, and it has wit, however intermittently. Above all, for the success of the author, it answered something in the temper of the age, a quality that it may be impossible ever to recover. The plot of *The Gentle-man Dancing-Master*, which was Wycherley's next play, was still uneven, and had incongruous elements. It descended too often into farce, with the tediousness that is also latent in farce for an intelligent audience. The plot turns on the device of the heroine who attempts to hide her lover by pretending that he is a dancing-master. The play has some satiric comment on the manners of the age, and there are characters in whom Spanish and French manners are parodied. *The Country Wife* has a stronger plot, and is a much more mature play, even if it is more unpleasant. The debt to Molière is considerable, yet, despite these derivations, the spirit and much of the conduct of the play are original. The tone is coarse in the extreme, but behind the lewdness one has the impression of a strong, sardonic mind. One feels in the presence of the satirist of Restoration comedy, though an incomplete satirist. The satirist should be one who does not accept the values of the society which he condemns. Wycherley's motives are not so integrated. It is contempt rather than moral condemnation which he expresses. Most often one feels that here is a sceptical mind which knows all that is most obscene in his age and contrives somehow to despise it and indulge in it simultaneously.

The Plain Dealer was the last and most effective of Wycherley's plays, and in this he shows that he was aware of the criticisms that had been made against the obscenities of *The Country Wife*. The play owes much to Molière's *Le Misanthrope*, though Wycherley's individual spirit still remains, and many of the values are changed. The central character is Manly, the Alceste of Molière's play; 'an unmannerly sea-dog', he shows a hatred for all men and yet conceals a very definite love beneath the hatred. Wycherley has given his play a much fuller movement of intrigue and incident than Molière found it necessary to employ. While Molière concentrates on Alceste, Wycherley adds to the story of Manly a varied and interesting movement of comic life. Wycherley was condemned by Macaulay for depriving Molière's play of its strength and beauty; but Wycherley had to adapt the figure of Alceste in the person of Manly to the condition of contemporary English society. A sympathetic French critic, Perromat, has realized this: 'If Manly had spoken the language of Alceste the picture of the century would not be real and the public would not recognize it.' Wycherley, like most of his contemporaries, is affected by the native influence of Jonson, as well as by Molière, and some of the characteristics of Manly seem to arise from a 'humours' conception. What ultimately contrasts him with other writers of Restoration comedy, apart from his ferocity and satire, is his interest in ideas, that he was ultimately, and however disguised, an intellectual.

William Congreve (1670–1729), was the last and greatest dramatist of this kind in the Restoration period. Like other famous writers of comedy, including Sheridan, Wilde and Shaw, he had an Irish background, though from an English family. He had been educated at Kilkenny School, and the University of Dublin, but as a young man he returned with his family to England, and the means of going to London were open to him. For the next few years he seems to have followed no definite profession, though he entered the Middle Temple in 1691: 'Law,' his biographer writes,[1] 'must have been as remote from his taste as the farthest Hebrides, but the Temple was an ideal home.' His first literary attempt was a novel, *Incognita*, published in 1692, though, in part, composed much earlier. Already his attachment to drama and to comedy had been aroused. A little later in the same year he published a volume of poems, a *Miscellany of Original Poems*. Then suddenly at the age of twenty-three he achieved fame with *The Old Bachelor* (1693). Only three comedies followed: *The Double Dealer* (1693); *Love for Love* (1695); and *The Way of the World* (1700). In the middle of these he wrote a tragedy, *The Mourning Bride* (1697). At the age of thirty his career as a dramatist was over. There is very little true comedy in English, and in that small circle Congreve is supreme. For comedy is more than farce, the play where untoward incidents render the characters ridiculous, and it is also more than a play of intrigue with a happy ending, which the histories of drama so often for convenience classify under comedy. Nor is it burlesque, for there the movement, however amusing, depends upon some life other than its own. Comedy, in its truest interpretation, depends, as Meredith saw, upon a conception of society, and the comic writer will hold up the mirror to his age, depicting its eccentricities, its deviations from some agreed norm. The society and the audience must be aware of the 'finer shades'. If the society is moral, the comedy will reveal the variations from a moral norm, but in Restoration comedy the errors are not those of a moral code but of deviations from wit and good manners.

[1] *William Congreve* by D. Crane Taylor, 1931

For such a comedy Congreve could draw on Ben Jonson and Molière. Ben Jonson, though he knew what comedy should be, never found the society with the 'finer shades', though he approaches it in *The Alchemist* and in parts of *The Silent Woman*. Molière lived in a different world, one of gentility, with its own elaborate and gracious conventions. A man might be commendable morally and yet fail in that world. He must conduct himself so that he is acceptable to society. This inevitable relation of comedy to society explains the licence of Restoration comedy, for if there was to be a comedy at all based on that society it had to be licentious. The theatre, as has already been suggested, was full of members of the court and of the looser elements amid the gentry, and the gallery of footmen and servants, and the women wore masks. They all knew what to expect.

Congreve, unlike Shakespeare, built only one world in his plays, and the same values hold for all his comedies. In his own age, so much was he admired, that he was compared to Shakespeare, even by Dryden:

> *Heaven, that but once was prodigal before,*
> *To Shakespeare gave as much, she could not give him more.*

If a character could walk from one play to another he would still find himself at home. There is a systematic conception behind that world. Tragedy and pathos must not enter in, and the display of emotion is rather bad taste. Elegance and wit are essential, and morality is tedious, and above all one must not speak from the heart. Much that has been written of Congreve is unhappy and untrue, and some critics, including Thackeray who should have known better, have indulged in mere vituperation. Some of the best things have been written by Swinburne: 'Congreve's intellect is clear, cold, and narrow; it has the force and brightness of steel; the edges of it, so to speak, are cut out hard and sharp. There is more weight and matter in Congreve than in any English dramatist since the Restoration; and at worst he is no coarser than his time. In Congreve all is plain and clear if hard and limited; he makes no effort to escape into the region of moral sentiment; if his world is not healthy neither is it hollow; and whatever he had of noble humour and feeling was genuine and genial. His style is a model of grace and accurate vigour, and his verbal wit the most brilliant and forcible in English literature. We do not say that it was pure and exalted; such properties belong to other times and other minds. But as a comic writer he stands above the best who came after him and beside the best who went before.' He owed much to his predecessors for they had invented this fashionable contemporary comedy, and defined its independence of morality and its dedication to wit. But Congreve surpassed them with his brilliance and with his creation of characters, which despite all changes, remain permanent in the theatre.

The Old Bachelor already shows something of Congreve's skill, though the action is excessively encumbered with intrigue. It is reported that Dryden, who admired the play, helped to give it 'the fashionable cut of the town'. That it was immediately popular is shown by the first run of fourteen nights at Drury Lane and the publication of three editions within two weeks. The title theme is the adventure of Heartwell, the old bachelor, who is nearly decoyed into marriage. Here, as often in Restoration comedy, there are two groups of characters, the 'wits', who claim our sympathy, and the 'gulls', the dull ones. The conclusion is not a triumph of good over evil, but of the keen over the stupid. Both sides may be equally bad, but that does not count in the play. The 'wits', whatever they may lack, do at least possess grace and style. They are never nonplussed and retain a certain attractiveness whatever they may do. The brilliance of the dialogue is defined in some early lines in the play:

Bellmour : Business!—and so must time, my friend, be close pursued, or lost. Business is the rub of life, perverts our aim, casts off the bias, and leaves us wide and short of the intended mark.

Vainlove : Pleasure, I guess you mean.

Bellmour : Ay, what else has meaning?

Vainlove : Oh, the wise will tell you—

Bellmour : More than they believe—or understand.

Possibly Congreve was told by his friends that the plot of *The Old Bachelor* was weak, for in *The Double Dealer* he was thinking excessively about plot and about the theory of drama. The plot becomes clear, though very complex, but too important for a comedy of manners. Congreve, in his dedication, seems to express his uncertainties. He affirms that 'he made the plot as strong as he could, because it was single; and he made it single to avoid confusion', and because he 'was resolved to preserve the three unities of the drama'. All this made the play heavier than the audience had anticipated. In result it was all closer to tragi-comedy than to Etherege's light-hearted comedy of manners. In compensation *Love for Love* is one of the best comedies in the language, and the enduring quality of its appeal was shown in the great success of its revival during the years of the Second World War. It is clear that there is one dominant intrigue and that all the others branch from it. Sir Sampson promises to pay the debts of his son Valentine if he will allow the inheritance to go to Ben, a younger sailor son. Ben refuses the match that Sir Sampson proposes, and so the old man thinks of marriage himself. His eye falls on Angelica, who is in love with Valentine, but has not declared her love. She falls in with Sir Sampson's wishes far enough to free Valentine from the stern plans of his father. There are excellent and well disciplined subsidiary actions, with clearly contrived characters, such as Mrs Foresight and Mrs Frail. The opening is inimitable. It is a conversation between Valentine and Jeremy, his servant:

Valentine : Jeremy!
Jeremy : Sir?
Valentine : Here, take away; I'll walk a turn, and digest what I have read.
Jeremy : (*Aside*) You'll grow devilish fat upon this paper diet. (*Takes away the books.*)
Valentine : And d'ye hear, you go to breakfast.—There's a page doubled down in Epictetus that is a feast for an emperor.
Jeremy : Was Epictetus a real cook, or did he only write receipts?

Throughout Congreve is in the happy exercise of all his powers. The audience is carried into the midst of the action on a stream of witty thought. If the author had the vigour of Shakespeare or Dickens a whole series of plays might have followed, but he was by nature indolent and self-indulgent, and an interval of five years separates this from his next comedy.

There followed in 1700 *The Way of the World*, the most elaborate and in some ways the most brilliant of Congreve's comedies. The plot is complicated and improbable, and misses the virtues of simple directness which *Love for Love* possessed. Congreve meditated long on the plot, and perhaps he meditated too long. He has rid himself of such devices as the aside and the soliloquy, which he had used so freely in *The Double Dealer*; but in doing so he left the movement of the action a little obscure. Much of the first act is occupied with the presentation of plot, particularly the theme of Mirabell's love for Millamant, the niece of Lady Wishfort. Millamant is to lose half her fortune if she marries without Lady Wishfort's consent. It is only when this tediousness with the mechanism of the action is over that Millamant, perhaps the most brilliant woman in English comedy, is allowed to appear. The scenes between her and Mirabell are the most excellent in the whole of the comedy of that age. The characterization has a subtlety which separates it from any obvious portrayal of type and gives to this play a delicacy all its own. Of its style George Meredith wrote: 'Where Congreve excels all his English rivals is in his literary force and a succinctness of style peculiar to him. He hits the mean of a fine style and a natural dialogue. He is at once precise and voluble. If you have ever thought upon style you will acknowledge it to be a signal accomplishment. In this he is a classic, and worthy of treading a measure with Molière.' Some critics have suggested that despite all Congreve's skill the play is not effective on the stage. But mid-twentieth century revivals show that this is not true. What it does require is superb acting both of voice and style.

In 1697 Congreve published his one tragedy: *The Mourning Bride*. This should properly be considered with the other tragedies of the age, with Otway and Rowe, though something may be gained by placing it here with the rest of Congreve's work. It is a good stage play, as one would expect from Congreve. To some extent it has been under-estimated, probably as a reaction against Samuel Johnson's extravagant praise in his life of Congreve. Johnson had asserted: 'If I were required to select from the whole mass of English poetry the most poetical paragraph I know not what I could prefer to an exclamation in *The Mourning Bride*.' Johnson refers to the description in the second act of an aisle in a temple which Almeria and Leonora are entering:[1]

[1] Act II, scene 1.

Almeria : It was a fancied noise, for all is hushed.
Leonora : It bore the accent of a human voice.
Almeria : It was thy fear, or else some transient wind
          Whistling through hollows of this vaulted aisle,
          We'll listen.
Leonora : Hark!
Almeria : No, all is hushed, and still as death. 'Tis dreadful!
          How reverend is the face of this tall pile,
          Whose ancient pillars rear their marble heads,
          To bear aloft its arched and ponderous roof,
          By its own weight made steadfast and immoveable
          Looking tranquillity! It strikes an awe
          And terror on my aching sight; the tombs
          And monumental caves of death look cold,
          And shoot a chillness to my trembling heart.
          Give me thy hand, and let me hear thy voice,
          Nay, quickly speak to me, and let me hear
          Thy voice—my own affrights me with its echoes.

Here was the generalized classical description which Johnson enjoyed, with the minute particulars discarded. The play was very popular and held the stage in the eighteenth century. The weakness lies in the inadequacy of the characters; one is left with a story of romantic incident dramatized, full of mystery and surprises, but lacking a powerful fable from which a true tragic crisis could emerge. It may have owed its popularity to the fact that it was a combination of all the modes, from the romance tragedies to the heroic play, with its scene distant in time, its setting in Granada, and its personages noble and full of exalted sentiments.

The vogue of the comedy of manners was partly affected by the attack in 1698 by Jeremy Collier (1658–1726) entitled *A Short View of the Profaneness and Immorality of the English Stage.* Collier was a clergyman who accepted a moral view of the drama: 'the business of plays is to recommend virtue and to discountenance vice'. Both Dr Johnson and Macaulay thought well of his intellectual qualities, but it was rather the strength of his case than his own merits that succeeded. His *Short View* led to a pamphlet warfare, and it was clear that however clumsily he conducted the argument there was something to be said on his side. Further, its publication coincided with the beginning of a change in public taste. Even Dryden, who had contributed his share to the lubricious comedy, confessed in 1686 in his ode *To the Pious Memory of Mrs Anne Killigrew* that his own 'fat pollutions' had added to the 'steaming ordures of the stage'. In the *Preface to the Fables* he wrote 'I am sensible as I ought to be of the scandal I have given by my loose writings, and make what reparation I am able by this public acknowledgment'. The manners comedy did not, however, disappear completely, for in the early years of the new century it was broadened and humanized by two competent practitioners, George Farquhar (1678–1707) and Sir John Vanbrugh (1664–1726). Farquhar began with two comedies of no particular distinction, *Love in a Bottle* (1699) and *A Constant Couple* (1699). These he followed by two far more interesting and mature comedies, *The Recruiting Officer* (1706) and *The Beaux Stratagem* (1707). He gives a wider portrayal of life than Congreve, so the recruiting scene in *The Recruiting Officer* and the opening of *The Beaux Stratagem* in an inn at Lichfield have a realistic interest such as is found in the eighteenth-century periodical essays and the novel.

Other elements also separate these plays from Congreve and give them a pleasing individuality. *The Recruiting Officer* occupies itself in part with the methods of recruiting. This may have a theatrical ancestry in Falstaff, but Farquhar is not relying on that source. He is satirizing the recruiting methods of his own time. In the scene before the Justices he employs a number of contemporary details, and these, with the satire, add to the realism of the comedy. Yet, while introducing these new features, he is faithful, in the main mood, to the manners type of presentation. He lacks the brilliance in dialogue of Congreve, though he shares his general immoral tone. He uses farce more freely, and he has a little of the sentimentality which was later to become dominant in the drama. The main plot is of how Silvia, a young heiress dressed up as a soldier, had strutted out impertinently and spoken as grossly as any trooper, so that she might marry Captain Plume of whom her father disapproved. The sentimental element appears when, suddenly and with some incongruity, Silvia makes a serious speech on marriage and the position of women. *The Beaux Stratagem*, a delightful play, which has always been given a welcome when it is competently revived, shares a number of features with *The Re-*

cruiting Officer. The main plot still has much of the quality of a manners play, but it is acted out with a greater variety of adventure. Two gentlemen with depleted fortunes, Aimwell and Archer, arrive at Lichfield. Aimwell gains the love of a charming and clever young lady, who is married to a sottish country squire named Sullen. There is a movement of farce in the plot, mainly supplied by Scrub, the servant of Sullen, but there is also a serious criticism of the hardship of marriage for women, when economic interests and not affection control. The difference of mood can be seen by a comparison of the discussion of marriage in the fifth act of this play with the witty, pre-marriage discussion of Milla-mant and Mirabell in *The Way of the World*. Farquhar has less wit, but the sentiment, which Congreve excludes, is here given a right of entry and leads to serious discussion. At the same time it would be erroneous to think that the whole play dwells in this atmosphere, for Farquhar had an independent mind. He was, as Bonamy Dobrée has suggested, an 'advanced rationalist', and, in support, Dobrée quotes some delightful lines from *The Beaux Stratagem*. Archer has captured the thief Gibbet, and threatens to shoot him rather than send him for hanging:

Archer : Come rogue, if you have a short prayer, say it.
Gibbet : Sir, I have no prayer at all; the government has provided a chaplain to say prayers for us on these occasions.

Dobrée adds the comment: 'one would not be surprised to find the remark in a page of Voltaire'.

Sir John Vanbrugh is a remarkable personality, whose range of achievement cannot easily be estimated, as it does not lie within the limits of any one art. His greatest contribution was perhaps as a baroque architect, for he was the designer of Castle Howard, his own Haymarket Theatre, Blenheim Palace and other great projects. He wrote a number of comedies of which the soundest is probably *The Provok'd Wife* (1697), as *The Confederacy* (1705), is the most immoral. The main plot of *The Provok'd Wife* turns upon the matrimonial cruelty of Sir John Brute, and on his wife's cynical attitude to virtue and faithfulness. The main movement of the play still arises from the same world as manners comedy, though a far more liberal use is made of farcical elements. The wit of Congreve is absent, but there is some compensation in the satirical attitude which is well maintained. It is found particularly in the portrait of Sir John Brute, a character who seems to look back to the 'humours' types of Jonson, and even of Massinger in *A New Way to Pay Old Debts*.

In a way the Restoration period was fortunate to have a comedy as elegant and distinguished as in fact it possessed. Immoral and licentious it may have been, but at its best it had style, wit and consistency. It was only when it attempted tragedy and heroic drama that it floundered into an unreal world and ultimately into dullness. At the centre of all this was John Dryden (1631–1700), who, apart from his genius in non-dramatic work as a satirist, culminating in *Absalom and Achitophel* in 1681, wrote comedy, heroic plays and tragedy. Of his comedy little need be said. He was unhappy in a medium to which he had been driven by economic considerations. Later, as has already been recorded, he apologized for his excesses. The best elements in his comedies are the lyrics, and in a well-known piece in *Marriage à la Mode* (1672) he sums up light-heartedly the whole spirit of Restoration comedy:

> *Why should a foolish Marriage Vow,*
> *Which long ago was made,*
> *Oblige us to each other now,*
> *When Passion is decay'd.*
> *We lov'd, and we lov'd, as long as we could:*
> *'Till our love was lov'd out in us both:*
> *But our Marriage is death when the Pleasure is fled*
> *'Twas Pleasure first made it an Oath.*

To this may be added the well-known and charming lines from *The Spanish Friar* (1681):

> *Farewell ungrateful traitor,*
> *Farewell my perjured swain,*
> *Let never injured creature*
> *Believe a man again*
> *The pleasure of possessing*
> *Surpasses all expressing*
> *But 'tis too short a blessing*
> *And love too long a pain.*

Of his comedies *The Wild Gallant* was unsuccessful on its first production in 1663; and of the others, and they are many, including *Marriage à la Mode* (1672), the most popular was *Sir Martin Mar-all* (1667), which derives in part from Molière.

He had an intellect beyond any of his contemporaries in the theatre, and his critical essays are outstanding as an assessment of poetry and drama. He was the first man of letters in English literature. Not until G. B. Shaw does one again discover a practising dramatist writing in such an illuminating way about his art. As has been suggested, it was economic circumstances that drove him into drama, and into the prefaces, and with a typical modesty he once wrote that he never thought himself 'very fit for an employment where many of my predecessors have excelled me in all kinds and some of my contemporaries even in my own partial judgement have outdone me in comedy'. Nothing in the whole period can touch his prose essays and prefaces, which began with *Of Dramatic Poesy, An Essay* (1668). He had grace, a conversational ease of style and, though the manner of his own imagination was very different, he seldom wrote better than of his predecessors: 'To begin then, with Shakespeare. He was the man who of all modern, and perhaps ancient poets, had the largest and most comprehensive soul. All the images of Nature were still present to him, and he drew them not laboriously, but luckily. When he describes anything, you more than see it you feel it too.'

Unfortunately when Dryden turned to tragedy he concentrated, in his best years, on the heroic drama, one of the most artificial forms to have engaged the English stage. These plays were in couplets, and most elaborately produced. In Dryden's mind they were the dramatic counterpart of the heroic poem, or epic, but epic that has also the qualities of tragedy. Many of the least profitable passages in his prose essays are devoted to expounding this theory. The motives displayed were those of heroic honour and heroic love. They were as far removed as can be imagined from the licentious realism of Restoration comedy. It was as if a society, knowing itself to be completely immoral, had preserved this one artificial form of art, where virtues it did not practise could be displayed in an exaggerated form, through the medium of bombastic couplets, and love and honour shown in the grand manner on an unreal scene. No one will revive these plays on the stage, and their importance would be small had not Dryden's powerful mind occupied itself with their composition and criticism. In *An Essay on Heroic Plays* he writes: 'an heroic play ought to be an imitation in little of the heroic poem'. For the actual origin of the species, Dryden would give some credit to Sir William Davenant, whose *The Siege of Rhodes* had been first introduced as a musical entertainment in 1656; it was then described as *The Siege of Rhodes Made a Representation by the Art of Perspective in Scenes, and the Story sung in Recitative Music*. Davenant revised it as an heroic drama. Dryden admits that the play lacked strength and characterization. He quotes boldly from Ariosto as his other inspiration, and states that love and valour and honour must be the motives of the action. Another influence was certainly the French romances, so popular in England in the late seventeenth century.

Roger Boyle, Earl of Orrery (1621–79), attempted heroic tragedy in unhistorical English history in *Henry V* (1664) and *The Black Prince* (1667). In the same period Dryden with Sir Robert Howard produced *The Indian Queen* (1664). Here the theme is of Montezuma, the conqueror of the Mexicans, just at his moment of triumph, and the action is in a very fanciful setting and based on heroic love. The play was successful and Dryden followed it immediately with the same scenes and dresses in *The Indian Emperor* (1665). Then in 1669 and 1670 came the most expansive and fanciful of all the heroic plays, *The Conquest of Granada by the Spaniards*, in ten acts. It was here that Dryden seemed most confident that heroic tragedy is the best form of drama produced in the most learned and elegant of ages:

> *If* love *and* Honour *now are higher rais'd*
> *'Tis not the poet, but the age is prais'd,*
> *Wit's* now *arriv'd to a more high degree*
> *Our native language more refin'd and free*

He affirmed that the conception of his hero, Almanzor, was based on the Achilles of Homer and on Tasso's Rinaldo, while some of the incidents were derived from the French heroical romances. Almanzor is the perfectly chivalrous warrior who maintains himself in the world of high honour with an unending supply of rhetoric, written in high-sounding couplets. Incongruous though the total effect must be, except to the audiences for which Dryden immediately wrote, there are many passages where his incisive powers as a poet re-assert themselves, as, for instance, in the lines,

> *'Tis war again, and I am glad 'tis so;*
> *Success shall now by force and courage go.*
> *Treaties are but the combat of the brain,*
> *Where still the stronger lose, the weaker gain . . .*
> *The minds of heroes their own measures are,*
> *They stand exempted from the rules of war.*

In 1675 Dryden composed *Aureng-Zebe*, the most sober and the last of his contributions to this type. The scene is set in India, the India of heroic drama. The play shows the nobleness of Aureng-Zebe as he struggles against the faithlessness of his father, his brothers, and indeed of all around him, and contains, again, individual passages of great skill including the well-known and memorable lines:

> *When I consider Life, 'tis all a cheat;*
> *Yet fooled with hope, men favour the deceit;*
> *Trust on, and think to-morrow will repay:*
> *To-morrow's falser than the former day;*
> *Lies worse; and while it says, we shall be blest*
> *With some new joys, cuts off what we possest.*
> *Strange cozenage! None would live past years again,*
> *Yet all hope pleasure in what yet remain;*
> *And, from the dregs of Life, think to receive*
> *What the first sprightly running could not give.*
> *I'm tired with waiting for this chemic gold,*
> *Which fools us young, and beggars us when old.*

It is clear from the prefatory verses to Aureng-Zebe that Dryden was growing tired of the composition of these grandiose heroic tragedies in rhymed verse. There was further in the 'seventies a change of taste that led back towards the more varied and real world of Shakespearian and Stuart tragedy. So Dryden, in bidding farewell to the heroic drama in *Aureng-Zebe*, writes:

> *And, to confess a truth, though out of time,*
> *Grows weary of his long-loved mistress, Rhyme.*
> *Passions too fierce to be in fetters bound,*
> *And Nature flies him like enchanted ground:*
> *What verse can do he has performed in this,*

Which he presumes the most correct of his;
But spite of all his pride, a secret shame
Invades his breast at Shakespeare's sacred name.

And so back from the couplet to blank verse! That Dryden himself
had deeply admired these earlier authors appears almost everywhere in his critical work. It is true that during the period of his
obsessive devotion to the heroic drama his affection was tempered
sometimes with a belief that they were 'the giant race before the
flood', not fully aware of the elegance and refinements that a more
modern age had introduced. Now in 1677 he returned to blank
verse, and in *All For Love* wrote a play on the Antony and Cleopatra theme. He indulged in no slavish imitation of Shakespeare's
play, though the composition shows again Dryden's admiration for
Shakespeare. Dryden breaks down the widely distributed scenes
of Shakespeare, and brings the theme as close to the unity of action
as its nature will permit. The picture of Antony is less generous
than in Shakespeare, for the emphasis is on the very last phase,
full of fretting and nerves and morbid suspicion. Nor has Cleopatra
the 'infinite variety' that she once possessed. *Antony and Cleopatra*
was the play in which Shakespeare approached the values of the
Restoration stage most closely, for this is the only one of his mature
tragedies in which love is made the dominant theme. *All For Love*,
of all Dryden's plays, is the one in which the Restoration motives
of love and honour are subordinated, and their place taken by
suspicion and jealousy. Much of the verse has an impelling imaginative quality combined with dramatic effectiveness. He returns also
to passages of reflection such as had been one of the few compensating features of the heroic plays:

> *Men are but children of a larger growth;*
> *Our appetites as apt to change as theirs,*
> *And full as craving too, and full as vain,*
> *And yet the soul, shut up in her dark room,*
> *Viewing so clear abroad, at home sees nothing;*
> *But, like a mole in earth, busy and blind,*
> *Works all her folly up, and casts it outward*
> *To the world's open view.*

Throughout the Restoration period there had been a strong

affection for the tragi-comedies of Beaumont and Fletcher. Other Elizabethan and Jacobean dramatists were frequently performed, though often in remodelled and amended versions. In the 'seventies this taste was emphasized not only by Dryden, for Thomas Otway and Nathaniel Lee adventured into the same field, and later, in the eighteenth century, they were followed by Nicholas Rowe. Of these the most distinctive was Thomas Otway (1652–85). He had begun with rhymed tragedies, following without any distinguishing excellence the fashion of the age in *Alcibiades* (1674) and *Don Carlos* (1676). He turned to blank verse with *The History and Fall of Caius Marius* (1679). This deals superficially with the quarrel of Marius and Sulla, but its main movement is an adaptation of *Romeo and Juliet* to a Roman setting. Previously *Romeo and Juliet*, 'revised' and played as a tragi-comedy, had not been a popular play on the Restoration stage. Pepys in 1662 had described it as 'the worst that ever I heard in my life'. Much of the attraction of Otway's version lay in the comic parts, particularly that of the Nurse, which was played by a man. Its interest lay in Otway's return, by a route however devious, from the conventional drama popular in his day, to Shakespeare. He followed his pastiche with two original blank verse dramas which are outstanding in the period, *The Orphan* (1680), and *Venice Preserv'd* (1682).

The Orphan is a tragedy of two brothers, Castalio and Polydore, who both love Monimia. She plans to marry Castalio secretly, but Polydore overhears this and, thinking their love illicit, plans to take Castalio's place. As a result of this action all the characters are overwhelmed by disaster. The weakness of the play lies in its characterization, for it is unexplained why Polydore should act so brutally, or why Castalio should remain so silent about his marriage. In compensation there is the strength of the pathos with which Monimia's position is portrayed. The play had sufficient appeal, particularly in its emotional scenes, to be for a long time a popular revival on the stage. *Venice Preserv'd* has a firmer dramatic basis. The play centres around the character of Jaffeir who is driven by debt into a conspiracy with Pierre and others against the State. He is drawn as a vacillating character who is led, first to swear his allegiance to the conspirators, and then, by the influence of Belvidera, the woman he loves, to betray them. After the capture of Pierre, Jaffeir feels a second remorse, and, as Pierre is on the scaffold, Jaffeir first kills him and then stabs himself to death. In the final scene the ghost of Pierre appears to Belvidera and she dies. The story may seem melodramatic and ineffective, but it has a strong theatrical quality, and again Otway is able to concentrate on emotion and the portrayal of pathos. It was in pathos also that Nicholas Rowe (1674–1718), gained his most notable effects in the early eighteenth century with *The Fair Penitent* (1703), *The Tragedy of Jane Shore* (1714), and *The Tragedy of Lady Jane Grey* (1715).

Among more miscellaneous pieces, a historical interest at least attaches to Buckingham's burlesque play of *The Rehearsal* (1671). The work may have been by a number of hands, but the main author was the Duke of Buckingham (1625–87), whom Dryden later satirized as Zimri. The features of contemporary drama here satirized and burlesqued are numerous. The central motive is the criticism of the heroic plays, and this appears mainly in the love of Chloris and Prince Prettyman, while a number of lines and couplets from plays of this type are parodied. Together with this there is a personal attack on Dryden who is accused of immorality, vanity and stupidity. Of other writers for the stage Thomas Shadwell (1640–92), can probably never escape from Dryden's brilliant satire of him in *MacFlecknoe*. If with modest talents one is to carry an unsullied reputation into posterity it is obviously wiser not to quarrel with or incense a master of verbal venom as was Dryden. Later critics have much to say in his defence, and to discover virtues in *The Sullen Lovers* (1668), and *Epsom Wells* (1672). He continued in a rather heavy-handed way with 'humours' comedy long after the vogue for it had passed. Mrs Aphra Behn (1640–89), deserves notice as the first woman to succeed as a professional dramatist. She had an adventurous career and was obviously endowed with intelligence and determination. She rescued herself from a debtor's prison by relying on her pen, and beginning with a tragi-comedy in *The Forc'd Marriage* (1670), she developed with some success into comedies of intrigue such as *The Rover* (1677, and second part 1680). Her plays have liveliness but they are neither as interesting nor as vivacious as her own life.

CHAPTER TEN

The Eighteenth Century

IT CANNOT be denied that the eighteenth century and the first fifty years of the nineteenth were, with the exception of only some half-a-dozen names, a dreary period as far as dramatic authorship is concerned. The whole of this vast and seldom elevated tract of drama has been explored in detail and with the accumulation of much fresh information by Professor Allardyce Nicoll, and anyone coming after him must acknowledge a debt; for he has orderliness and patience in making a reasonable chronicle of years when dullness often reigns in unchallenged supremacy over the theatre.

A number of reasons may be advanced for this declension. As has been noted, Dryden died in 1700 and in the same year Congreve retired from the theatre. The careers of their contemporaries were ended, and, as if to mark a conclusion, Jeremy Collier's *A Short View* appeared in 1698. The physical conditions of the theatre itself were unfavourable. In the Restoration period London, by which must be understood the Court and its adherents, was content, as has been seen, with a very limited number of theatres. In the early eighteenth century several little theatres developed, and in these some excellent performances were given. Then, as has already been discussed, in 1737 the Licensing Act cut at the very heart of drama, and all regular dramatic presentations were confined to Drury Lane and Covent Garden. The little theatres continued their underground activities and Garrick made some of his early performances in one of them. Such were the conditions which prevailed until the act of 1843 made the opening of new theatres possible. The audience widened in the early eighteenth century, and the citizen or middle-class elements were no longer tolerant of the moral laxity of the Restoration audiences. At the same time, it must be confessed that these earlier audiences had taste and discernment and a dread of dullness which the middle-class patrons of drama in the eighteenth century most notably lacked.

There developed in contrast to the hard cynicism of manners comedy a drama of sensibility, in which pathos and delicacy and refined sentiments found a place, and where moralizing was restored to a central position. Colley Cibber, for instance, in such a play as *The Careless Husband* (1704), while he retained much that belonged to the manners tradition, superimposed moral and didactic elements. More important than Cibber was Sir Richard Steele (1672–1729), who wrote a number of plays of sensibility: *The Funeral* (1701), *The Lying Lover* (1703), *The Tender Husband* (1705), and *The Conscious Lovers* (1722). *The Funeral* has a number of manners elements with moralizing as a sort of addendum. In *The Lying Lover* he sets his aim with greater precision: 'to banish out of Conversation all Entertainment which does not proceed from Simplicity of Mind, Good-Nature, Friendship and Honour'. Despite these declarations and motives, a number of the moods of manners comedy are retained, though their direction is modified finally to an edifying conclusion. In *The Tender Husband* the sensibility motive was more completely fused into the play as a whole. The conception of *The Conscious Lovers* is based on Terence's *Andria*, but the plot is transformed beyond recognition in the cause of sentimentalism, and at the conclusion of the second act Steele abandons his Latin model altogether. The plot does not sound very encouraging. It depends on young persons who wish to marry otherwise than their parents would suggest. This ancient theme Steele employs to exploit his campaign against forced marriages and duels. He confessed that he was mainly proud of a scene in which the hero rises above the desire to fight a duel. Judged in one way it is a priggish scene, and over-written, yet it must be remembered that Steele and his followers had a definite influence on restraining the practice of duelling; here was one of the few occasions where drama had a direct effect on human conduct. Morally the play is most commendable, and it may be recalled that Parson Adams in Fielding's *Joseph Andrews* found that as a Christian he could commend it as 'containing some things solemn enough almost for a sermon'. Yet from the point of view of the theatre it misses the brilliance and glitter of the manners comedy of the Restoration.

There were numerous other practitioners of sentimentality in the theatre. Mrs Centlivre for instance, a picturesque figure, and the eighteenth century counterpart of Mrs Aphra Behn, had much success. Of her early life little is known. After her first husband was killed in a duel she took to the stage as an actress and later married Joseph Centlivre, chief cook to Queen Anne and George I. She died in 1723. A number of her plays had appeared, without much distinction, before she gained success with *The Gamester*, in which the evils of gambling were displayed and the whole action made dependent on the moral. The heroine promises to marry the hero if he will abandon the tables and ultimately shocks him into such action by dressing up as a man and so outwitting him that she wins from him her own picture.

More effective than the exaggerated moods of this sentimental play was the genuine domestic tragedy which constituted some of the most satisfactory dramatic production of the first fifty years of the eighteenth century. As has been seen, this type of play had gained a certain vogue as early as the Elizabethan period with *Arden of Feversham*, *A Yorkshire Tragedy*, and *A Woman Killed with Kindness*. In the eighteenth century it developed a new realism with a direct and genuine attempt, though most often with a melodramatic emphasis, to represent some aspect in the lives of the middle classes, who were constituting an ever increasing part of the audience. One of the most successful of these writers was George Lillo (1693–1739), a Londoner, brought up to his father's trade as a jeweller. Lillo was familiar with the earlier tradition of domestic drama, as can be seen by his adaptation of *Arden of Feversham*. With *The London Merchant; or The History of George Barnwell* (1731), he had an apprentice as hero and introduced into the eighteenth century a new prose drama of domestic life. To such a degree did Lillo match the temper of his age with this tragedy that it had a European reputation. That Lillo is deliberately making an appeal to a less elevated social sphere appears in his prologue to *The London Merchant*. Unfortunately he gives his characters, both in dialogue and soliloquy, a rhetorical and unnatural expression; sometimes it sounds like an heroic drama in prose. Yet his intention was otherwise: tragedy he says has dealt with great characters in Rowe or Otway:

> *Forgive us then, if we attempt to show,*
> *In artless strains, a tale of private woe,*
> *A London 'Prentice ruin'd is our theme.*

In England the play was long popular in the theatre. Whatever its limitations and its crudity, it seemed to open up the promise of new dramatic possibilities. Lillo followed it in 1736 with *Fatal Curiosity: A True Tragedy*, which is a stronger play. He has given up prose for blank verse, which he also used, not very successfully, in his tragedy *The Christian Hero* (1735). *Fatal Curiosity* deals with a rural couple who are overwhelmed with poverty. Their son who has been successful in the Indies returns to them in disguise and they kill him for his riches. When the error is revealed the husband kills his wife and then commits suicide. The play has many sentimental elements, as for instance a certain luxuriating in emotion. An outstanding example is the melodramatic incident of the son's return in disguise so that later he may have additional pleasure in revealing his true identity to his parents. At the same time one feels that here is a drama, honestly composed, with a stern tragic intention which triumphs over any excesses of expression and situation. Lillo answered some need not only in his own countrymen, for his influence spread to France and to Germany.

While the sentimental drama and domestic tragedy constitute the most original contribution in the first half of the eighteenth century other and more traditional types also had their place. The success of Nicholas Rowe (1674–1718) has already been noticed. He made a link between the Restoration age and the eighteenth century. Trained for the bar he found his way, as many others had done, into the theatre. In *The Fair Penitent* (1703), and in his later plays he was looking back towards the tradition of tragedy of Otway, for whose work he expressed an admiration. The theme is derived from a play of Massinger's entitled *The Fatal Dowry*, and, though the plot is domestic, in the sense that it deals with a crisis in a number of private lives, it has a background that is romantic, and even heroic. The interest lies with the female character, who dies for the sake of love, and here emphasis is given to the pathos of her position. The play, written in an agile blank verse, had a great success in the theatre and was still being played in the third decade of the nineteenth century. Later, in *The Tragedy of Jane Shore* (1714), which was 'written in imitation of Shakespeare's style', Rowe gave to the domestic or private theme some gestures of an historical setting. It is difficult to discover the resemblances to Shakespeare, but it was an effective play for the stage and gave

Mrs Siddons one of her greatest parts. The emphasis still lies on a woman and the pathos of her position. The same elements combine in *The Tragedy of Lady Jane Grey* (*1715*). Rowe had gifts as a poet and as a dramatist, but at times he seems uncertain as to whether he will restore older forms of drama or capitulate to the new tendencies which have developed in his age; on the whole he decides to capitulate as a dramatist of the post-Jeremy Collier period.

While Rowe attempted to compromise between two worlds others maintained firmly a classical tradition in tragedy. Ambrose Philips (1675–1749) in 1712 produced with success *The Distressed Mother*. The first four acts are little more than a translation of Racine's *Andromaque*, and after this Philips contrives a sentimental ending. Both Steele and Addison helped to give the play its popularity and it will be recalled that Captain Sentry took Sir Roger de Coverley to see it and the knight was surprised that in a tragedy 'there was not a single sentence that I do not know the meaning of'. There followed in 1713 Addison's *Cato*, based on Plutarch's life of the younger Cato. The popularity of Addison's tragedy is now difficult to understand, for the verse is stiff, the theme has little dramatic vitality, and the characterization is uninteresting. Its verse contained the two notorious lines spoken by Cato's son, Portius;

> *'Tis not in mortals to command success,*
> *But we'll do more Sempronius, we'll deserve it.*

Yet the enthusiasm for this heavy classical tragedy was unbounded, and, on its translation into Italian, German, and French, it met with considerable approbation on the Continent. At home, political motives contributed to the success, for both parties wished to claim virtue and liberty as their own distinguishing qualities, and, apart from this, the portrait of a philosoper had interest to the men of the Age of Reason. Abroad the phenomenon of a regular classical play composed by an Englishman must have been a motive of curiosity that increased interest. Despite Addison's success, while Shakespeare and the older dramatists remained popular, the production of new work in the tradition of high tragedy declined. Samuel Johnson in 1749 brought the blank verse tragedy of *Irene* with him to London as part of his literary assets, but, despite the acting of his old pupil Garrick, the play was not successful. Thus, while much practised throughout the first half of the century, audiences became decreasingly receptive of the heroic and classical tragedy. Had some man of genius been associated with its history, its fortunes might have been otherwise, for the continued devotion of audiences to Shakespeare showed that there was a public for tragedy in the grand manner, when it had character and liveliness and a command of the theatrical art.

The contemporary attitude to the excesses of the diction of classical and heroic tragedy and the improbability of the situations can be seen in a number of parodies and burlesques. Of these the most effective was the burlesque tragedy of *Tom Thumb* (1730), by Henry Fielding, the author of *Tom Jones*. This entertaining piece, which was later reworked as *The Tragedy of Tragedies or The Life and Death of Tom Thumb the Great* (1731), touched upon all the weaknesses in the more ambitious tragedy. Though in his own plays Fielding had little of the strength which marks his work in fiction, he certainly possessed a genuine sympathy with the more sentimental and domestic types of drama. *Tom Thumb* had great popularity and encouraged Fielding to other burlesques, and to topical satires in the manner of Gay. *Pasquin* (1736) was followed by *The Historical Register for 1736* (acted 1737) with its satiric references to Sir Robert Walpole, and this was ultimately responsible for the Licensing Act of 1737. So without much exaggeration one may say that Fielding was responsible indirectly for all our absurd modern censorship of the drama in England.

Fielding was probably led to entertainments such as *Tom Thumb* by the success of John Gay's ballad-opera *The Beggar's Opera* (1728). This is one of the outstanding achievements of the English stage in the early eighteenth century. Its immediate aim was to satirize Walpole in the person of Macheath, the highwayman. But it had a more subtle design in transferring the whole grandiose apparatus of opera to the precincts of Newgate. Gay may have begun the notion innocently, and modestly enough, from a chance suggestion 'of a Newgate pastoral' given him by Swift, but he had fallen upon a new dramatic form, which had great charm, and on an idea which was effectively satirical, and in an unintentional way, half-revolutionary. *The Beggar's Opera* belonged not only to those things in the theatre which are original, but to that very small group of plays which are permanent, and have success whenever they are competently revived to intelligent audiences.

If the first half of the eighteenth century was weak in drama it could claim to have some outstanding figures among actors and actresses. The tradition in the early years of the century favoured excessive gesture, turgid declamation, and the extravagant exploitation of farce. This was modified by a few men of outstanding genius. With them the actor became more important than the play. A step in the right direction was taken by a remarkable figure, Charles Macklin, who, if the records are to be trusted, lived to be over a hundred, and was engaged actively on the stage for over sixty years. He brought some degree of naturalness into the interpretation of Shakespearian parts. For instance, in the early years of the eighteenth century Shylock had been played as a comic part. While Macklin was not bold enough to destroy this tradition, he had brought to it elements that were pathetic, so that one member of his audience wrote that 'the Jew's private calamities made some tender impressions'. David Garrick was the most memorable figure in the whole eighteenth-century theatre. This pupil of Samuel Johnson, who came with him to London, won his way with nothing except his histrionic talent to a place of national fame, with a fortune and a funeral at Westminster Abbey. He is, unquestionably, the greatest figure of the English stage. Many actors seem to have no character of their own: they are empty places to be filled by one imagined personality or another. But Garrick had a talent outside the stage as his letters show. He could hold his own with the great ones, with Johnson and Burke. Of his power over audiences and of his great range and talent there can be no doubt. It might be urged that he subdued everything, author, play, and all to the actor. His career shows a notably varied range of performances of Elizabethan and other classical plays, but he performed them in his own versions. Great as were many of his interpretations of Shakespeare's characters it can be questioned whether he fully appreciated the greatness of Shakespeare's genius. He would have been a more faithful servant of the drama as a whole if he had been less ready to adapt the plays to his own liking, and if he had performed the plays in Stratford instead of setting in motion that strange masquerade of the 'Shakespeare Jubilee'. But Garrick is dead, and for the actor, unlike the author, the wonder passes as soon as he leaves the stage for the last time. It is easy for those who have not seen him to write critically, but had we been among the audiences of his time we should also have succumbed to the spell. He belongs to an age when the actor dominated the theatre, and that is not a healthy condition, for the theatre can only truly flourish when all the partners to the play work in unison.

The conditions in the later eighteenth century do not differ materially as far as the audiences and their taste are concerned from those in the earlier decades of the century. The prevalent demand was for sentimentalism and pathos, and these the dramatists supplied with outrageous extravagance. Such drama can contribute nothing to the permanent tradition of the English theatre; while it remains important only to the student of taste, the student of the theatre may wish to be warned of the dangers and excesses which surround the art. Two of the most egregious practitioners were Hugh Kelly (1739–77), whose *False Delicacy* (1768) had an enormous success, and Richard Cumberland (1732–1811), who was equally if not more popular in plays such as *The West Indian* (1771). Kelly was the son of a Dublin tavern-keeper and it was there that he first met actors and gained some knowledge of the theatre. When he came to England he presented his first play, *False Delicacy*, to Garrick, who produced it at Drury Lane. In it he presents a number of lovers who owing to their complications are maintained in a continuous emotional fret, from which neither they nor the audience are released. The action is full of moral platitudes and the play itself states that 'the stage should be a school of morality'. It answered something in the mood of the age, and, apart from its theatrical success, three thousand copies were sold in a day. Nor was the taste insular, for the play was applauded in Paris and Lisbon. He followed it in 1770 with *A Word to the Wise*, a play on a similar theme.

Richard Cumberland (1732–1811), was from a distinguished family: his father became an Irish Bishop and his grandfather was Richard Bentley, Master of Trinity College, Cambridge. He turned to the stage after an official career as secretary to the Lord Lieutenant of Ireland. In *The West Indian* he portrays a young man who delights in intrigue but is full of 'nice feelings' and finds his motives in conflict when he attempts to seduce a young lady;

he offers his 'love free, disencumbered, anti-matrimonial love'. After a number of complexities the 'nice feelings' prevail. He is portrayed as the natural West Indian, with strong primitive feelings. As he describes himself: 'in short, I am a West Indian; and you must try me according to the charter of my colony, not by a jury of English spinsters'. Ultimately he concludes an honourable alliance with the lady he had tried to seduce only to discover by one of those chances, more common in the theatre than in life, that she is an heiress. Cumberland brings the vigour and sincerity of the allegedly uncorrupted life of the plantations into contrast with the manners of the city. With audiences satisfied with plays such as these there seemed no future for the theatre, or at least no future unless some man of genius appeared. Fortunately two such did arise in the persons of Oliver Goldsmith and Richard Sheridan, and, suddenly, they make the 'seventies of the eighteenth century one of the distinguished periods in English drama.

All that criticism need say of Oliver Goldsmith (1728–74) is contained in the phrase in Samuel Johnson's epitaph: 'there was no type of writing that he did not attempt, and each type that he attempted he adorned'. With natural genius few men can have been so richly endowed, but the application and capacity for taking pains, which are necessary auxiliaries if genius is to be effective, were sadly lacking. In turn he produced essays, a novel, and poems in the heroic couplet, and into each genre he seemed to instil, by some effortless means, an original element which was the outcome of his own personality. In none of these forms did he persist. For instance, *The Vicar of Wakefield* is so fresh and human amid the fictions of the eighteenth century that one would imagine that the author would be impelled to go on and repeat his success. For him it was only a volume that, with the help of Johnson, he might sell to some rascally bookseller, and so escape from debt, and he seems all unconscious of the possibility that before the end of the next century over a hundred new editions of his masterpiece would be printed.

Goldsmith seems equally casual in his entry into drama. His own work is so full of genuine and recognizable emotions that one can easily understand that he had a deep antagonism to the false excesses of sentimentalism. When he came into the theatre with *The Good Natur'd Man* in 1768 it was with the deliberate intention of exposing the strained emotionalism of Kelly and Cumberland. Much in the play shows that Goldsmith is new to the stage, and some of the scenes and motives seem not wholly to have detached themselves from the type of drama which he is out to attack. Still the satire was keen enough to be recognized by eighteenth-century audiences and they opposed a play in which their emotional indulgences were parodied. Goldsmith was a clear-sighted reformer who asked 'Which deserves the preference, the weeping sentimental low comedy, so much in fashion at present, or the laughing and even low comedy, which seems to have been last exhibited by Vanbrugh and Cibber.'

Admirable in its period, *The Good Natur'd Man* has not the qualities to lift it into that small group of plays whose power of entertainment remains potent from one generation to another. It was otherwise with *She Stoops to Conquer, or The Mistakes of a Night* (1773), for this has given pleasure whenever it has been reproduced. It survives rough handling by the rawest of amateurs and yields a new vitality when the best of theatrical talent is devoted to it. The critics have found many faults in it, but then how easily the critics do discover these blemishes in great works of art. The most memorable thing that T. S. Eliot said about *Hamlet* was that it was imperfect, while A. C. Bradley once permitted himself the sentence that 'something of the confusion which bewilders the reader's mind in *King Lear* recurs in *Antony and Cleopatra*, the most faultily constructed of all the tragedies'. The task of criticism should be supremely to define the quality which has given certain dramatic works an abiding vitality. In *She Stoops to Conquer* this can be discovered first in the fable, which, whatever its improbability or its absence of originality, is full of strong dramatic situations, easily intelligible, and all contributing towards a main design. This central story, endowed with an atmosphere at once natural and romantic, is full of that geniality and warmth which are continually such pleasing qualities in Goldsmith's work. The characterization is strong and unmistakable, but within well-defined types an element of novelty has been introduced. The whole combines to make a comedy, never pretentious, never over-subtle, but arising so solidly from what is fundamental in human nature that audiences in succeeding generations have always recognized its quality.

As has been emphasized more than once in this volume, there is very little English comedy that lives on from one generation to another. With the single exception of G. B. Shaw, those who have produced it, Congreve, Goldsmith, Sheridan, Wilde, all have been active in the theatre only for short periods. Of these one of the most brilliant is Richard Brinsley Sheridan (1751–1816), and his career is perhaps the strangest, as, unfortunately, it is one of the shortest. He was the son of an actor, and was sent to Harrow for his education. There, according to Lord Holland, 'he was slighted by the masters and tormented by the boys as a poor player's son'. As a result he had an aversion for the stage. If he refused to act in a theatre he became in real life involved in an adventure which has all the motives of an eighteenth-century comedy. To save the beautiful Elizabeth Linley from an undesirable suitor he eloped with her and went through a form of marriage. As a consequence he had to fight two duels to save his reputation, and later he fell in love with the lady whom he had been previously platonically protecting. In 1772 when they settled in London, in the centre of the world of fashion, sheer indigence forced Sheridan to turn to that world of the theatre which he had attempted to avoid.

Sheridan's later career is less well-remembered. He abandoned the stage for politics, becoming, at one time or another, Under Secretary for Foreign Affairs, Secretary to the Treasury, and Treasurer of the Navy. One could willingly have spared every one of those honours for ten years of comedy. As it is, all that is important comes within four years: *The Rivals* (1775), *The School for Scandal* (1777), and *The Critic* (1779). To these can be added the short farce of *St Patrick's Day* and the lively and successful comic opera *The Duenna*, both of which belong to 1775, the same year as *The Rivals*. In 1777, a few months before *The School for Scandal* was enacted for the first time, he prepared an adaptation of Vanbrugh's *The Relapse* under the title of *A Trip to Scarborough*.

Of *The Rivals*, which is a miracle as a first play, Sheridan's own opinion was very modestly expressed, and Moore, in his Diary, goes as far as to affirm that 'Sheridan always said *The Rivals* was one of the worst plays in the language and he would have given anything he had, not to have written it'. It is a comedy which acts far better than it reads, and this accounts for the patronizing tone of the opinion expressed by some contemporary periodicals.

A typical example of this critical myopia appeared in *The Gentleman's Magazine*: 'The dialogue of the comedy is, in general, natural and pleasing; as to the plot, though we have often heard of younger brothers and fortune-hunters assuming fictitious titles and estates as credentials to rich heiresses, it seems very unlikely that real rank and fortune should be deemed an objection, and therefore disclaimed as in the piece before us. Here the marvellous and the romantic seem to lose sight of the natural and probable.' The immediate popularity lay partly in the skill with which Sheridan combined the wit and elegance of a manners comedy, freed from all immodesty of the Restoration pattern, with scenes of sentimentality which could be played 'straight' or treated ironically. It is more difficult to account for the permanent power which the play has possessed over audiences in the theatre. Sheridan seemed to have some innate knowledge of the conventions of the stage. His characterization is broad, and, indeed, in Mrs Malaprop it may be urged that it is too broad. Still it consistently gives magnificent opportunities to the players. The plot, which would not serve for a novel, holds together admirably in the theatre. Basically, it returns to the theme of classical comedy, of the quarrel between parents and children. A father and an aunt try and arrange a match for a son and a niece, while the young people have already found each other and are secretly in love. The exposition is quickly, even entertainingly given and the purely comic plot is mingled with the sentimental. The whole has elegance, and one is again reminded that while morals make men good, it is manners that make them interesting. Often one is reminded of Shakespeare's handling of comic situations. One of the most original things in the play is the dialogue. This is Sheridan's own invention. It is sometimes said that Shaw makes all his characters witty or at least amusing, but so do Congreve and Sheridan and Wilde. If the characters talked as they would in real life they would be unbearably dull, but a 'nice derangement of epithets' makes them entertaining, and despite the fact that Sheridan is writing in prose he would seem to have learned from Shakespeare this way of giving a wash of fine words to the play.

As *Love for Love* is to *The Way of the World* so is *The Rivals* to *The School for Scandal*. The later play is more considered, more subtle, more perfect even, but less spontaneous. The farcical

elements have been removed; the characterization is firm, penetrating and human and, above all, the plot is one of the most
perfect in the whole range of English comedy. Congreve, who had
long considered the plot of *The Way of the World*, allowed his
pattern to become so elaborate that elements of obscurity intruded,
but Sheridan maintains a complex movement with complete
clarity, and shows the strength of his command, particularly in
episodes such as the famous screen scene. The characters, too,
are penetrating portraits so that one must go back to Congreve,
and sometimes beyond Congreve to Shakespeare, to find the like
of Charles Surface and Lady Teazle. *The Critic* is a less ambitious
play. It is a general burlesque on dramatic absurdities bringing
up to date the parodies which in the previous century Buckingham
had invented so successfully in *The Rehearsal*. Augustan tragedy,
the sentimental drama, the incongruity of mismanaged stage
effects, all these Sheridan burlesqued. It can still give entertainment as modern revivals have shown. There is no play which
reveals more fully how Sheridan understood the stage and its
conventions. English drama would have been far richer if he
could have served it longer.

However uneven in dramatic creation, the late eighteenth and
the early nineteenth century had some outstanding figures among
their actors and actresses. Garrick was retiring by the time that
Sheridan had captured the stage, but he wrote an admiring prologue to *The School for Scandal*. Edmund Kean was finding his
way to the stage as a child player before the century had ended,
and in the early nineteenth century gave commanding performances
of the great Shakespearian roles, particularly Shylock, Richard III,
Hamlet, Othello and Iago. Roger Kemble formed his own company as an actor and a manager in 1753, and through his marriage
with Sarah Ward, became the father of one of the most distinguished of all English theatrical families. John Philip Kemble, his
son, was an actor of the declamatory school, and played in all the
major Shakespearian roles. He was overshadowed by his sister
Mrs Sarah Siddons, one of the great figures of the English stage.
She had been engaged by Garrick in the 'seventies to play Portia
at Drury Lane, and from then until 1812, when she gave a farewell
performance in Lady Macbeth, she was a figure of incomparable
power. Her friendship with all the great literary authors of the day,

and the esteem in which she was held by the Royal Family did much to elevate the social status of the actor in the community, where unfortunately the theatre itself as an institution had but little standing. These were not healthy conditions, for as has already been suggested the theatre depends on a multiplicity of efforts all aimed at one end, and the lack of this cannot be compensated by the excellence of one contributor, however brilliant that may be.

CHAPTER ELEVEN

The Nineteenth Century

THE EARLY nineteenth century is one of the most unrewarding periods in the English theatre. It was a great era in poetry and fiction, but men of letters when they came into the theatre seldom found themselves in a congenial atmosphere. The audiences were content with farce and melodrama and extravagant displays, and no management had the courage to attempt any elevation in their taste. The legitimate theatres had been constantly enlarged so that natural acting was no longer possible, and spectacle and declamation could alone appeal to the large and sometimes unruly audiences that filled the vast auditoria of Covent Garden and Drury Lane. The players, apart from the brilliant exceptions, were too often a group isolated from ordinary society, and without adequate taste or education. The great players such as Mrs Siddons and Kemble found the audiences gross and unrewarding.

All the poets of the romantic period showed some interest in the theatre, but failed as dramatists. Robert Southey did not succeed with his plays on a revolutionary theme *The Fall of Robespierre* and *Wat Tyler*. Nor was Samuel Taylor Coleridge much more successful with *Remorse* (1813), a revision of an earlier play: he thought well enough of his attempt to send it to Sheridan with an eye to production, but that master of the stage could not discover any theatrical validity in the melodrama. William Wordsworth, like Coleridge, under the influence of Schiller's *The Robbers*, attempted the drama in *The Borderers*, but the blank verse would have been heavy enough to weigh down the play, even if the theme had been theatrically successful. Shelley's *The Cenci* (published, Leghorn, 1819; London, 1821) is the most notable dramatic achievement of the romantic poets of his period, and, if the incestuous theme had not been so forbidding, the tragedy would probably have had a greater success on the stage. Coleridge and Wordsworth were far too self-centred and introspective to be successful in the theatre.

On the other hand, Byron, despite a formidable egocentricity, showed genuine knowledge of the stage and of its possibilities in plays such as *Manfred* (1817) and in 1821 *Marino Faliero, Cain, Sardanapaulus* and *The Two Foscari*. He continued with *Werner* in 1823. Yet his skill as a dramatist is never fully related to his lyrical and imaginative power. It is ironic that *Manfred*, which is poetically the most profound, has the least chance of theatrical success. Keats delighted in the theatre, and had he lived he might well have matured his knowledge into a successful dramatic talent. He wrote with Armitage Brown a play, *Otho the Great*, which was actually accepted for performance at Drury Lane, though it was not produced. Neither in the verse nor in the theme does Keats match his non-dramatic achievement.

Part of their lack of success rests with the romantic poets themselves, and with their deliberate cult of individualism, and an isolation from society. Further there was the dead-hand of a false Elizabethan tradition, the belief shared by many of these poets, as with Charles Lamb in *John Woodvil*, that stretches of blank verse would themselves constitute a play. But as has already been suggested, whatever the limitations of the poets themselves, the conditions in the theatre were invariably discouraging. Popular taste was attracted not by the best things in romanticism, but by gothic tales and horror themes and the ravings of the more lurid elements in German romantic tradition.

The failure of the early romantics did not deter poets later in the century from attempting success in drama. Robert Browning seems at first sight to have the right talents; his dramatic monologues have, at times, a Shakespearian quality, and he could command a vivid blank verse. Further he had a distinguished actor, Charles Macready, to encourage him towards the stage. It was Macready who asked him to write *Strafford* in 1837, but, though the play has a certain nobility, it fails in dramatic cohesion. Undeterred Browning returned with *King Victor and King Charles* (1842), and *The Return of the Druses* (1843) and later plays. Lord Tennyson's outstanding reputation as a non-dramatic poet and the help of Sir Henry Irving and others led to the acceptance on the stage of *Queen Mary* (1876), *Harold* (1877) and *Becket* (1879). A. C. Swinburne devoted much of his time to blank verse drama, including his gargantuan tragedies on the life of Mary Queen of

Scots, but he was not thinking so much of the theatre as of book publication.

It is a commonplace that in the second half of the nineteenth century there was a renaissance of taste and of dramatic writing in the English theatre. All this can be admitted without unduly exaggerating the quality of the work through which the improvement was achieved. In order to maintain standards it is well to remember that, in Norway, Ibsen's *Catiline* was written as early as 1850, and *Pillars of Society* by 1877, and it is a sobering exercise to compare these with the best that was being written in England at the same dates. In England itself a number of new conditions contributed to improvement. By an Act of 1843 the restriction which had kept the approved performance of plays to the patent theatres was removed. Strangely enough the new liberty was not immediately realized, but in the 'sixties and in the 'seventies a number of new theatres were built. Unhappily it was not one of the choicest periods in English architecture, but whatever the structural deficiencies, conditions developed in which there was a freer trade in the presentation of plays. Further, an improvement, though only a modest one, could be observed in the quality of the audiences, while the delight of the Queen in dramatic entertainments tended to give the theatre a social standing which it had not possessed in the early years of the century. The position of the dramatist improved when from the 'sixties onwards he contrived to substitute a profit-sharing basis for a lump payment. The change made the profits of the dramatist comparable with those of the popular fiction writers, and had the system existed earlier in the century, men such as Dickens and Thackeray might have been drawn to the theatre. Further, there existed, especially from the 'sixties, an increasing awareness of social problems, and some of this found expression in drama.

The earliest of the reformers who modified drama from the fustian of stale romantic themes, farce and extravaganza was T. W. Robertson (1829–71). He brought scenes into his plays which had a contemporary realism, and employed more modern methods of production on the stage. He had begun as a dramatist as early as 1845, but there was nothing to distinguish his work from that of other popular exponents of farce and melodrama. A fresh quality became apparent in *David Garrick* (1864), based on one of his own novels, and *Society* (1865), where he began his conscious attempt to introduce naturalism into the drama. The play was successful, and he was encouraged to give his intentions fuller definition in *Caste* (1867). This play when read seems to be full of gross exaggerations, but it has a dramatic quality, immediately apparent, when it is revived on the stage. Robertson has given the play direction by adding to its comedy and sentiment a strong central theme based on social ideas. A working-class girl, Esther Eccles, has married George D'Alroy who in rank is far her superior. The characters are grouped around these two personalities who represent social extremes. On D'Alroy's side is the haughty De St Maur, and the reasonable Captain Hawtree. Among Esther's associates, apart from her inebriate father, there is her sister Polly with her solid working-class lover, Sam Gerridge. *Caste* is not a great play, but it is an enormous improvement on the theatre of its time, and it seems to set the drama on the task of social criticism in which during the next half-century some of its greatest triumphs were to be won. Robertson had achieved much both in theme and in the effective production of plays, yet it is sobering to remember that Ibsen's *Peer Gynt*, the greatest drama, perhaps, of the modern theatre, belongs to the same year.

Robertson was followed by Henry Arthur Jones (1851–1929), a playwright of good intentions and some melodramatic skill, for whom excessive claims have been made by the historians of the drama. He started life as a commercial traveller but turned to the theatre with great success. In 1882 he produced *The Silver King* in collaboration with Henry Herman. The play deals with a protagonist who falls on evil ways as a result of unhappy influences but makes good in America and returns to deal out retributive justice and revenge. Lest one should gain any exaggerated conception of the merits of this sentimental melodrama it is again well to remember that Ibsen's *An Enemy of the People* was produced in the same year. Jones's talent in the plays which followed is uneven, often pretentious and solemn; heavy and bombastic when he is serious, but with a talent for comedy when he is in his easier moods. In *Saints and Sinners* (1884) and in *Michael and his Lost Angel* (1896), he made his most serious attempts to deal with social and religious themes. Through Michael he shows a clergyman falling in love with a girl whom he has previously condemned. There is a fundamental unreality in the main conception despite theatrical effectiveness in individual scenes. This is true again of a play such as *Mrs Dane's Defence* (1900), which has an admirably conducted cross-examination scene, though the theme as a whole never intrudes beyond melodrama into the theatre of the imagination. More effective is *The Liars* (1897), where he treats of love and marriage and the conflict of emotions without the excessive self-seriousness of some of his other plays. It must be admitted that little either in his plays or in his personality remains attractive, but his contemporaries saw him as one to whom 'belongs a generous share of the credit for restoring the drama in England to its rightful position as a civilized and civilizing art'.

A far more engaging figure was Sir Arthur Wing Pinero (1855–1934). He had a very long career which began in the late 'seventies and continued to *The Enchanted Cottage* of 1922. In fifty-five years he wrote fifty-four plays of one sort or another. His wide range extended from farce in *Dandy Dick* (1887), to sentimentality in *Sweet Lavender* (1888): these were plays in the popular tradition and it can at least be said that the action was already far more skilfully deployed than in the work of his contemporaries. Stronger than these was *Trelawney of the 'Wells'* (1898), a play, which, with its portrait of the young Tom Robertson, under the name of Tom Wrench, has proved to possess an enduring quality. Pinero in looking back at the theatre earlier in the century has allowed a warm and generous mood to instruct the action, and, though sentimentality may be dominant, the whole has a genuine humanity which audiences have recognized whenever the play is revived. Influenced by Ibsen's ideas but not yet comprehending Ibsen's theatrical skill he had approached the more serious social and personal problems already in 1889 with *The Profligate*, but his greater success in this type of drama came later with *The Second Mrs Tanqueray* (1893), with Mrs Patrick Campbell playing the leading role, and *The Notorious Mrs Ebbsmith* (1895). By comparing *The Second Mrs Tanqueray* with *The Profligate* one can discover what an English writer could learn on the technical side alone by the study of Ibsen. The whole management of a modern theme with a natural movement of the characters within a well-constructed plot has now come within the powers of an author who earlier had to rely on 'asides' and coincidences and innumerable entrances and exits. This increased skill in construction combines with a firm and sober treatment to make *The Second Mrs Tanqueray* one of the best social or problem plays in the nineteenth century. Paula, the wife of Tanqueray, is a woman with a past, who is led ultimately to suicide, and, though a modern audience may feel that the emotions are forced, they remain effective in the theatre, and Pinero, as usual, offers ample opportunities to the players. As St John Ervine has suggested, Pinero's fame decreased as that of Shaw rose, but he has left something permanent to the theatre.

While Henry Arthur Jones and Pinero were aiming at a play in which contemporary problems and conditions could be seriously explored, other traditions were also finding a new vitality of expression. William Schwenk Gilbert, who began his career as a writer of farces, developed an individual type of poetic and satiric comedy in *The Palace of Truth* (1870). The motive of the action lies in the fantasy that within the Palace of Truth each character must speak precisely what is in his mind. The play had a powerful dramatic influence. Gilbert employed it again, though not in such an obvious or direct way, in *Engaged* (1877), and it remained the dominant motive in a number of Shaw's early comedies such as *Arms and the Man*. Gilbert might well have developed into a considerable dramatist of a regular type had he not discovered a new medium for his talents. In 1875, he wrote *Trial By Jury*, and from then onwards he worked in collaboration with Arthur Sullivan on the 'Savoy' comic operas. The wit and brilliance of these made contemporary dramatists realize that if they were to compete they must improve both in plot construction and in verbal dexterity. The English stage had not been so brilliantly entertained since Gay's *The Beggar's Opera*. The work of Gilbert and Sullivan has suffered from too frequent repetition, and there would be much to be said for the institution of some voluntary self-denying ordinance limiting the number of performances of the Savoy operas. Yet their very popularity is evidence of their appeal and of the fact that in English there is nothing that matches them.

Before the nineteenth century closed, one writer of comedy for a few years adorned the stage, and then tragically disappeared. On the work of Oscar Wilde (1856–1900) criticism still maintains considerable dispute, and yet whenever his comedies have been revived they have pleased audiences, even those whose minds were not held when they read the plays in the unrevealing pages of a book. Apart from his French play *Salome* (1892), his reputation depends on a small group of comedies: *Lady Windermere's Fan* (1892), *A Woman of No Importance* (1893), *An Ideal Husband* (1895), *The Importance of Being Earnest* (1895). Wilde's comedy is an intimate expression of his own personality. From some critical standards the plots may be deficient, and in the earlier plays he is occasionally beguiled into episodes which are sentimental, and even a little solemn. But from the first he is working out towards a comedy that shall be all compact of elegant artifice, and this ultimately he achieved in *The Importance of Being Earnest*. It was a return, not by any direct imitation, but by some innate sympathy, to the spirit of Congreve. But Wilde was hampered because his fashionable and well-bred audiences would not permit the dramatist to employ the amorous themes which Congreve pillaged as motives for entertainment. Wilde had to preserve a strait-laced decorum and yet achieve gaiety and wit. That he succeeded is a measure of the brilliance of his dialogue. Further he endowed comedy with a sense of good-natured amusement, of fun, of gay irresponsibility, so that his plays have not their like on the English stage. The dramatic critic may complain about construction and discover that Wilde employed the antiquated device of the 'aside'. But in a comedy where all is artifice why should a complaint be lodged if in addition the dramatist uses the artifices of the stage itself? The solemn have shown with ponderous efficiency that Wilde had not the serious and moral aim which was developing in the social drama of his time. It would indeed have been inappropriate had he allowed these elements of the real world to intrude into this pattern of gaiety and entertainment. The test of drama lies ever in the theatre and any who will submit to that test with Wilde's comedies are likely to succumb. Those who mix up considerations about Wilde's life with his comedies are confusing two unrelated issues. As far as the drama is concerned, the tragedy of Wilde's life is that it removed him from the theatre when his contribution might have been so much more ample and varied. The degree of advance in *The Importance of Being Earnest* from the earlier plays shows how far his talent might have extended if circumstances had permitted.

CHAPTER TWELVE

G. B. Shaw

THE GREATEST figure in the English drama of the late nineteenth and the twentieth century has been George Bernard Shaw (1856–1950). Though this statement is made thus categorically it would not meet the approval of the younger writers and critics of the 'fifties and the 'sixties. They have written disparagingly about Shaw, or neglected him altogether. When the English periodical *The Twentieth Century* in February 1961 devoted an issue to the contemporary theatre with articles by playwrights, actors and directors, there was only one reference and that a contemptuous one to Shaw. A typical comment, but one less extreme than many was made in 1962 by A. R. Jones in another publication.[1] While he admires much of what Shaw achieved he concludes: 'The modern dramatists' debt to him is considerable, for the popular plays that hold the London audiences, the plays of Terence Rattigan or Peter Ustinov, for example, are derived directly from Shaw and it is this whole tradition that the contemporary dramatist has repudiated.' Some assessment of the 'contemporary dramatist' in England will be found at the conclusion of this volume. Here let it merely be stated that Shaw's work has a range and brilliance with which none of his younger successors has been able to compete. The neglect of him is comparable to the neglect of H. G. Wells by critics of the novel; the disparagement of both is only a temporary and arrogant phenomenon. It arises from the excessive praise in some quarters of certain contemporary dramatists, above all of those who think they have broken away from tradition without having adequately schooled themselves in the tradition from which they think they have broken away. Against this it may be asserted that in a period when, on the whole, drama in England has not reached the eminence attained by some American and Continental writers, Shaw stands out as the only English

[1] *Stratford-upon-Avon, Studies 4*, 1962

dramatist with a world reputation. Further, he has survived the supreme test that his plays still remain on the stage in a period which began nearly eighty years ago. They have survived transference into the mass medium of the film and in his life-time he exercised such great authority that on the screen his own dialogue was retained. What he would have thought of the popularization of *Pygmalion* into the successful musical of *My Fair Lady* is more difficult to say, but that the execution was possible shows the dramatic strength with which he had portrayed the fable in the original play.

His career was the longest in the British Theatre, for his first play, *Widowers' Houses*, was begun as early as 1885 while *Buoyant Billions* appeared in 1949 over sixty years later. The massive list of plays written between those dates gives only a part of his literary output, for he was active as a political pamphleteer and a critic. Born in Dublin, he came to England in 1876 and early emerged as a leading figure with Sidney and Beatrice Webb in the Fabian Society. The Fabians aimed at penetrating government gradually with socialistic institutions by non-revolutionary means, and Shaw was a prominent contributor to *Fabian Essays* (1889), where some of their proposals are set out. William Archer, the dramatic critic, has described how he saw Shaw, as a young man, in the British Museum Reading Room, with Marx's *Das Kapital* and the score of *Tristan and Isolde* set out before him, one on each side of the desk. Such a picture symbolises his interests. He was never a Marxist, but his mind was constantly stimulated by ideas; socialism, religion, sex, medicine, vegetarianism, education, there was no aspect of human activity that he was not prepared to think out afresh. On the other hand, he was deeply moved, possibly as an inheritance from his mother, in music, and through music in opera and drama. It may be questioned whether this awareness extended to the visual arts. One of his most individual achievements was to bring his two interests together and use drama in the service of ideas.

In his early years it was his knowledge of the arts that supported him as a professional critic. In the new evening newspaper the *Star*, which sold for a halfpenny, he had his column as a musical critic, and used the generally radical policy of the paper to incorporate his views on many topics including himself. He came to the theatre first as the dramatic critic of the *Saturday Review*, and his articles, written weekly from 1895 to May 1898, are collected in *Our Theatres in the Nineties* (1931). The amount of dramatic criticism of play productions, that has any survival value is depressingly small. Shaw's essays are among the most brilliant and painstaking series of notices of the contemporary drama ever composed in England. Nor did his comment on matters theatrical end here, for, as one of the first in England to announce the greatness of Ibsen, he composed as early as 1891 *The Quintessence of Ibsenism* (revised, 1913). Further, the published volumes of his correspondence with two great actresses, Ellen Terry and Mrs Patrick Campbell, reveal not only much about his personality but a great deal about the art of acting.

His earliest work in drama was directed towards the statement and criticism of contemporary social evils: in *Widowers' Houses* (1892) he dealt with slum landlordism; in *Mrs Warren's Profession* (1893) with prostitution; and in *Arms and the Man* (1894) with the romantic conception of the soldier. In *Widowers' Houses* he had, admittedly, made an uneasy start, and *The Philanderer* (1893, not performed until 1895), in which misconceptions of Ibsenism are mingled with a certain egocentric display, is only of ephemeral interest, and is the worst of his plays of the early period. By *Mrs Warren's Profession* he had proved to himself, though not immediately to the general public, that he was a dramatist of great power and originality. The play was censored, though its theme is profoundly moral: it displays the wealthy prostitute in her relations with her hard, unromantic daughter, whom she had educated to a world of refinement and culture. With *Arms and the Man* he had attracted attention, if not as yet any massive acceptance. To compare this comedy with the plays of Jones or Pinero is to realize the degree of advance he had already made. From Ibsen he had learned how to manage plays with a contemporary setting, and scenes which admit the discussion of ideas as well as action. Further, he had an intellectual equipment far beyond that of any English dramatist since Dryden. From his predecessors in England there was little for him to learn except to discover that with Wilde he shared a brilliance in dialogue. Unlike Wilde he was determined to employ this verbal gaiety, not merely for entertainment, but to explore every known problem, social, moral, political and religious.

He had an ear for all the rhythms of speech, and his friendship with
Henry Sweet, the philologist and phonetician, led him to study the
ways in which dialogue could be made as natural in movement as
it was witty in content. It was this special interest in language that
led him to *Pygmalion*, first produced Vienna 1913, and to the
desire to bequeath his whole fortune to the reform of the alphabet,
should this be found feasible.

In the presentation of character as opposed to the employment
of language, he seemed at first to work a little more to a formula.
He studied the conventional conception of a character as it appeared on the stage and in the minds of the public, and then
inverted it for the purposes of his own challenge to the lethargy
in contemporary thought. For the romantic courtesan he substituted the hard-headed business woman, Mrs Warren, and for
the guardsman of Ouida, who emerged from action with his
uniform in parade-ground perfection, he showed the mercenary
who knows hunger, fear, dirt and despair. It was as if all his
characters were passing through Gilbert's 'Palace of Truth', and
disclosing themselves unashamedly as they were. The satiric effect
of his characterization was undoubted, even if it was obtained at
some loss of human depth and variety. Yet *Arms and the Man* is
rich enough in comedy to admit of frequent revivals. A warmer
and fuller conception of character was obtained in *Candida* (first
performed in the provinces in 1897), a play in which he subjected
himself more deeply than before to Ibsen's influence. It was
through the production of *Candida* in New York in 1903 that
Shaw began to capture the theatre, and the American success led
Granville-Barker to introduce the play into a series of matinées
at the Royal Court Theatre. From this date onwards Shaw had
acceptance as a dramatist, though, in the early stages, Germany
and America were more receptive than England. Even if the theatre
would not always immediately accept his plays, he found a public
by volume publication. In so doing he transformed the presentation of the printed play. Instead of the dull stage directions,
normally found, he gave lively descriptions of character and scene,
so that the reader could follow the action. To the printed plays he
added dissertations, which were themselves substantial works, and
the whole was produced in a gracious format which he himself
designed.

In the next phase of his development Shaw departed from the contemporary scene to portray historical figures though maintaining the same formula of inversion as he had first employed in *Mrs Warren's Profession*. The 'nineties had almost worshipped a romantic conception of Napoleon, and so in *The Man of Destiny* (1897) Shaw presented a satiric portrait of the young Bonaparte which mocks at the grandeurs and idealizations. In *The Devil's Disciple* (first performed, New York, 1897) he showed how melodrama could be converted into a play through which thought and discussion could be conveyed, and then in *Caesar and Cleopatra* (1898, not performed in London until 1907, published 1901) he made his most considerable attempt up to this period in the presentation of an historical character. His mind had turned toward Shakespeare's writing down of Caesar in *Julius Caesar* and to his magnificent and romantic portrayal of the mature Cleopatra in *Antony and Cleopatra*. Shaw allowed himself a more ample plot than he usually employed. He gave a conception of Caesar which is, at once, comic and impressive. In a part originally designed for Mrs Patrick Campbell, he introduced high comedy into his portrait of a young Cleopatra of the pre-Antony period.

Already, as the portrait of Caesar showed, his mind was moving towards philosophical problems. He had worked out for himself a dynamic conception of evolution in which man need not be idle in the settling of his destiny. If any man would be but alert and active, the life force would use him in the unsteady and uncertain fight towards Progress. Still indulging in an atmosphere of luxuriant comedy he explored these ideas in *Man and Superman* (1901–3), one of the most brilliant of all his plays and unclouded by the deeper vision which appeared after the war of 1914–18. The play was a success in both England and America, and Shaw, on publishing the play, seemed to give proof that his genius was inexhaustible by adding a third act 'Don Juan in Hell', and an 'Epistle Dedicatory', with a 'Revolutionist's Handbook', and 'Maxims for Revolutionists'. The philosophical life-force theme gained a briefer, but dramatically an effective, presentation in *The Shewing-Up of Blanco Posnet* (1909), and here a touch of sentimentality, very rare in the plays, gives a human quality to the action; this did not prevent the play being banned, though performance at the

Abbey Theatre, Dublin, was possible as there the Lord Chamberlain had no power.

Shaw's other plays before 1914 gave evidence of great versatility. Already in *You Never Can Tell* (1896, published 1898) he had shown that his comic genius could have an almost irresponsible exuberance. In the later plays the exuberance remained even when a social theme was elaborately explored. So in 1906 there was gaiety in *The Doctor's Dilemma*, where the Shavian attack on the medical profession is presented, and again in *Misalliance* (first performed 1910), where, on a basis that is nearly farcical, education and the oddities of society are discussed. In 1912 *Androcles and the Lion*, with its massive preface on Christianity, gave an entertainment which is highly comic without ever abandoning its main purpose of exploring the nature of religious faith. Some urged that in these years the plays were merely brilliant speeches. This was altogether to miss the skill with which discussion had been made dramatically possible by a great command of the stage. Nowhere was this more clearly shown than in *Getting Married* (1908), where action, as ordinarily understood, was reduced to a minimum, while the dialogue and interplay of the minds of the characters maintained the interest of the audience.

Three plays of this period showed a more solid narrative basis in plot. *John Bull's Other Island* (1904) was Shaw's dramatic exploration of the Irish problem. *Major Barbara* (1905), looking back towards the methods of 'inversion' in character portrayal, showed the ways of a millionaire munition manufacturer and his Salvation Army daughter, and their several contributions to society. Of more permanent interest, in that its theme was detached from social and political problems and rested in the human personality as such, was *Pygmalion* (1913). This play may have begun with the jest that phonetics are a clue to class distinction, but it seized with Shavian transmutations on the old fairy-story theme of the poor girl who became a princess.

During the war years 1914–18 it would seem that Shaw did not write a new play. He came back to the stage with *Heartbreak House* (completed in 1918; performed New York, 1920; London, 1921), a satiric comedy in which he had used his study of Chekhov's *The Cherry Orchard* to give his impression of how Heartbreak House, which is England, drifted into ruin in 1913. As Captain Shotover says: 'The Captain is in his bunk, drinking bottled ditch-water; and the crew is gambling in the forecastle. She will strike and sink and split. Do you think the laws of God will be suspended in favour of England because you were born in it?' Though audiences in England failed to detect it, there was an increased depth of vision in the play which resulted from all that Shaw had felt and contemplated during the war years. *Heartbreak House* has been frequently revived and was presented on the London stage as late as the early 'sixties.

In 1919–20 with *Back to Methuselah* (first performed, New York, 1922) he produced his most elaborate dramatic creation, in which he went back to the very beginning of things, and forward as far as thought could reach, in order to show the nature of the life force, and its effect on the destiny of man. Shaw, in his preface, reviewed his past achievement in drama, and regarded this series of plays as its culmination. He confessed that he had intended *Man and Superman* to be a dramatic parable of Creative Evolution, but 'being then at the height of my invention and comedic talent, I decorated it too brilliantly and lavishly'. Now he abandoned Don Juan for the Garden of Eden and, in a more tragic period of human history, offered man a new myth without the erotic associations of the previous theme. The play was produced in all the main centres of theatrical activity in the world, and it aroused such interest that its appearance marked the height of Shaw's reputation as a dramatist. The series of five plays which constituted the work cannot be easily performed in the theatre in a run of less than three evenings, and it is a tribute to Shaw's genius and reputation that managements and public have on several occasions combined to revive the cycle. In its scenes he moved from comedy to a movement of rhetoric which has in it an element that is solemn and almost sublime: so here in the concluding speech of Lilith; 'Of Life only is there no end; and though of its starry mansions many are empty and many still unbuilt and though its vast domain is as yet unbearably desert, my seed shall one day fill it and master its matter to its uttermost confines. And for what may be beyond, the eyesight of Lilith is too short. It is enough that there *is* a beyond.'

In 1923 *St Joan* was produced, first in New York and a year later in London, and this was perhaps the most popular of all Shaw's plays, and continues to be frequently reproduced. In the person of the 'Maid' he had constructed a character which served all the purposes of his thought, and yet remained an attractive and credible human person. The complex historical actions with which she was concerned he had simplified into six superbly clear dramatic scenes, and only in his 'epilogue' did he revert to his normal practice of the permitting of ideas, presented in comedy, to be supreme over characterization. He allowed a quality warmer and more romantic than is usual in his work to suffuse this play. In the last group of plays, *The Apple Cart* (1929), *Too True To Be Good* (1932), *The Millionairess* (1936), and *Geneva* (1938), discussion increases and action declines. Of these *The Millionairess*, which he wrote originally with the thought that Edith Evans might play the main role, is a comic fantasy which has been frequently revived. *The Apple Cart* had a topicality in its exploration of democracy and dictatorship and its immediate impact was considerable. In 1949 he continued his career, and at the age of ninety-three had produced at the Malvern Festival, a play, *Buoyant Billions*, and a puppet·show, *Shakes versus Shav*.

To his own generation he was a great figure and he gave more delight in the theatre to the world at large than any man of his time. His limitations are obvious. He did not touch tragedy, possibly because he had a certain physical fastidiousness, which amounted almost to a fear of any world which could not be controlled by his own thought. His brilliance of dialogue sometimes led him beyond the bounds of dramatic propriety. Further in some of the later plays, such as *Geneva*, his dramatic devices lack the earlier ingenuity. He kept romance and colour out of his plays deliberately, and so, with the possible exception of *St Joan*, he failed to give the visual artists of the theatre, the designers and costume-makers, the opportunities of collaboration which they would have delighted to possess. It is churlish, possibly, to insist too sternly on this side of the balance-sheet for one who has given so much delight. His philosophy and his basic attitude of mind were formulated in a period when man still had some underlying faith in progress and in reason. When his age entered a more tragic period he was less at his ease, and he wrote some things about dictatorships which one could prefer unwritten. The century entered into a tragic period, and the great master of comedy seemed less appropriate. It was this change in values that led some of the generation of the mid-century to turn against him. Against all this must be assessed his achievement as a whole. Fortunately it can still be studied in the frequent revivals of his work. This, after all, is the great test of a dramatist; the survival on the stage of his plays after his own lifetime, instead of as textbook pieces. How few English dramatists have gained continuing acceptance by theatre audiences. Of Shaw it can be said, with certainty, that some of his plays will enter into the permanent repertory of the English theatre.

CHAPTER THIRTEEN

The Background of the English Theatre in the Twentieth Century

OF ENGLISH drama in the twentieth century this at least can be said that it is better than the drama of the nineteenth century. Shaw's contribution, which is mainly of the twentieth century, would alone establish this fact. Yet throughout the period the art of the theatre has worked uneasily inside the entertainment industry. It has suffered from the inroads of speculators and commercialism, and from the increasing costs of production, particularly in the West End of London. While there is this basic background, conditions have varied from one decade to another and the great dividing line is the period of the war of 1939–45. In 1940 the severe German air-attacks on London led the theatres to be closed. Only one remained open, the Windmill Theatre, which continued with its programme of non-stop Variety, and did so until recently. By 1941, after Hitler had diverted his main effort to his attack on the Soviet Union, London had some degree of slackening in air-attacks, and in 1942 many London theatres were re-opened, though under difficult conditions. On the whole, audiences preferred revivals of well established plays rather than untried works of new dramatists. One of the earliest and most brilliant of these war-time productions was Sir John Gielgud in *Macbeth*, a tragedy which discovered a moving topicality in its portrayal of tyranny. The public, though venturing into the darkness of the blacked-out city, wished to be home as early as possible, and so the time of opening was advanced from eight-thirty to seven-thirty or even to seven. In the post-war period many London theatres have retained seven-thirty as their time for opening. The old pre-war theatre catered, in its more expensive seats, for an audience that had already dined and was prepared often to change into evening dress for a visit to the theatre. In the 'twenties and the 'thirties there was a definite social distinction between the audience of the stalls and the dress circle and the audience of the pit and the gallery. In post-war England, as an aspect of the 'affluent' society, that distinction no longer exists. The effect on the drama itself was not as profound and beneficial as might be expected. True, the commercial theatre of the 'twenties and the 'thirties had to attempt, above all, to fill the stalls and the dress circle, and the successful dramatists, of whom Somerset Maugham and Noel Coward were supreme examples, aimed at an elegant and sophisticated drawing-room comedy. The ordinary West End audience may be socially more mixed, but there is nothing to suggest that it is more discriminating. Many of these new theatre-goers come in large organized parties at the end of a day in London, and such intelligence as they have is diminished by fatigue. It is this new element that has led to the exceptionally long runs of popular plays, a development in itself unhealthy for the theatre: as this chapter is being written (1964) one play in London, Agatha Christie's *The Mousetrap*, has been playing for twelve years.

Throughout the period the theatre has failed as a whole to gain a vital place in the community. Theatre-going is not a natural or necessary part of the life of even the more cultured members of the community. There are many towns of considerable size in England today without a resident professional company of any sort, and children often 'complete' their education without seeing a play performed on a live stage by professional actors.

In the twentieth century the theatre in England, as in other countries, has had to meet severe competition from new media. First, and very powerful, was the film. After its pioneer days the film housed its audiences far more comfortably than did the theatre and the hours of performance were more extended and con-venient. In an intermediate period, theatres were taken over and used for film productions. It has been estimated that as a conse-quence some five hundred theatres have been closed or pulled down in the last forty years. The film had an actuality and a range of scene with which the theatre could not compete, and it is not enough to say that this was an appeal solely to the less sophisticated parts of the audience. These factors were emphasized when later the film was able to incorporate both sound and colour. One effect of this competition is that, fortunately, the theatre has given up the old type of clumsy spectacle which had once been among its most popular appeals. A type of this entertainment was *Chu Chin Chow*, popular with audiences in the war of 1914–18, and surviving the war to create a record with two thousand performances on 29 December 1920. In the same year another popular spectacle, *The Garden of Allah*, based on Robert Hichens's novel, proved so popular at Drury Lane that the traditional 'Lane' pantomime had to be taken to Covent Garden. Further, it was to some extent the influence of the film that has led to the brilliant improvement in production décor and lighting which has marked the twentieth-century theatre.

Television has introduced a second and even more insidious competitor to the living theatre. A single television performance, given the size of English audiences, might reach as many people as would be represented by twenty thousand performances in the theatre. As yet it is difficult to calculate the effect in England of television on the living theatre. As far as the production of traditional drama, such as Shakespeare, is concerned the theatre has a magnificence for which the diminished screen is but a poor substitute. Younger dramatists have not taken easily to the medium and some of them view it almost with hostility. Thus John Osborne writes: 'I'd love to write something for a circus, something enormous and immense, so that you might get a really big enlargement of life and people. What's so boring about television is that it *reduces* life and the human spirit. Enlarging it is something that the theatre can do best of all. That's one reason why I'm not interested in writing for television. Economically, it has nothing to offer, considering the amount of work involved.'[1] So far, television drama has been left mainly to television dramatists, and, with some exceptions, their more serious productions have been of a realistic, almost documentary, character in contemporary social settings. It is always possible that this may change. For instance, a most promising young dramatist, John Arden, won his first success with a television play *Soldier, Soldier*, which won the Italia Prize in 1960.

Despite the conditions that have been imposed on it, the theatre in England in the twentieth century has survived and developed. There has been, for instance, almost continuously a theatre which

[1] *The Twentieth Century*, February 1961.

was not dependent on the commercial stage of the West End of London. Early in the century there were repertory companies maintained by private patronage; such was that of Miss Horniman in Manchester and that of Sir Barry Jackson in Birmingham. Nor was Sir Barry a remote patron who merely found finance: he directed plays, encouraged new dramatists, actors, and producers. Sir Barry was also able to make successful raids on London with plays such as Shaw's *Heartbreak House* and *St Joan*. In addition, during the 'thirties, he established the Malvern Festival, mainly devoted to Shaw, but also successfully introducing to the London stage plays such as 'James Bridie's' *The Sleeping Clergyman*. It was under Sir Barry Jackson's direction that the Stratford-upon-Avon company gained its major development after the war of 1939–45. Earlier than anyone else in England he saw that a successful theatre depended on a group of actors, directors, and designers who worked constantly together. Liverpool also had a repertory theatre with a distinguished record of achievement. In London, early in the century, Miss Lilian Baylis developed at the Old Vic, and later at Sadler's Wells, an organization for the performance of Shakespeare and the classical drama, as well as for opera and ballet. After the Second World War Government funds were made available to strengthen this whole organization, which is now functioning as a basis for the development of a National Theatre. The London public has shown itself prepared to go out as far as the Lyric Theatre, Hammersmith, when such a delight as the revival of *The Beggar's Opera* was prepared for its entertainment. Since 1945 there has been a new civic interest in the possession of a theatre. Here Coventry led the way with the Belgrade, and similar plans are actually in operation or contemplated by authorities at Nottingham, Leicester, Cardiff, Newcastle-under-Lyme, Croydon and Scarborough.[1] Also, mainly out of his own resources, Bernard Miles in recent years has constructed the Mermaid Theatre in London. Yet all this represents a number of isolated enthusiasms rather than the expression of a national need for drama, and compares sadly with the German construction since the war of nearly a hundred new theatres for opera and drama.

[1] Much of the information on these new developments is derived from Stephen Joseph's *Arenas and All That*, *The Twentieth Century*, February, 1961.

As has already been indicated,[1] the main period for construction of new theatres in England was in the eighteen-sixties. Many of these were designed for spectacle and all of them had a proscenium stage. It is difficult to adapt them for modern lighting and for conceptions of modern production. Until recent years the architect has had no place in the English theatre, for no new theatres were built and any lively tradition of theatre architecture was impossible. Some of the boldest experiments of the 'fifties and the 'sixties have had to be conducted in what Stephen Joseph has called 'the old and inadequate Royal Court Theatre, and at the ancient (but enchanting) Theatre Royal at Stratford in East London'. Certain younger artists today would like to see a departure from the proscenium stage to a theatre in the round and Sir Laurence Olivier has made experiments towards this end with the new 'open stage' theatre he helped to create and direct at Chichester, which is designed to hold 1400 people. Some young English theatre designers have looked with envy at the experimental architecture of University and other theatres in the United States, such as the Casa Manana Theatre at Fort Worth in Texas.

In each decade of the twentieth century new and enterprising experiments have been established, though none of these is a substitute for a theatre that had the close relation to the national life that existed in Elizabethan times. When speculation forced up the rentals of theatres in the West End of London in the 'twenties and the 'thirties, making the production of classical and experimental plays a dangerous venture, actors, who are devoted to their profession, arranged for Sunday productions of financially impossible ventures. H. Granville-Barker had commenced such Sunday performances through the Stage Society as early as 1898, and some of these proved sufficiently impressive to tempt West End managers to offer regular 'runs'. The Royal Court Theatre, in Sloane Square, which was later in the 'fifties and the 'sixties to become such a lively home of experimental drama, was used as early as April 1904 for a season of bold experiments in the whole art of play production by J. E. Vedrenne and H. Granville-Barker. It was during that season that Shaw gained an opportunity of reaching larger audiences in the theatre. There were frequent examples of the inability of commercial managers to assess the

[1] See page 145.

best in popular taste and one of the most successful plays of the whole period, R. C. Sheriff's *Journey's End* (1928), with a setting in the First World War, and with an all male cast, was rejected by almost every commercial management in England. The First World War produced very little drama. Sheriff had dealt with trench-warfare. Clemence Dane in *A Bill of Divorcement* (1921) dealt with problems following the aftermath of the war. In an adroit and moving action she reflected on problems of insanity and divorce with the consequences of the First World War as a background. The deep human interest of the theme and the skill of its dramatic presentation gave the play great popularity. Already well known as a novelist, Clemence Dane found herself famous as a dramatist. She essayed the stage again, as in the ingenious *Will Shakespeare*, but never with equal success.

Throughout this volume the indifference, and often the active hostility, of official and government sources towards the theatre has been apparent. This changed, in a typically English way, almost by accident as it were, during and after the war of 1939–45. In 1940 the State found funds of a modest character for C.E.M.A. (Council for the Encouragement of Music and the Arts) to assist in wartime, and under the conditions of evacuation, the wider distribution and the improvement of standards in Music, Drama and the Visual Arts. In 1946 C.E.M.A. was incorporated as a permanent body entitled the Arts Council of Great Britain, under the Chairmanship of Lord Keynes. The funds made available have greatly increased. Possibly the major impact of the Council has been on the display of the visual arts, but its influence on the theatre has been considerable. It contrived to assist in the removal of the Entertainment Tax on theatre tickets for companies who qualified under the somewhat clumsy formula that their work was 'educational, or partly educational'. Fortunately the Customs authorities interpreted this formula in a very generous way. The Council was also able to put its own funds at the disposal of the Old Vic and Sadler's Wells organization and greatly to strengthen the range and possibilities of production in those two companies. A further development of support for the theatre on a national scale followed an Act of Parliament of 1948 which permitted localities to spend a six-penny rate in England (rather less in Scotland) on the arts. In 1961 £250,000 was raised in this way, though the sum represented only a sixtieth of the amount the local authorities could have spent if they were so minded. The Arts Council was also able to convert Covent Garden into a national centre for opera and ballet, though, unfortunately, only at the expenditure of a considerable portion of its budget. From this new approach instituted by the Council, there emerged, as a practical possibility, what had long been a dream in the mind of many actors, namely the establishment of a National Theatre. English artists have often admired organizations such as the Comédie Française, the Moscow Art Theatre, and the Berliner Ensemble, and wished that they had some similar centre which on a national scale could give prestige and continuity to their art. The Old Vic and Sadler's Wells had been an approach, as in its own way had the Stratford-upon-Avon Theatre, which under the direction of Peter Hall had companies both at Stratford and London. Under the Chairmanship of Sir Laurence Olivier and with its preliminary base, as has already been indicated, on the Old Vic organization, it would seem that after innumerable delays the National Theatre has been established, though it will be a long time before it has its own buildings. It is proposed that there shall be two auditoriums, one of which will have an open stage, and a site has been assigned on the South Bank of the Thames.

Meanwhile in the 'fifties and the 'sixties the independent theatre has continued in new forms. The most important of these has been the work of the English Stage Company, under the direction of George Devine, at the Royal Court Theatre, the centre, as earlier noted, for the experimental seasons of Vedrenne and Granville-Barker. Devine, who has had long experience both as actor and director, began work with the London Theatre Studio in 1936, and from 1940 to 1946 was director of the 'Young Vic'. He has done much to open out new directions in the English theatre. Without attempting to impose his own personality on all the productions he has rather created a group, and within it expected close co-operation from author, director and actor. Asked what his own policy was, Devine once defined it as 'the right to fail'. Fortunately both he and the Royal Court have had some outstanding successes as well as failures. On 8 May 1956 John Osborne's *Look Back in Anger* was produced, and proved a turning-point in the theatre. The play had been submitted in the ordinary way after an appeal by the Royal Court for new plays. It became a commercial success, as did the film based on the play and produced by Tony Richardson. It was followed in 1957 by *The Entertainer* which was again a great commercial success. The merits of these and other plays of this new movement are discussed in the next chapters, all that is noted here is that great financial success came to the author and the theatre on the basis of these two plays and this, in turn, provided the Royal Court Theatre with Devine's 'right to fail'.

The other outstanding experimentalist has been Joan Littlewood with her Theatre Workshop in the theatre at Stratford East. Joan Littlewood, unlike Devine, imposed her own strong and highly imaginative personality on the plays she directed, so that some of them were re-shaped in rehearsal. She, again, had a commercial success that must have been almost embarrassing in its degree. From what was the left-wing theatre of the East End plays came to the commercial theatres of the West End in almost continuous succession. Thus in 1959 two Theatre Workshop plays were outstanding features of the West End season: Shelagh Delaney's *A Taste of Honey* and Brendan Behan's *The Hostage*. In a somewhat similar way Samuel Beckett's *Waiting for Godot* had its first English performance at the Art Theatre Club, but when transferred to the popular stage at the Criterion Theatre proved a powerful attraction. It is difficult to tell what can be deduced from this phenomenon. The commercial managements have obviously not the courage of the experimental and group theatres. Nor could plays such as those mentioned be contrived within the conditions of West End management and direction. A play such as *A Taste of Honey* demands the activist direction of a Joan Littlewood and the concentrated co-operation of an organization such as she controls. Seldom has quick financial success awaited an author so readily through a single play or two plays, especially if a film follows the theatre production. The conditions under which Shakespeare had to produce some two plays a year for thirteen years before he was a man of property at Stratford no longer prevail. Whatever the effect on the author, it may be surmised that the effect on the experimental theatres themselves cannot be a completely happy one. It is true that these spectacular successes give them the resources with which to continue, but some of their original impulses must be dispersed. A healthier condition would prevail if the theatre were not thus divided within itself, if, in fact, one were back with the Shakespearian conditions of a fellowship of players, which had cohesion and continuity, and addressed itself with the same plays to the Court and to the popular audiences.

This brief account of the background of the English theatre in the twentieth century would not be complete without some reference to the great development of the art of acting and stage production and direction in the period. When the century opened the era of the actor manager was still at its height. He would choose his own plays, to a large extent finance them, and above all he would play the main roles, and public attraction would centre around his personality. The most memorable figure here is Sir Henry Irving (1838–1905), who began his stage career as early as 1856 by playing Gaston in Bulwer Lytton's *Richelieu*. He became famous for his interpretation of the main role in a melodrama *The Bells* and finally he had a prolonged season at the Lyceum Theatre from 1878 to 1902 with Ellen Terry. One can see from Shaw's *Saturday Review* criticisms and from his letters to Ellen Terry what a tyranny this system could become, when the play, the other actors, and all that might pass under the name of production, were subdued to the authoritarian mannerisms of a single player, who himself was subject to no criticism. He neglected contemporary drama and contented himself with elaborately mounted productions of Shakespearian and other classical plays. A younger and more versatile example of the same breed was Sir Herbert Beerbohm Tree (1852–1917). He did at least include Ibsen, Wilde and Maeterlinck in his productions, but the same insidious defects were there. For two long periods he had first the Haymarket Theatre and then from 1897 Her Majesty's under his personal direction. The productions became ever increasingly more lavish and the mannerisms more pronounced. A virtuous variation on the type of personal domination was afforded by Sir Frank Benson (1858–1939), who provided the Festival at Stratford for thirty-three years with a Repertory of Shakespearian plays. He directed all but two of Shakespeare's plays. It was possibly fortunate that he had little money for his productions. Though he was the un-questioned leader of his company, it was in a genial way and his great generosity of personality led him to encourage young actors.

It is difficult to assess all the influences that broke down the enervating tradition of Irving and Tree. Shaw must have contributed something, and one can see in his theatre notices and his letters his distress that the beauty and talent of Ellen Terry should be wasted on the methods and tyranny of Irving. Also Shaw's dialogue, which responds to the natural idiom of the language as easily as did that of Swift, made highly mannered acting inappropriate. A wider influence, as has been suggested, was the film itself, for all the lavishness of stage production of the great actor managers could not begin to compete with the range and diversity of the film. Ibsen was again an influence in breaking down the old tradition, and, though it was long before his plays had any popular success, as so often happens the experimental theatre had its influence on the popular stage. One who proved a brilliant theorist of stage reform was Gordon Craig, and his influence was considerable though his temperament was not adjusted to the frustrations of actual production. His *The Art of the Theatre* appeared as early as 1905 and was followed by a number of volumes such as *The Theatre Advancing* (1921). His autobiography *Index to the Story of my Days* was published as late as 1957. A reformer who worked more within the theatre itself was Harley Granville-Barker (1877-1946), whose seasons at the Royal Court Theatre have already been mentioned. Granville-Barker's productions of *The Winter's Tale* and *Twelfth Night* in 1912 and of *A Midsummer Night's Dream* in 1914 set a completely new approach to Shakespearian production and had a wide influence. It is to be regretted that after his second marriage Granville-Barker became much less active in the theatre, for his *Prefaces* written between 1923 and 1946 show what he might have achieved; they have remained a powerful influence on younger directors.

In the training of actors, even in the belief that formal training is necessary, England has been backward. One step in the right direction was the founding in London of the Royal Academy of Dramatic Art through the initiative of Shaw and others. Unfortunately this lacked funds until it began to benefit from a bequest of the third of Shaw's estate; so that it can be justly said that if young actors and actresses are now trained under better conditions it is largely owing to the profits on *My Fair Lady*. The main training ground for actors in the twentieth century has been the Old Vic, particularly since Miss Lilian Baylis gained complete control in 1912. The tradition was continued after her death in 1937, and after the Second World War, the organization in London was supplemented by a company in Bristol. Apart from the Old Vic the provincial companies have provided wide experience to many of England's leading players. The fact that the Old Vic was such an important centre has meant, fortunately one may think, that England's outstanding actors have been trained in the classical tradition. This is memorable when it is recalled that the major tradition with new authors from the 'forties onwards has been in plays of a contemporary setting, and often with an emphasis on the sordid.

Space permits the mention of only a few names. The most representative figure of the contemporary generation of English actors is, possibly, Sir Laurence Olivier. His early days were spent with the Birmingham Repertory Company, but in 1944 he began a period of co-direction of the Old Vic with Sir Ralph Richardson, another actor in the best classical manner, and their productions were among the most outstanding in living memory. Olivier succeeded in making three films of Shakespeare's plays, *Henry V*, *Richard III* and *Hamlet*, which brought an awareness of Shakespeare's work to a far wider audience than ever before. The cancellation by his financial backers of his proposed film on *Macbeth* may have been crucial in his own career as it was in the history of dramatic taste. His versatility is shown in that he could turn from the great tragic roles to the brilliant interpretation of the broken down actor, Archie Rice, in John Osborne's play *The Entertainer*. More recently he has rendered Othello in a manner incomparable in living memory; and many have tried. He has taken an interest in the whole business of the theatre; a leader in the organization of the National Theatre and the prime mover in the experimental theatre in the round at Chichester. By common consent the figure that stands with Olivier is Sir John Gielgud, whose first stage appearance was at the Old Vic in 1921: he has brought supreme intelligence, subtle interpretation, and a beautiful speaking voice to the rendering of a large number of classical roles, and extended his range into contemporary drama, both in tragedy and comedy. One feels that a certain fastidiousness of personality would daunt him if he had to face interpreting Archie Rice in *The Entertainer*. Among other actors in this great tradition have been Sir Alec Guinness and Sir Michael Redgrave, both of whom have had connections with the Old Vic. Guinness has proved himself one of the most versatile of actors, both of theatre and film, but whether he will add something fundamental to the art, as Olivier and Gielgud have done, remains to be seen.

It might well be argued that the last three decades in England have had greater players than playwrights, for apart from these actors there have been great actresses; Sybil Thorndike who has had the longest stage career of the twentieth century and who could claim to have played a hundred parts in twenty-five plays in Shakespearian Repertory in America before she joined with Horniman's company in 1908; Edith Evans who since 1912 has played a large range of roles, Shakespearian, Restoration and modern; and Peggy Ashcroft who began with the Birmingham Repertory Company in 1926 and, often acting with Gielgud, has brought the same sensitive interpretation to many classical and modern parts.

The best of the talents of these and other great actors have been employed in revivals, in Shakespeare above all, but also in Restoration and other classical roles. Yet as the century proceeded drama in England began to be increasingly concerned not with the great themes and the historic figures but with contemporary settings and the meaner ways of life, and playwrights exorcized romance as if it had been a plague. It seemed that they had little use for the talents of many of the great artists of the theatre that were available in their time.

CHAPTER FOURTEEN

English Drama in the Twentieth Century

IN CONSIDERING the plays of the twentieth century in England it must be admitted that the younger dramatists and critics see a complete break in the conception of drama in the 'fifties and the 'sixties. This attitude is stated in its extreme form in the comment of Richard Findlater[1] that 'the first night of John Osborne's *Look Back in Anger* at the Royal Court on 8 May 1956, was a turning-point in the history of the modern British theatre'. Similarly John Russell Taylor writing in 1962 in *Anger and After* affirmed that 'the whole picture of writing in this country has undergone a transformation during the last five years or so' and once again the decisive event is alleged to be the first night of *Look Back in Anger*. This attitude is confirmed by the approach of some of these younger dramatists to their own work. Naturally these considerable claims have not gone completely unchallenged. For instance, Harold Hobson, the dramatic critic of the *Sunday Times*, who has shown a discriminating interest in the new drama and who could not possibly be described as a reactionary, wrote in 1959: 'It is time someone reminded our advanced dramatists that the principal function of the theatre is to give pleasure. It is not the principal function of the theatre to strengthen peace, to improve morality, or to establish a social system. Churches, international associations and political parties already exist for these purposes.' Another similar assessment comes from Allardyce Nicoll, who has shown his capacity to appreciate drama in all its manifestations. In the *Stratford-upon-Avon Studies* of 1962 he contributed an essay entitled 'Somewhat in a New Dimension'. His aim, while giving full appreciation to new achievement, is to show the merit of what had been produced earlier in the century. His attitude is identical to

[1] *Twentieth Century*, February, 1961.

that which is maintained later in this volume. He demonstrates how much of the work of the 'fifties and the 'sixties had been anticipated before 1930. Arnold Wesker, for instance, in commenting on his play *Chips with Everything* had said that there was a whole scene in the play 'in which absolutely nothing is said'. It is clear that Wesker considers this as an original invention. Nicoll points out that 'the now unduly neglected John Galsworthy excited London audiences with just such a wordless scene when he produced his *Justice* in 1910'.

All assessment of work that has been produced in one's own lifetime is difficult, but the attempt here is made, with as much objectivity as is possible, to deal with the plays of the last sixty years and to avoid the bitterness that has entered into much criticism. A single example may be quoted from many. In 1919, soon after the war of 1914–18, there was produced at the experimental season at the Lyric Theatre, Hammersmith, to which reference has already been made, a poetic play, entitled *Abraham Lincoln* by the now despised Georgian poet, John Drinkwater. It can be readily admitted that its success depended largely on the appropriateness of its theme in that particular post-war period. It drew large audiences and those of the more intelligent elements in the population. It was widely acclaimed and was superior to most plays that were appearing on the London stage at the time. Yet all that a younger critic such as Kenneth Muir could say of Drinkwater's language in the play is that it shows 'the putrescence of a dead romanticism'. To speak thus is to lose all touch with historical perspective. It is merely to express some personal conflict, some individual and private wound. Probably Drinkwater's play will never return to the stage, but then that is true of most of the plays mentioned in this volume, but that it could once have moved large audiences of intelligent playgoers suggests that it should be considered without contempt.

In the first decade of the century a number of dramatists continued the tradition begun by Robertson, Jones and Pinero of dealing seriously in the theatre with contemporary social problems. Shaw's contribution has already been assessed, and Ibsen was now available as a guide. Among these writers was Harley Granville-Barker (1877–1946) whose work as a critic and producer has already been a theme of comment. As early as 1899 he had completed *The Marrying of Ann Leete* (produced in 1902). In this comedy a young girl of an upper middle-class family rejects her official suitor for a match with her father's gardener. A certain air of fancy which surrounds the play is missing from the grim outlines of *The Voysey Inheritance* (1905), which deals with a young lawyer who discovers that his father has been misapplying the funds entrusted to him by his clients. He determines to continue the fraud in order to save his father's reputation. William Archer, the dramatic critic, saw the merit of this play on its first production and commented: 'A great play, conceived and composed with original mastery, and presenting on its spacious canvas a greater wealth of observation, character and essential drama than is to be found in any other play of our time.' *Waste* (1907) in which an illegal operation causes the death of the mistress of Henry Trebell, a brilliant young politician, proved too strong a theme for the censor. The play itself, which ends with Trebell's suicide, has an atmosphere of unrelieved gloom. *The Madras House*, which followed in 1909, proved the most successful of all Granville-Barker's plays. Complex in theme, bold and original in treatment, it may be best described as a satire on the thwarted lives led by women in England in the first decade of the century. Granville-Barker's theatre may not be completely satisfying, but it is so original that one could wish that he had persisted. His *Prefaces*, to which reference has already been made, are but little compensation for the loss incurred by his defection from the theatre after his second marriage. It has been suggested that a relentless gloom dominates *The Voysey Inheritance* and *Waste*, but that Granville-Barker could have developed into other moods is shown in *Prunella*, a romantic play where he collaborated with Laurence Housman.

John Galsworthy (1867–1933) came to the theatre after he had established some success as a novelist and his first play, *The Silver Box*, was performed in 1906 the same year as the publication of *The Man of Property*, the earliest volume in his successful series of novels, finally published under the title of *The Forsyte Saga*. For the next quarter of a century London West End managements accepted his plays and found them reasonably popular with audiences. Since his death Galsworthy's reputation has suffered a remarkable collapse, and revivals, which are the only real test of an author's continuing dramatic survival, have been very infrequent. It is true that in his own lifetime excessive claims were made for his achievements, and further, in any objective and critical reckoning, he will be found more effective as a novelist than as a dramatist. In England, at least, radio renderings have extended the audience of *The Forsyte Saga*, while the dramatist remains neglected and unacted. Yet on any historical assessment such as has been the approach throughout this volume, his achievement appears considerable. Place his work against that of Pinero and Jones and one can see how he had advanced in the art of play-making, apart from the increased seriousness and depth of his themes. Nor must it be forgotten that his plays were not being performed in a coterie theatre but to the regular audiences in the West End of London. Galsworthy's aim is to state a single theme, developing it in a plot of great simplicity of design. So in *The Silver Box* the plot has an almost mathematical precision. A domestic worker in a wealthy middle-class house is wrongly accused of stealing a silver box. From this Galsworthy is able through a number of neatly related incidents to show how unjustly life operated between different social groups. In 1906 it must have appeared as a play of much originality of thought with adroitness in dramatic execution. Its weaknesses are those which pursue Galsworthy throughout his dramatic work. His desire to illustrate some social theme in each of the plays leads to rigidity in design that can descend to the mechanical, and at times even to the obvious. From this closely designed plot the characters seldom emerge into any independence; they are rather 'humours', characters in the Jonsonian sense of the word, as if each person had to show but one aspect of himself and as if his speeches were controlled by the development of a single argument which is under the personal supervision of the dramatist himself. At the same time, though Galsworthy remained within that range of social realism, his talents as a dramatist developed markedly as he matured in his work. Among his most memorable plays were *Strife* (1909), *Justice* (1910), *The Skin Game* (1920), *Loyalties* (1922) and *Escape* (1926). Of these *Strife*, which deals with the struggle in industry between employers and employed, is the clearest example of his tendency to over-simplify a problem and to achieve this with an element of sentiment. *Justice* was among the most effective of his plays; it exposed the less desirable features of the British prison system, and Winston Churchill, who was Home Secretary, and so in charge of prisons, was led to initiate some reforms after he had seen Galsworthy's drama. Of all his plays *Loyalties*, which explores some of the more subtle forms of anti-semitism, has probably the best chance of survival, and it has been revived since Galsworthy's death. Its attraction lies not only in his treatment of the theme, but in the larger independence of action that he has allowed to the characters.

Galsworthy served an immediate purpose in awakening contemporary audiences to the urgency of the social problems that he explored, though as Harold Hobson reminded younger dramatists, in a passage already quoted, this is not the primary purpose of drama. Beyond this, Galsworthy gave to drama a depth and integrity that it did not generally possess on the English stage at the time. Yet Galsworthy remained in the plays, as in his novels, ultimately fixed, in a solid way, within the values of the world that he criticized. He had compassion, intellect to some extent, and a vision of a more just world, yet all of this did not disturb a certain unconfessed conviction that the upper middle-class to which he belonged was something permanent. His drama was held in tightly with materialism and the limited conception of realism that dealt solely with the contemporary scene.

This tradition of bourgeois drama was a strong one and it found expression through a number of writers. E. C. St John Hankin (1869–1909) wrote a number of plays with a frankness and realism that had previously not been found on the contemporary English stage. His earliest success was *The Return of the Prodigal* (1905) where he showed himself a successful satirist of the English middle classes. This was followed by a number of similar plays, including *The Charity that Began at Home* (1906) and *The Cassilis Engagement* (1907), which proved to be the most popular of all his works. He had a fresh approach, and he contributed to the development of the drama in England, but he had not the strength and originality to give his plays a permanent place in the repertory of the English theatre. A similar playwright was Stanley Houghton (1881–1913), who was discovered by Miss Horniman's Repertory Theatre in Manchester to which reference has already been made. Houghton knew conditions in Manchester at first hand, for he had been engaged in his father's cloth business. With a certain mild influence from Ibsen, and in the climate of the social realism of his time, he wrote *Hindle Wakes* (1912), which gave effective expression of the revolt of youth against the dinginess of its narrow provincial and middle-class background. While *Hindle Wakes* was his most notable achievement, he also had some contemporary success with *The Dear Departed* (1908), *The Younger Generation* and *The Master of the House* (1910).

A dramatist in the same tradition, but with a somewhat wider range, was St John Ervine (b. 1883), who has had a very long career both as critic and dramatist. Born in Belfast, his early dramatic career was associated with the Abbey Theatre, Dublin, where some of his early plays were produced; but London soon became the centre of his activities. He raised the play of social interpretation out of the area of social commentary into grim prose tragedy, as in *Jane Clegg* (1913), and *John Ferguson* (1915). These are plays memorable in their time, but, with the harsh realities of the theatre, standing very little chance of ever being seen on the stage again. Yet in his own age he has had a real influence on the theatre not only as a dramatist but as a dramatic critic in *The Observer*. He gave much pleasure in his own time, and to the most exacting of contemporary audiences. *The First Mrs Fraser* may not be a great play, but the author is not alone in creating the effect of a play in the theatre and audiences who saw that great actor Henry Ainley (1879–1945) walk on to the stage on the first night in 1929 may cherish it as a memorable theatrical experience.

On the whole, it was to the period before the war of 1914–18 that this drama of social realism properly belonged. It continued with success into the 'twenties, but by then more imaginative minds were aware, as was shown in *Heartbreak House*, that there were other problems more fundamental to the existence of civilization to be explored. Thus while Galsworthy continued to the end of the 'twenties with a succession of new plays, and St John Ervine had *The Ship* produced in 1922, and while an interest attached to a new-comer such as 'C. K. Munro', who in *At Mrs Beam's* (1921) gave a comic portrayal of a London boarding house, the main original impulse of this drama had been supplemented by other forms. Already, as early as 1908, John Masefield (b. 1878), an artist of whose dimensions the present generation has, as yet, made no true assessment, had produced *The Tragedy of Nan*. The play, possibly with some influence from Synge, gave an imaginative, even a poetic quality, to a drama of rustic realism. There is a certain incongruity between the grim, domestic setting and the prose medium on the one hand, and the rhythms and imagery of the language on the other, which seem to look back to the Elizabethan playwrights. Masefield's tragedy was a major protest against the social realism of the 'Manchester' school, and those who regarded the stage as a medium for exploring middle-class problems. Masefield continued his dramatic experiments in *The Tragedy of Pompey the Great*, and in *Philip the King*, and in the free blank verse of *A King's Daughter* and *Tristan and Iseult*, but these had less success.

There was a figure, who after some initial failures (*Ibsen's Ghost*, 1891; and *Walker London*, 1892) long maintained a seemingly effortless conquest of the London stage, and he was one who had never admitted that the theatre could be held within the confines of realism. Sir James Barrie (1860–1937), the son of a hand-loom weaver of Kirrimuir, Forfarshire, was educated at Glasgow, Dumfries, and at Edinburgh University. He made his way to London as a journalist, and established himself as a writer of humorous and descriptive pieces, such as *Auld Licht Idylls* (1888) and *A Window in Thrums* (1889) and as a novelist with *The Little Minister* (1891), before he made his way successfully to the theatre with *The Professor's Love Story* (1894), a play which had much popularity in the United States. For nearly thirty years his success was continuous, culminating in *Mary Rose* (1920) and *Shall We Join the Ladies?* (1922). Only later with *The Boy David* did he seem to lose contact with the audiences of his time. During the decades of popularity Barrie produced a great variety of drama. With *Peter Pan* (1904) he invented a new child's mythology. To see his plays now, and they are occasionally revived, is to realize that they belong to a mood which is strange and repellent to the 'sixties. They are part of a lost world of kindliness and of more gentle emotions; they are shot through with sentimentality, which in its less restrained moments could be united to the whimsical. Yet few writers of his age have had such a complete mastery of the stage, or had such a certainty in the effects that they wished to produce. He had a real skill in dialogue, particularly in comic dialogue, while the way he could adroitly dispose of his characters on the stage and control their entrances and exits is shown in his unfinished play *Shall We Join the Ladies?* One of his plays which has good possibilities of survival is *The Admirable Crichton* (1902); here he dealt in a mood of high comedy with the problem of social castes and individual worth. Robertson had used a similar theme in *Caste* more than half a century before. While Barrie may miss Robertson's attractive earnestness, his desert island scene with the butler becoming the universally recognized leader of the group has a dramatic adroitness which Robertson did not possess. *Quality Street* (1902) was a frankly sentimental comedy where he created a world that was peculiarly his own. One of his greatest successes was *What Every Woman Knows*, where in a social comedy he depicted a Scottish character from a background that he knew so well. *Dear Brutus* (1917) showed many of his distinctive qualities at their best. The theme, that for the most part it is ourselves and not circumstances that settle our fate in life, is developed in scenes partly of domestic comedy but linked with a fantasy that is cunningly related to the rest of the play. *Mary Rose* had great popularity with audiences in England after the war of 1914–18: it combined fantasy with a comment on the future life and it had a wide, topical appeal to many who had lost friends and relations in the war. Yet it is difficult to see the conditions under which it would reach the stage again. One may speculate how Barrie's genius might have developed if he had come to a theatre less commercial and less conventional. He might well have achieved something in greater depth if he had had an atmosphere, such as surrounded Shakespeare, of a congenial group which might have stretched his genius and deepened his vision. As it is, in some of the plays he seems to be holding himself back as if anxious not to over-tax the intellect or the imagination of his audience. Still, some two or three of the plays, as has been indicated, may find a permanent place and there is always *Peter Pan* with its annual revival.

The element of poetry and fantasy, present in different ways in Masefield and Barrie, gained a far stronger expression as one of the manifestations of the Abbey Theatre in Dublin. The whole movement has been admirably described in Ellis-Fermor's *The Irish Dramatic Movement*. One of the founders was Lady Gregory

(1852–1932), who was herself a playwright and poet and was a director of the theatre from its beginning in 1904 until 1932. With her were two writers, W. B. Yeats and J. M. Synge, who must rank high in the English achievement in the twentieth century, if for this purpose dramas written in Ireland and on Irish themes may be included as part of the English theatre. W. B. Yeats (1865–1939) is the greatest poet to have written in England throughout the modern period. In his plays, he probably remained a lyrical poet even in the theatre, and audiences are likely to enjoy *The Land of Heart's Desire* (1894), *The Countess Cathleen* (1899), *The Shadowy Waters* (1906), and the later plays, more for the beauty of their language than for dramatic situations. Unlike Synge, and, later, unlike O'Casey, he and Lady Gregory had a theory of what drama should be, and with Yeats this theory became more important to him in his later years. He and Lady Gregory had rejected J. T. Grein's Independent Theatre in 1891 because of its excessive attachment to social realism. They had written their memorandum on the poetic drama as early as 1898 and *The Countess Cathleen* had been produced in Dublin in 1899 five years before the Abbey Theatre had been established. In his later phases, Yeats became interested in the ritualism of the Japanese Noh plays and dreamed of an idealized theatre. In *Plays and Controversies* he wrote: 'My blunder has been that I did not discover in my youth that my theatre must be the ancient theatre that can be made by unrolling a carpet or marking out a place with a stick or setting a screen against a wall. . . .' Ultimately these views, particularly in his dealings with O'Casey, as recorded later, were to prove unfortunate for the Abbey, but this must not diminish any estimate of the major contribution that he made. As Ellis-Fermor has written of him: 'the Irish drama had not only a founder, and an acute business man and a courageous fighter, but, something without which these would have been barren, a visionary poet'.

One of Yeats's great services to Irish drama was his discovery of J. M. Synge (1871–1909). They met first in Paris in 1899, the year after Synge had visited the Aran Islands. Yeats had the wisdom to persuade him to revisit the Aran Islands, which he did annually from 1899–1902 to study the rhythms of unadulterated primitive speech. In this way Synge discovered that strange imaginative language which informs the beauty of his plays. He had a genius for comedy and tragedy: the one appears in *The Shadow of the Glen* (1903) and *The Playboy of the Western World* (1907), and the other in *Riders to the Sea* (1904) and *Deirdre of the Sorrows* (1910). It may be unwise to attempt to distinguish between the merit of two gifts so original and valuable as the comedy and tragedy of Synge, but it may without ingratitude be confessed that the comedy wears better. The tragedy seems a little self-conscious, even sought after, but the comedy has a virile and permanent quality, and remains as impressive and original as when it was first conceived. *The Playboy of the Western World* has often been revived, and it is difficult now fully to appreciate the controversies associated with its first production at the Abbey Theatre. Synge, apart from Yeats, remains, with O'Casey, the most original and distinguished artist that the Abbey Theatre produced.

While Synge's contribution was outstanding, the Irish theatre produced other playwrights of merit. Lennox Robinson, the author of a number of plays, captured the London stage with his comedy *The White-Headed Boy* in 1916. Lord Dunsany, a picturesque figure and an accomplished poet, while he relied on a less directly Irish inspiration, still maintained in plays such as *A Night at the Inn* (1916), a world removed from the stubborn realism which held captive much in English drama. Further, Lady Gregory, while her main inspiration lay in the encouragement of others, was, as has already been mentioned, herself a writer of plays. These were minor writers as far as drama is concerned.

The sole remaining major figure, and one comparable with Synge, is Sean O'Casey[1] (1880–1964). As a child he knew the slums of Dublin, and he was impressed not only with the memory of Parnell, and the political leaders, but with Jim Larkin who came as a labour agitator to Dublin in 1908. The sordidness of the Dublin of his childhood he was never to forget. He involved himself with the Irish Citizen Army, whose history he wrote. As a dramatist he was largely self-taught. In 1923 *The Shadow of a Gunman* was produced at the Abbey. It was a highly original drama, a mixture

[1] There is a good study by David Krause, *Sean O'Casey*, 1960, from which some of the material in this chapter has been derived.

of comedy and tragedy, with the rich and varied vocabulary of one who knew Shakespeare as well as he knew the language of the Dublin slums. In 1924 *Juno and the Paycock* appeared at the Abbey and was a great success, nothing of so original a quality had appeared on that stage since Synge. In 1926 there followed *The Plough and the Stars*, the performance of which, exploring both religious and patriotic prejudices, led to a riot in the theatre. O'Casey was himself a rebel, yet against the background of the Dublin tenements he could see the vain-glorious elements in some of those who exploited rebellion. The tragedy was that Ireland, the home of so much originality in drama, was censorious of free speech, and in 1926, with the award of the Hawthornden Prize, O'Casey withdrew to London. There he composed a remarkable play *The Silver Tassie* which was completed in 1928. The play is set in the period of the First World War and its mood is definitely anti-heroic. In the first scene, Harry Heegan is shown as the hero of the football team and the winner of the Silver Tassie; he is secure in his own innocent prowess and in his love of Jessie. He and two comrades leave for the war, one of them in a riotous Irish way, breaking up the home and beating his wife before he goes; and Mrs Heegan, Harry's mother, at the close says with a deep sigh of satisfaction: 'Thanks be to Christ that we're after managin' to get the three of them away safely.' The second act, which led to a profound controversy, is in the war zone; it is in complete contrast, poetic, abstract, and without any of the characters of the first act. In the third act we go back to the characters with which the play began; Heegan is half paralysed, Jessie has deserted him, and his riotous friend is blind. This play has been summarized in some detail for it is a turning point in the Abbey Theatre and in much else in the drama. For when O'Casey submitted it to Yeats he rejected it and Lady Gregory agreed with him. Much later when, as an old lady, Lady Gregory saw the play in London, she wrote to Yeats regretting her decision. Yeats felt this moving and imaginative play was too far from the ritualistic drama to which his mind was moving. The rejection of *The Silver Tassie* was the end of the most imaginative period in the Abbey, and though it was not the end of O'Casey as a dramatist, much must have been lost from his art through this major set-back. The Abbey relented over *The Silver Tassie* in 1933 but it was then too late. It was after

O'Casey had been turned down that the Abbey rejected Denis Johnston's *The Old Lady Says 'No'* in 1929. O'Casey, during his exile in England, ran into financial problems; he wrote books and plays but he seemed in a vacuum. In *Within the Gates* (1934) the symbolic elements increased in a play which is a criticism of religion. He no longer had actors around him and the atmosphere of the theatre. He was writing for a publisher, and this leads to the diminished dramatic quality of his anti-fascist play *The Stars Turn Red* (1940). Fortunately, his old talents returned in *Red Roses for Me*, performed in London in 1942; in this moving play all his best qualities seem to combine, the poetry, the symbolism, the Dublin tenements and the humour. He seems to re-live his Dublin youth and yet at times to bathe it in a light that belongs to Shakespearian drama. Similarly he indulges in comedy, even farce, and yet holds his audience with profound sentiment that ranges from the ironic to the tragic. At his best, he has a great command of the stage, and over language he exercises a compelling power, so that cascades of bright words seem to overflow from his plays. Since 1939 O'Casey was engaged on a gargantuan autobiography of which the first volume was *I Knock at the Door*. One cannot help feeling that had the dramatic atmosphere been more promising all this energy might have been turned into drama.

Much in the theatre of the 'twenties and the 'thirties is ephemeral; it was not worth doing at the time and is not likely to be remembered. It is surprising what skilled actors can make of incompetent scripts, but those who had to attend the theatre regularly in those decades must often have wished that something better could be offered. At the same time, there is much that is interesting in this period. The admittedly popular entertainers produced some writers of great skill; the regular, but more ambitious, theatre, is served by some writers who have, at least with part of their work, a possibility of survival, and there were new and successful experiments in verse drama.

It is difficult in a history of drama to know what space to give to popular entertainment. In the early periods all is gathered in for there is so little material that everything is valuable. Possibly in contemporary periods the danger is to neglect these aspects of dramatic art, or to hand them over to the clinical survey of the sociologist. The outstanding example of the man of the theatre, in a gifted but popular sense, in the period between the two wars was Noel Coward (b. 1899). He, above any other man of his generation, understood the whole instrument of the modern stage, and he showed himself equally competent in films. He had this at least in common with Shakespeare, that he mastered every aspect of his profession. He was an accomplished actor and played not only in his own plays, but in major roles such as that of King Magnus in Shaw's *The Apple Cart*. He wrote successful comedies and musical comedies, and he gave great pleasure to countless playgoers of his generation, and, often in his work, he seems to indicate that he could have done so much more, if the theatre had been closer to the centre of society in his time. *The Vortex* (1923) first gave him a reputation as an actor and author, and showed that he could write with a study of character and a concern for a problem. He did not, however, develop in depth from *The Vortex*, but in the 'twenties mainly applied himself to such light-hearted comedies as *Fallen Angels* (1925), and *Easy Virtue* (1926). When after the economic crisis of 1929 the mind of the country became more serious, Coward responded with a spectacular musical piece *Cavalcade* (1931); this will never see the stage again, but it had a profound effect on the generation for which it was written. He showed here, as in his earlier operetta, *Bitter Sweet* (1929), that he had the whole mechanism of the theatre under his control. It is very easy to underestimate the contribution of a writer such as Coward, for whatever the narrower and more intellectual judgement may be, it must be conceded that he probably gave more pleasure in the theatre to a larger number of people than any other man of his generation. It is difficult to say whether any of his comedies will survive the age for which they were written, yet *Blithe Spirit* (1941), to instance only one, has a verbal dexterity that approaches that of Wilde.

A writer who had reached popularity much earlier than Coward, and who retained his hold on the public throughout the 'twenties and the 'thirties, was Somerset Maugham (b. 1874). His earliest work was as a short-story writer and as a novelist, but as early as 1903 he was writing for the stage and soon no London season was complete without one of his plays and, indeed, two were often available at the same time in West End theatres. These were nearly all comedies of elegant life in which cynicism mingled with commentary. It must be confessed that nothing in the plays approaches the depth of some of his novels, such as *Liza of Lambeth* (1897) and *Of Human Bondage* (1915). He had an accomplished control of dialogue and managed stage situations neatly. He never made his audiences exercise their intelligences excessively; he did not offend their taste, and though his cynicism might arouse them, it was only in a way that meant they were not deeply disturbed. What he could achieve within this formula is shown in plays such as *Caesar's Wife* and *Home and Beauty*, both of which were produced in 1919. In *Sheppey* he departed from his formula, but the play was not a success. At his best, he recalls Restoration comedy, and this is true of *The Circle* (1921), the most accomplished comedy that Maugham wrote. The play, ultimately, lacked the gaiety and the wit which Congreve commanded. Maugham seems to have despised the society he portrayed, and a play such as *Our Betters* (1923) shows how heartless and degenerate is the world in which his cunningly contrived comedy so skilfully moves. If one returns to Swinburne's praise of Congreve,[1] one can see the difference between the two men and the societies they portrayed. Swinburne, it will be recalled, wrote: 'if Congreve's world is not healthy neither is it hollow; and whatever he had of noble humour and feeling was genuine and genial'. Maugham seems often to despise the puppets who provide the wit, and whom he contorts with a not wholly genial malice. He has not on the one hand the moral energy to deepen the portrait into satire; on the other hand he does not accept his world with Congreve's witty and gay nonchalance. Possibly he made too easy a capture of the commercial managements, and succumbed to supplying what he knew they required, instead of stretching his considerable talents. His success was extended beyond the 'thirties into the 'forties. *The Circle* has been revived, and may continue to hold a place in the theatre, but it would be optimistic to suggest that this is true of his other comedies.

Among the new dramatists of the 'thirties were two promising but contrasting figures 'James Bridie' (O. H. Mavor) (1885–1959) and J. B. Priestley (b. 1894). 'James Bridie', who was a member of a distinguished group of Glasgow personalities, gave up medicine for the theatre. His Scottish background often appears in his plays,

[1] See pages 115–6.

and his imagination in its depth and boldness is far removed from anything that was happening in the conventional English theatre. The most direct and potentially the most enduring of his plays is *The Anatomist* (1931), which was based on the careers of Burke and Hare, the body snatchers: it has a deeply moving theme and, though it has not been recently revived, would stand the test. Usually Bridie's imagination sought more unusual themes, and in these he was most successful in the miracle play plot of *Tobias and the Angel* (1931); this proved popular and was frequently revived. As often in his work a brilliant opening led to a conclusion of an unfinished character, as if he had become weary of the work in hand. His range as a dramatist was wide; in *The Sleeping Clergyman* (1933), one of the most elaborate of his plays, he dealt with the lives of three generations; while in *Mr Bolfry* (1943), which delighted wartime audiences in London, he seemed to transfer the Faust story to a Scottish setting, exploiting fully the resultant situations with humour. Among his later successes was *Daphne Laureola* (1949). Bridie was genuinely devoted to the theatre. He helped to make Glasgow an independent centre for the drama by his work for the Glasgow Citizens' Theatre. As a dramatist he did not fulfil all that had been hoped of him; for, at its best, his imagination seemed so effective dramatically and so strong. It was very different from that of Barrie; it had a craggy element, as of one who has seen the sinister and the satanic in life. On the other hand, his humour had a fine, individual Scottish quality. It may have been that he never felt at home in the London theatre, for his real loyalties were to Scotland, and above all to Glasgow; and yet, unfortunately, as a dramatist it was to London that he had, ultimately, to look for his audiences.

J. B. Priestley is a writer who has achieved great success, and yet his talent has been much underestimated, partly because of his facility and the size of his output, and also, it would seem, as a reaction against his immense popularity. He had shown himself an essayist and critic of distinction before he came to the novel, and he had won a leading name for himself as a novelist before he turned to the theatre. *The Good Companions*, which was later dramatized in collaboration with E. Knoblock, was published in the year of the depression in 1929, and marked an epoch in the history of the modern novel. He seemed to recapture the immense audience which Dickens had discovered in the nineteenth century. It was after the success of this novel, and of *Angel Pavement*, which followed so quickly afterwards in 1930, that he turned to the writing of plays. Some thought that he had come only accidentally into the theatre, but he soon showed that he was there to stay. Priestley was born in Bradford, and he has cultivated the image of the down-to-earth, forthright Yorkshireman. Yet all that is best in his literary work denies this: he has a sensitive imagination with intermittently, a half mystical element, as was shown in his early essay *Dissolution in the Haymarket*. It was this now which entered into the plays. He had a pre-occupation with the idea of time, and the reality of experience, and all these notions gave originality to themes, which were admirably constructed with recognizable characters. An interest in the time theories of Dunne and Ouspensky may not seem the best preparation for a dramatist, but the study of these philosophers had come because they touched something deep in his experience which could in turn stimulate him as a dramatist. He had an immediate success with *Dangerous Corner* (1932) and this he followed with a series of notable plays including *Laburnum Grove* (1933), *Eden End* (1934), *I Have Been Here Before* (1937), *Time and the Conways* (1937) and a farcical comedy *When We Are Married* (1938). In 1939 he produced a more ambitious expressionist play *Johnson Over Jordan*, which though not wholly successful showed that he was prepared to experiment boldly in new ways. The half concealed poetic element, which is present in his character, was revealed in the symbolism of this play as it was in *They Came to a City* (1943). Here was the promise of something beyond the studies of character, the social settings and the comedy of a number of the earlier plays. The war of 1939–45 interrupted his work as a dramatist at what might seem to be a crucial stage. He had later successes, particularly *An Inspector Calls* (1946), but this, instead of developing from *Johnson Over Jordan*, returned to the mood of the earlier plays; it had a contemporary theme, exposed characters in a social context, and employed a further manipulation of the time theme. When the whole of his dramatic work is reviewed his contribution is seen to be considerable and the personality behind the plays, as has been suggested, is far more complex than either his public image or the comments of much criticism would suggest. That the

Yorkshireman is there one need not deny: it appears in his bold characterization, and a solid comic dialogue such as Dickens might have enjoyed. It is, however, the other elements that have given a highly individual quality to his art, his consciousness that all that seems so solid may be evanescent and uncertain, and with this uncertainty, which is linked with his metaphysical interest in the concept of time, there is a compassion for men and women, finally exposed and defenceless however confident they may feel.

CHAPTER FIFTEEN

Contemporary Drama

ONE OUTSTANDING feature of the drama of the 'thirties was the development of a new verse drama which had a success in the theatre. As has been noted, many poets wrote plays, but few of them were acted, and indeed some of them were written with no thought of production in mind. Thomas Hardy wrote his great epic drama of *The Dynasts* for the theatre that each individual reader could imagine for himself, yet he showed here and later in *The Tragedy of the Queen of Cornwall* that he had genuine dramatic gifts. The English theatre would obviously be far richer if conditions had permitted its exploitation by men of genius who were led away into the novel or into non-dramatic verse. An early experimenter in the 'thirties in a poetic drama definitely designed for the theatre, and ultimately the most successful, was T. S. Eliot (1888–1965). In his early verse, and chiefly in *The Waste Land* (1922), Eliot had shown that he had a gift for dialogue and above all for adapting the natural rhythms of speech into verse. His experiments in dramatic verse began as early as 1924 with a number of isolated fragments and gradually these he united into a play *Sweeney Agonistes* (1932). This was not long enough for performance in the ordinary commercial theatre, but it was performed under other conditions, and Eliot must, in this way, have become aware of his dramatic gifts. He was already established as a poet and some important volumes were still to follow, including *Ash Wednesday* and *Marina* in 1930, and *Four Quartets* (1943), which was, possibly, the most memorable of all his works. Yet it can be said that from the early 'thirties to the late 'fifties his main concern was with the theatre and the attempt somehow to conquer the popular stage with actable poetic plays. The first attempt was incidental. By this time Eliot was an Anglican in religion and a pageant play was required by a church, and so for *The Rock* (1934) he composed a scene and some choruses. It cannot be claimed that in itself *The Rock* is important, but it confirmed in Eliot's mind his own dramatic powers and it brought him into contact with audiences who obviously appealed to him. He was fortunate for his next attempt to find not only a strong theme, closely adapted to his interests, but an audience that was alert, intelligent and sympathetic. So he came to write *Murder in the Cathedral* (1935), for performance in the Chapter House of Canterbury Cathedral. This remains the most popular of his works, and though it has not frequently found its way back to the commercial stage, it is often performed. It may be said to have entered into the permanent repertory of the English drama, and deserves to have done so. The death of Thomas Becket had given him the opportunity of writing a play on a Christian theme and of exploring again, though possibly in a simpler way, some of the motives of his non-dramatic verse. The play has a chorus of the poor women of Canterbury, who express in moving lines the helplessness of the individual if left to his own resources amid the strength of temporal powers. It gave great encouragement to those who longed for a return of poetic drama to the English stage. Eliot himself must have felt committed to this attempt, for he proceeded to write *Family Reunion* (1939), which was first performed not in the West End, but in one of London's more intimate theatres. What one could have wished was that he might have proceeded from *Murder in the Cathedral* to a theme even more generally intelligible; but this was not to be. There remained a close relationship between his non-dramatic work and his plays, and the problems which he was exploring in *Four Quartets* enter into *Family Reunion*. The play is complicated, and its design depends to some extent on the myth of Orestes pursued by the Furies. This classical myth has, not without an element of incongruity, been transferred into a contemporary setting, which was puzzling to audiences seeing the play for the first time. Further, the influences of *Four Quartets* led him to transform the motives of the classical myth into a Christian theme of redemption, and the result, though interesting, is, it must be admitted, a little confusing. It is difficult to see how in the future *Family Reunion* can ever hope to appeal to audiences in the theatre, and that is after all what plays are for. Yet it has a distinction of mind and a quality in the writing far beyond what was being produced in England at the time. If ever there is a theatre where more difficult and complicated work can be produced, then *Family Reunion* will be part of its repertory. Eliot himself, one may surmise, was not entirely satisfied. He wanted to make his assault on the commercial theatre, to capture the popular stage. There was a gap of ten years before he was prepared to make the attempt. The war of 1939–45 is mainly responsible but one must also remember his considerable labours with *Four Quartets*. Then there appeared a series of plays all produced, and with success, in the West End of London; these were *The Cocktail Party* (1949), *The Confidential Clerk* (1954), and *The Elder Statesman* (1959). Eliot would seem, whether consciously or not, to have made considerable concessions in order to come to terms with the audiences of the contemporary theatre, the type of compromise that he would not think of making in his non-dramatic verse, and which Shakespeare did not have to make to Elizabethan audiences. For instance, all the plays are given a contemporary setting, so that, although the action is very different, the setting looks like that of a drawing-room comedy. The chorus, with which he had been experimenting with some success, is abandoned, except for a single chant in *The Cocktail Party*, and this, when now left in isolation, is definitely incongruous. The verse is most skilfully deployed, but increasingly from one play to another the obviously poetic element is reduced, so that in *The Elder Statesman* it is difficult to know that one is listening to verse until the text is examined. It is true that much poetic drama had been rendered ineffective for the stage by the use of a fustian verse rhetoric, and Eliot's subtle comprehension of the natural rhythms was, as has been suggested, a most important part of his skill. In *The Cocktail Party* he does make the union with some success though when the poetic element is emphasized the audience may be puzzled to assess what is gained in the employment of verse by characters placed in a modern setting. Ultimately it appears that the play is not vitally dramatic but a vehicle, as are the non-dramatic poems, for his own ideas. There is something of *The Wasteland* and *Four Quartets* in *The Cocktail Party* with the ideas and the language simplified and spoken by characters on the stage. Coleridge in writing of Shakespeare's *Venus and Adonis* says that one of the signs of genius 'is the choice of subjects very remote from the private interests and circumstances of the writer himself'.

This, it may be said, Eliot achieved in *Murder in the Cathedral*. It is the lack of this element that limits his achievement in *The Cocktail Party*. To judge thus is to judge severely, but an artist of Eliot's dimensions must be assessed by the highest standards. When first performed in London *The Cocktail Party* seemed both moving and profound. In his distinctive language the characters explored that spiritual waste which Eliot had discovered in Western European life, and the sense of personal helplessness of men and women without a faith. The play exposes, at the same time, his own belief in a Christian solution, which could be the basis of an ordinary life lived in a routine way and equally of martyrdom; though again it may be suggested that with this modern drawing-room setting the references to martyrdom are not made wholly convincing. It is difficult to speculate whether *The Cocktail Party* will survive as a play acceptable to succeeding generations in the theatre. It can never recapture the excitement of its first presentation, for much in Eliot's thought had a topical character, and there was then the promise, as with *Murder in the Cathedral*, that he might develop and that a great tradition of poetic drama might be restored. Both the succeeding plays have considerable dramatic skill and knowledge of how to handle the stage: *The Confidential Clerk* exploits the theme of mistaken identity while *The Elder Statesman* has in part the design of a melodrama. Yet neither can be ranked as an advance on *The Cocktail Party*; the verse is often so near to prose as in the theatre at least to be indistinguishable, and the themes, though clever and entertaining, have not that depth of vision which Eliot at his best possessed.

All this was, however, very different from what the West End theatre was normally producing and for this reason alone was very welcome. Nor was Eliot the only dramatist attempting to bring verse back into the theatre. W. H. Auden (b. 1907) had become the leader of a group of poets in the 'thirties who were all 'committed' to using verse for political ends. They were Marxist or near Marxist though ultimately by devious ways Auden returned to Christianity. Auden was a poet of great lyric power, and a number of these pieces are not affected by his political loyalties. He had experimented in conversational vocabulary and rhythms in his verse, and had to some extent been influenced by Eliot. In his dramatic work he collaborated with a close associate Christopher

Isherwood (b. 1904), whose main success was to be in two novels set in pre-war Nazi Germany: *Mr Norris Changes Trains* (1935) and *Goodbye to Berlin* (1939). Their plays were *The Dance of Death* (1936) and *On the Frontier* (1938). These could not have had a success in the commercial theatre, but they were performed, and as dramatists these two writers had considerable influence on their generation. One is first impressed by the liveliness of the verse. Auden had been interested in popular art and in the music-hall, and his perceptive mind had found many new and interesting rhythms, and further there was an entertaining use of dancing and mime and movement on the stage. One would suppose that the main contribution came from Auden, for so much of the text resembles that of his non-dramatic verse. It is difficult to know what might have happened if the war had not made a break in his career and led to his permanent residence in the United States, for his genius, despite his sense of rebellion, was very English, and a part of it could not flourish away from the English scene. There was certainly here a dramatic talent, and it was at its best when it was at its most carefree and amusing. But it was not Auden's mood to remain untroubled when faced with the problems of his uneasy decade, and the mood had deepened with him, as with all his associates, after the opening of the war in Spain. It is this compelling unrest that led to the most ambitious of these plays, *The Ascent of F6*. The nominal theme is of an expedition that has been sent to conquer a peak that has previously defeated all climbers. The action offers a ready medium for comment on the problems of the decade of anxiety, and much of the incident is symbolic in character. Auden and Isherwood never reached the originality of imagination or thought that Eliot achieved. What they showed was great promise but it was a promise not to be fulfilled. Some of Auden's lyrics, particularly the non-political ones, will enter into what is permanent in English literature, but this cannot be said of his dramatic work.

The activity in poetic drama did not end here, for Christopher Fry (b. 1907), whose work seems to have no contact with either Eliot or Auden, gained considerable success, particularly in the years immediately following the war of 1939–45. The dates of publication of some of his major plays, which differ from the dates of production, are: *The Boy With the Cart* (1939), *A Phoenix Too*

Frequent (1946), *The Lady's Not For Burning* (1949), *Venus Observed* (1950), *A Sleep of Prisoners* (1951) and *The Dark is Light Enough* (1954). Part of Fry's success arose from the fact that unlike Eliot or Auden he had a long and exacting experience in the theatre. He had been a director of provincial repertory companies at both Tunbridge Wells and Oxford, and had thus familiarized himself with every aspect of stage technique. After his experiment with *The Boy With the Cart* he became associated with the Arts Theatre in London and it was for them that he wrote what proved to be his most successful play *The Lady's Not for Burning*. Such was its popularity that it was transferred to one of the major West End theatres. It is important to remember that these years immediately after the war were notable for a number of most distinguished Shakespearian revivals; the glamour of the settings and the magnificence of the verse seemed in complete contrast with the drabness that had been imposed on civilian life by war conditions. The rationing of food and clothes, the limitation on travel, the denial of light and colour, indeed the absence of all variety in life, led audiences to welcome, with exceptional readiness, the romantic excitement that the Shakespearian plays could provide. Christopher Fry's success was largely due to the fact that he seemed the living and contemporary counterpart to all this exuberance. He had a fascinating control of words, which had a compelling interest for him as they had for Shakespeare, and all that he wrote was in vivid contrast to the plain prose of realistic drama. Words seemed to brighten in his hands, until they became illuminated and the words themselves were extended into images of a brilliant, even exotic daring.

As one approaches so close to the contemporary scene it is difficult to make valid judgements: these works have not been sorted through the exacting test of the appraisal of successive generations. One can record the deep impression that a play such as *The Lady's Not for Burning* made on its first audiences, and something like a debt of gratitude to an author who could produce words that were so resplendent in a theme that was so moving. But all that is to record impressions of audiences in the late 'forties. By the 'sixties, critics and young dramatists were suggesting that those audiences were deceived and that these bright verbal lights, by which they were attracted, were a delusion. Nor did Fry develop into any greater maturity. *Venus Observed* had the benefit of a brilliant caste, but its theme, in which an elderly man gathers together his mistresses and reviews his past life, is artificial, without any strong compensating elements. He went back to his earlier type of inspiration in *A Sleep of Prisoners*, which, whatever its defects, must be assessed as his most ambitious and serious work. The theme is of four English soldiers, locked in a bombed church, whose minds are interpreted through their dreams. The action is not solid enough to sustain the words and despite all the author's sincerity there is ultimately a hollowness in this play. On Christopher Fry many hopes for the English theatre had rested but unfortunately they were not completely fulfilled; he remained only an interval of brightness against the mediocrity of the commercial productions. That he understood the stage and had theatrical skill was shown by his adaptations of plays by Giraudoux and Anouilh.

From these writers one comes to the English stage of the postwar period, particularly the stage of the 'fifties and the 'sixties. Some of the importance of these new developments has been suggested in the chapter dealing with the background of the theatre in the twentieth century; it now remains to consider the plays themselves and their importance. As has already been suggested, to many members of the present generation the first night of John Osborne's *Look Back in Anger* at the Royal Court Theatre on 8 May 1956 was a turning point in the English theatre. This may be admitted to be true, without any accompanying assessment that *Look Back in Anger* is a great play, or that it will pass that final test of entering into the permanent repertory of the English theatre. Its success was enhanced by the high praise given it by Kenneth Tynan, the most dynamic of the critics of Osborne's generation. John Osborne (b. 1929) was himself a new phenomenon, not only in the theatre, but in English society. As far as the theatre was concerned, his experience was familiar enough; he had toured in numerous provincial companies and he had worked in Repertory. He knew the stage intimately before he came to the writing of plays. It was his social background that was different, or rather his approach to it. He had been to a minor public school, but this had only led him to be a rebel against the whole centre of power in England, the Establishment, as it was coming to be called. There had been writers such as O'Casey, whose protest was definitely proletarian, but this was far from being Osborne's case. He found the whole class structure in England indeterminate. He did not know where he was, but he knew that many shared his predicament. Much of the fiction of the period and its plays were still being written in the illusion that the old system existed, that England was still an Imperial power and that people dressed for dinner. Yet Osborne knew that all this was not true, and part of his originality was that he was able to find a dramatic medium for this perception. Further he belonged completely to a post-war generation. He was sixteen when the war ended; he was not old enough to be a soldier, but he was old enough to have endured evacuation, rationing, and all the dreariness that the war brought into social life in England. His generation which grew to manhood in the 'fifties began to ask what had been gained. It need not be suggested that they posed the questions in a logical or systematic way for, indeed, as the title of Osborne's *Look Back in Anger* suggests, their approach was highly emotional. Yet their attitude is capable of a rational definition. Instead of the war bringing some release, it had ushered in the nuclear age, with the threat of cosmic destruction. It had brought into the great cities more over-crowding and sordidness. The younger generation had a baffled sense of purposelessness, a feeling that it had no roots in the past, and no hope for the future. Further, young rebels had always in the last reserve wanted the Empire, for it gave them a theme for protest, but now with the Empire going if not gone, they found themselves angry and emotionally frustrated. That Osborne intuitively realized all this, and that he found in *Look Back in Anger* a dramatic medium for it, is the measure of his achievement, and it is considerable. His central character, Jimmy Porter, symbolizes all that has been suggested above. Jimmy is weak, neurotic and capable of an almost indefinite amount of self-pity. There is no ordered society into which he can enter, no tradition which he can inherit. The war has left him a derelict character, and he sees society, such as it is, as something hostile. All the old standards have broken down, and the old opportunities are missing. Jimmy has had some sort of university education, but society is so mixed and he himself so weak, hysterical and rudderless that he is unable to make any use of it. As if to emphasize the upheaval in the classes in society,

Osborne portrays him as living in a mean ineffective way with a friend on the proceeds of a sweet stall. Yet the remnants of the old well-defined class society are still there. Jimmy is married to Alison who comes from an Anglo-Indian family, so belonging to one of those great traditions that had sustained the middle-classes in England from the middle of the nineteenth century onwards. Dramatically, the most effective conflict displayed by Osborne is that while Jimmy hates all that Alison represents it is a hatred mingled of jealousy and despair, and, whatever its violence, it leaves him ultimately very dependent on her, and she in a strange and perhaps less credible way on him. Whatever its ultimate merit, here was a play fresh to the English stage. The social protest of Galsworthy had been written as a compassionate observer from outside; Shaw had penetrated deeper, but, except in *Heartbreak House*, he had written, whatever might be the opinions expressed, as one emotionally secure in the society in which he lived. They may have written better plays but here was something new, for here was the image of post-war England as it appeared to a post-war generation, with gentility submerged, with the Empire lost, with the war seen as an ugly deceit, and with no hope or grace anywhere. It may, by some sober minds, be said to be exaggerated, even false, or at best only the portrait of the worst and most self indulgent in that generation. Yet the immediate response it gained, particularly from men and women of Osborne's own age, showed that the play had a symbolic relation to its period. Osborne had the good fortune to follow *Look Back in Anger* with *The Entertainer* (1957), and equal good fortune to have Sir Laurence Olivier render the part of the broken-down actor, Archie Rice. *The Entertainer* has more opportunities for humour than the earlier play, though in both Osborne shows his genuine gift for dialogue, which seems as if it were an epitome of contemporary speech. *The Entertainer* made a profound impression on audiences when it was first produced, though some of that impression was compact of hostility. It is a subtle play and one that can be interpreted at different levels. The most obvious theme is that of a character study of Archie Rice himself, an old music hall actor who drinks too much and is capable of every kind of self-deceit, with moments of absurd buoyancy and elation and with memories of past successes, or, possibly, imagined successes, and with hints of somewhat inactive debaucheries. He is, of all Osborne's characters, the most rounded and effective. With Archie are his family and others forming in all a sordid and ineffectual group and through them Osborne somehow contrives to image a larger theme. If *Look Back in Anger* symbolizes the post-war generation, *The Entertainer*, though this may be more difficult to understand, has a relationship with the crisis following Egypt's nationalization of the Suez Canal and Osborne's own complex love-hate relation towards England. Archie Rice and all the miserable and defeated creatures around him somehow symbolize that lowest and most bewildered moment in England's post-war record. Laurence Kitchen in *Mid-Century Drama* described the play as 'a kind of *Cavalcade* in reverse', and noted that Osborne was influenced by Arthur Miller's *Death of a Salesman*. Dramatically effective the play must readily be consented to be, but it is difficult to know what is ultimately Osborne's attitude. Does he have in his heart an image of the England that has departed, would he wish to restore some different but positive image, or is it all contempt and a half concealed egoism? It is difficult to enter the record wholly on the positive and favourable side.

Though it was *Look Back in Anger* that brought Osborne his popularity, he had written earlier plays, and one of these, *Epitaph for George Dillon*, was produced at the Royal Court Theatre in 1957. The central character is George Dillon himself, and he has this in common with Jimmy Porter that he is rebellious and lost, without loyalty or vision. Dillon had once planned to be an artist, but all ambition had been drained out of him by the very sordid dreariness of life. It may be an unexhilarating picture but it is cunningly conveyed and with much conviction. Once again Osborne's dialogue is brilliant; he, somehow, finds a medium for conveying contemporary conversation, with all the half-finished phrases and abrupt transitions. The background is in an unrelieved way the lower-middle classes in the post-war period at their lowest; nowhere is there grace or elegance or hope. So compulsively does he portray this world that it might seem to be the only world that Osborne knew, and it was one that some of his contemporaries were to imitate.

At this period in his career he made an experiment that moved entirely from contemporary settings; in 1961, at the Royal Theatre,

Nottingham, was produced his new play *Luther* and, instead of the Jimmy Porters of contemporary England, the scene goes back to the Germany of the sixteenth century. This change from the contemporary to the historical appeared at first sight as a profound development in the range of Osborne's art, yet the underlying values are ultimately unchanged. Still occupied with insecurity and protest, and with the hatred of power, Osborne remains with some compulsive, half-confessed admiration of force and strength. Nor is the strange and incongruous element of sentimentality far away, and with such a mood the play is led to its unsatisfactory conclusion. It is too early to assess Osborne's place as a dramatist; one may hope that a great deal of his career lies before him, and indeed this is confirmed by the production of *Inadmissible Evidence* (1964).

He has obviously made a profound impact on his own generation, and, as has been recorded, his own success has made possible the production of work by other young dramatists at the Royal Court Theatre. Yet after *Luther* his work was, for a time, disappointing. His unevenness and descent to triviality was shown in 1959 in *The World of Paul Slickey*, which he described as a 'comedy of manners with music' and had as its theme the newspaper world of the writer of a personal gossip column. Osborne himself has expressed a contempt for television and when he made his own attempt in this medium in *A Subject of Scandal and Concern* it was a failure. Sometimes one felt that Osborne, having expressed the protest of his generation, or at least a part of it, is now voicing some private grievance about a world that has conspired against him personally. As was suggested in the chapter on the contemporary theatre, when success comes to a dramatist on a big scale and when his works are turned into films, the rewards are very large indeed. Such has it been with Osborne. Not for him the Shakespearian conditions that exact two plays a year. One can only hope that some period of readjustment will be effected for he has shown the potentiality of a talent that the English theatre should not lose and *Inadmissible Evidence* is a happy augury for his future development.

One dramatist was remote from all these movements, and the new theatre regarded him with open hostility. Charles Morgan (1894–1958) had a distinguished career as a novelist, essayist, and the dramatic critic of *The Times*. He turned to the theatre as early as 1938 with *The Flashing Stream*, and this was followed some years after the Second World War with *The River Line* (1952) and *The Burning Glass* (1954). It is said that he wrote *The Flashing Stream* in a period when he found progress with a novel difficult, and his early naval training gave him the opportunity of an exciting plot, dealing with service secrets. It seemed that his intrusion from fiction into the theatre was incidental, but the play was a great success, and so he followed it, seven years after the war, with *The River Line*. This, in many ways the most successful of his dramatic achievements, deals with events on one of the escape routes contrived by the French Resistance for Allied prisoners. The ultimate theme is the problem of loyalty, and the conflicts it arouses. It could be argued that Morgan explores this in an intellectual rather than in a dramatic way. *The Burning Glass* dealt with the moral responsibilities of a scientist to society when he is conscious that he possesses great destructive powers. The desire to develop his own thought contrasts with the dramatic presentation of the theme. The abstract intellect controls the characters. Morgan's work has a certain impressive quality, a 'high seriousness', and in his own time the theatre readily accepted him.

The new theatre of the 'fifties and the 'sixties, in which Osborne played a conspicuous part, had certain general features, very far removed from anything that Morgan with his distinguished but decorative thought was exploring. Many of the writers were of working class origin, and there was a common element of protest and a background of Left Wing politics. A pleasing feature was the recognition of the drama of other countries: Clifford Odets was an influence with *Waiting for Lefty*, Arthur Miller in *A View from the Bridge* and *Death of a Salesman*, and Tennessee Williams in a number of plays. The influence of Eugene O'Neill continued and as late as 1958 *The Iceman Cometh* had a welcome in London. Further, plays of Sartre and Brecht were performed in London, were most admired, and were part of the active background of the younger playwrights. Among younger writers a considerable importance was attained by the Rumanian, Eugène Ionesco, whose plays were welcome at the Royal Court Theatre. In 1958, in *The Observer*, Kenneth Tynan accused Ionesco of being 'a self-proclaimed advocate of *anti-theatre*: explicitly anti-realist and by implication anti-reality as well'. He was moving away, Tynan added, from realism, 'from the theatre of Gorki, Chekhov, Arthur Miller, Tennessee Williams, Brecht, O'Casey, Osborne and Sartre'. To this Ionesco made a vigorous response, saying that he was not a messiah, and that to save the world was the business of the founders of religions, of moralists, and politicians: 'a playwright simply writes plays, in which he can offer a testimony not a didactic message'. He added, 'an ideological play can be no more than the vulgarization of an ideology'.[1]

Some of these intentions may have affected Samuel Beckett, born in Dublin in 1906, who had a surprising success, first at the Royal Court and then in the West End. Beckett had an ordinary Protestant middle-class background, but as a young man he went to Paris and met James Joyce, an encounter which deeply affected his life. Though for a time he was a lecturer in Dublin, he concluded that all routine would ruin his talent, and, still under Joyce's influence, he lived at Montparnasse throughout the war and in the post-war years. Those post-war years were his most productive period, when he wrote novels and plays, all in French. Asked by a student, why in French, he replied: 'Parcequ'en français c'est plus facile d'écrire sans style.'[1] Success came with *Waiting for Godot*, performed at the Theatre de Babylone in 1953; in London, first at the Arts Theatre and later in the West End with great success. The play made a profound impression both on the public and on other dramatists. When asked what the play meant, and what he meant by Godot, Beckett said: 'If I knew, I would have said so in the play.' The scene is of two old tramps, Vladimir and Estragon, who are waiting, and at the end of the act they are told that Godot for whom they are waiting cannot come but will come tomorrow; it is the same at the end of Act II. As Act I ends Estragon says: 'Well, shall we go?' and Vladimir replies: 'Yes let's go'; and the stage direction reads: 'They do not move.' *Waiting for Godot*'s ultimate importance was that through some never clearly defined symbol it showed how different the post-war world was from the pre-war world. The tragedy and despair of man came out through Beckett's two tramps. This is why he was successful, and this is why his dramatic contribution

---

[1] See *The Theatre of the Absurd* (1962) by Martin Esslin.

is important. Joyce and others may have been in the background, but the achievement was his own, and a wonderful combination of those two old and distinguished civilizations, the Irish and the French. One needed someone to give a dramatic image of how far contemporary Europe, with the scarifying experiences of the war, the diminished place of culture, and the minor voice of the intellect in the violent affairs of the explosive incoming world had become removed from the solid and placid Europe of the period before the Second World War. Beckett's two tramps and Godot who never arrives have done this more effectively on the stage than has any play of this whole period. There is an element in them of two cross-talk comedians of the cabaret or circus and that gives the action a sustaining element, but most observers found something more profound, a symbol of the world as it is, not a precise symbol, but one of almost indefinite reference. Apart from its effect on audiences, the play had a deep effect on writers. It was William Saroyan who said: 'It will make it easier for me and everyone else to write freely in the theatre.'

As has been already suggested, some modern dramatists have disappointed those who are attached to the theatre because they do not seem to advance from one success to something that is more profound. There may be no single reason for this, but it is in various ways true to Eliot and Fry and for a time it seemed true of Osborne. Sometimes it seems to arise from a distrust of contemporary audiences, and an excessive desire to compromise, sometimes it is the insidious temptation of economic success and sometimes it is just a failure of vision. The situation with Beckett seems entirely different. Having written a challenging play with *Waiting for Godot*, he does not retreat but goes ahead into a play that requires an even greater and more exacting attention from his audience. If one may take the analogy of his master James Joyce, he has moved from *Ulysses* to *Finnegans Wake*. *Endgame*, produced at the Royal Court in 1957 makes *Waiting for Godot* seem like a child's primer. A blind old man, Hamm, sits in a wheel-chair; he is paralysed and cannot stand. His servant Clov cannot sit down. In two dustbins near by are Hamm's legless parents, Nagg and Nell. They are alone these four. Hamm's parents lost their legs cycling in the Ardennes; they are doltish and sentimental and Hamm hates them. Esslin, in the study to which reference has already been made, suggests that the whole of the play may be a monodrama: 'Is Clov then the intellect bound to serve the emotions, instincts and appetites, and trying to free himself from disorderly and tyrannical masters, yet doomed to die when the connection with the animal side of his personality is severed. Is the death of the outside world the gradual receding of the links to reality that takes place in the process of ageing and dying. Is *Endgame* a melodrama depicting the dissolution of a personality in the hour of death.' This is ingenious and sympathetic criticism, but one has first to ask whether *Endgame* is a play at all. Is it any more a play than Joyce's *Finnegans Wake* is a novel? And Joyce has remained for Beckett the major influence. In one passage Hamm asks: 'We're beginning to . . . to . . . mean something?' And Clov merely laughs: 'Mean something! You and I mean something!' This is perhaps the final comment on *Endgame* and the title is not without significance. This is as far down this particular road as you can travel, as *Finnegans Wake* was in the novel. If you have reached this point you must turn and do something entirely different. Joyce in the novel never did, but Samuel Beckett, with his comparative youth and his undoubted dramatic talent, may yet have new and different achievements. It remains to be seen, but this is certain, that they will have to be different.

Beckett had the effect of introducing a sense of adventure into a number of young writers, even if their motives and methods were very different from his. Most of them are still in the early stages of their careers, and all that can be done here is to give a summary of their work. They all had their first success in the experimental theatre or on television but most of them have graduated to the West End theatre. One of the more original is Harold Pinter (b. 1931), the son of a Jewish tailor, originally of Portuguese family, who grew up as a boy in wartime Britain. Those conditions and his own personality made his early years irregular and incohesive with a period of vagabondage. He made his way ultimately to provincial repertory and to the writing of verse. Then, finally, in 1957, he broke through into dramatic form with *The Room, The Dumb Waiter* and *The Birthday Party*. These bore no relation to the plays in which he had acted in Repertory. They were all an image of his own early uncertainties and of his desire to hide this personality from the world. *The Room* reached the stage of Bristol University, and this, in turn, led to a performance of *The Birthday Party* in London, which was a failure. Pinter was now at the end of his resources and for a time was the caretaker of a Notting Hill basement. Then, after some success in television plays and revues, he produced *The Caretaker* in 1960 and his success was made. Obviously Beckett's drama had touched his imagination and it has been suggested that he was also influenced variously by Sartre and Brecht and particularly by Ionesco. But though Ionesco and Pinter both belong to what Martin Esslin has called the 'Theatre of the Absurd', there is a profound difference between them; if one accepts Tynan's argument, then Ionesco employs language to show that language does not work. As John Bowen has written,[1] 'Mr Pinter's buses really run, his observation may be appalled but it is exact,' and he adds that Pinter's characters use language 'as a cover for their fear and loneliness.' In describing his own work Pinter says that he began as a poet before he became a dramatist. He confesses that he does not find anything very strange about *The Caretaker*; he has merely taken a situation and let it develop, without any preconceived position either politically or religiously and without any audience in mind; 'I take a chance on the audience.' Yet he is conscious of the audience and comments that *A Night Out*, a play he wrote for television, was performed before an audience of sixteen million people. He has also written for sound radio and suggests that it is 'more flexible and mobile' than any other medium. In speaking of his sound radio play *The Dwarfs* he comments,[1] 'I was able to go the whole hog and enjoy myself by exploring to a degree that wouldn't be acceptable in any other medium. I'm sure the result may have been completely incomprehensible to the audience, but it isn't as far as I am concerned to me.' There might appear to be here a sort of built-in arrogance. It is rather that Pinter, like a number of writers of his generation, is conscious of having parted from tradition, of being associated with something that is new. He wrote,[1] '*The Caretaker* wouldn't have been put on, and certainly wouldn't have run before 1957. The old categories of comedy and tragedy and farce are irrelevant, and the fact that managers seemed to have realized that is one favourable change. But writing

[1] *The Twentieth Century*, February, 1961.

for the stage is the most difficult thing of all, whatever the system. I find it more difficult the more I think about it.' These last sentences contrast with all he had written about the audience. They show an awareness which allied to the fluid condition of his mind may yet lead to new and interesting things in the theatre. Yet it must be admitted that he has not been very productive in recent years and, as with some of his contemporaries, success has dispelled the conditions that originally gave an impulse to his art.

Another figure identified with the new movement in the theatre is Arnold Wesker (b. 1932). He is the son of an East End tailor and worked through a variety of jobs, a seed sorter, a plumber's mate, a kitchen porter and a pastry cook in Paris. He was influenced by the Free Cinema Movement through the London School of Film Technique, and so came to writing a play, _The Kitchen_ (1959), which is set in the kitchen of a large restaurant. It was with _Chicken Soup with Barley_, which in 1958 was produced by the Coventry Belgrade Company at the Royal Court, that he first began to attract critical attention. This play is contemporary realism, far removed from the imaginative improbabilities of Pinter's drama. Wesker portrayed a family of East End Jewish socialists, using a background with which he was most familiar. After this production the Arts Council helped Wesker with a bursary, and during this period he composed _Roots_, which dealt with some of the characters of the earlier play, but in a Norfolk setting. _Roots_ was staged at the Royal Court in 1959 and was widely praised; it was clear that Wesker had developed considerably since the days of _Chicken Soup with Barley_. In 1960 he wrote _I'm Talking About Jerusalem_, which was produced at the Royal Court and so he completed a trilogy of plays about the same characters, though no character appeared in all three of them. Taken together they represent a major contribution to contemporary English realism. Wesker served a two-year period with the R.A.F. and after his trilogy he explored the effect of social differences in a service background in a play entitled _Chips With Everything_. It is difficult to see that this marks any major development in his work. The main setting to Wesker's plays has been one of sordidness and the tragedy of despair, but this is not accompanied by a negative attitude. As _Chicken Soup with Barley_ closes the mother, despite all her personal tragedy, says to her son: 'You'll die, you'll die—if you don't care you'll die.

Ronnie if you don't care you'll die.' Wesker, like some of his contemporaries, seems to gain an excessive exhilaration in his independence from the theatre that preceded him, yet his social realism
has more contact with that tradition than, say, the plays of Pinter.
In one revealing passage he writes:[1] 'I have always said, right from
the beginning, that if I have any importance at all, it is not because
of my style, but because of what I am saying. And then one comes
up against the old argument, "But content and style are one and
the same thing. If your style is stale, then what you are saying is
stale." The old styles have suited me perfectly, and the fact that
I have been conventional has not detracted from the importance
(granting the importance) of what I had to say.'

Social realism, with its sordid settings, is now so strong a
tradition that much in contemporary drama seems to have become
attached to it. There is, for instance, Shelagh Delaney, a writer
with, again, a genuine proletarian background. Her father was a
bus inspector and her grandfather had been in the old Keir Hardie
Labour tradition. She had been brought up in Salford, in one of
the urban centres developed and despoiled by the Industrial
Revolution. She had left school at seventeen to be a shop assistant,
a clerk in a milk depot, an usherette, and a worker in the research
photography department of an electrical firm; and she wrote *A
Taste of Honey*, a strangely moving play, based one must assume
largely on her own experience, of twisted domestic situations and
of appealing but abnormal people. It had great success, but
nothing of note has followed. It may be that with all these writers
success is disconcerting, for it removes them from one way of life
to another and it relieves them of the hazards of insecurity; at the
same time it takes them away from the background on which their
art depended. Somewhere in this world is the strange and independent character of Brendan Behan (1923–64). His success as
a playwright was closely associated with Joan Littlewood's Theatre
Workshop with all its Left-Wing and revolutionary contacts.
Behan seemed in his own life the genuine revolutionary, wild,
disordered, often not very sober, and to complete the credentials
with greater authenticity, one who had served 'time' in an English
prison for Irish revolutionary activities. *The Quare Fellow* was
produced by the Theatre Workshop in 1956: it is dominated by

[1] *Twentieth Century*, February, 1961.

that compulsive concern with capital punishment, which some in this generation seemed to isolate as the sole theme worthy of moral argument. A liveliness and satiric quality can be found in the dialogue, as when one of the warders describes a prisoner as 'the fellow beat his wife to death with the silver-topped cane, that was a presentation to him from the combined Staffs, Excess and Refunds branch of the late Great Southern Railways'. A more succinct example is the description: 'What's a crook, only a business man without a shop.' *The Hostage*, again produced by Joan Littlewood's Theatre Workshop appeared in 1958 and to some seemed to mark a development in dramatic technique. The compulsive theme was the Irish Revolution, perpetual and ultimately dreary but relieved by a sympathetic treatment of the English hostage and some irony for his Irish captors. Whether Behan had a talent that might have developed is a theme solely for speculation. His way of life decided ultimately that there was to be no future.

Though Wesker gave an emphasis to social realism, and caustic and unjust critics said that the English drama concentrated on the kitchen sink, there were other traditions. John Whiting, whose death at a comparatively early age is much to be regretted, had a poetic quality of imagination and much dramatic originality without ever gaining any major success with audiences. He was older than the writers who have been considered above and, born in 1918, he had six years wartime experience in the army. He began his theatrical career as an actor and when he turned dramatist he was highly critical of his own work. He first appeared on the London stage with *A Penny for a Song* (1951) to be followed by *Saint's Day* (1951) and *Marching Song* (1954). None of these plays was a commercial success, though they attracted much critical attention. In *A Penny for a Song* he showed that he had a highly individual imagination, with an element of humour and fantasy. He was led away from the stage to write for the film, but in 1961 Peter Hall commissioned him to write a play, *The Devils*, based on Aldous Huxley's *The Devils of Loudon*, and this had a greater success than any of his original works. Among the younger writers who are independent of the tradition of social realism and upon whose work great hopes are placed is John Arden. Some of his success has been made through television and his play for this medium, *Soldier, Soldier*, won the Italia Prize in 1960. In the theatre he has had an association with the Royal Court, which has produced *Serjeant Musgrave's Dance*, *Live Like Pigs* and *The Happy Haven*. He has not yet achieved a commercial success, but he is working in a world of imagination far removed from that of Osborne or Wesker.

The work of all these writers demonstrates that whatever the ultimate assessment of their plays may be, a new lively and independent theatre has developed in the 'fifties and 'sixties; that the independent managements have become far more adventurous in their production of new plays and that often this initiative has led to success in the commercial theatre to a degree that is puzzling. Meanwhile the commercial theatre has continued. Among those who have served it with much skill and success has been Terence Rattigan (b. 1911). He began with a successful farce *French Without Tears* (1936), but his most reputable plays were studies of character and social situations such as *The Browning Version* (1948), *The Deep Blue Sea* (1952) and *Separate Tables* (1954). When he attempted a more ambitious play on the theme of Alexander the Great he did not succeed. Probably he was at his best in *Separate Tables* where he analyses a group of characters, all clearly if somewhat obviously drawn, in the life of an English boarding house.

As one concludes here this record of English drama it is difficult to assess the present situation with any precision. The existence of the Royal Court Theatre and the presence of new and adventurous writers might at first sight suggest a renaissance in the theatre. This would be to assume too optimistic a view. The enthusiasm for the new theatre is still confined to limited sections of the cultivated population and much of it, whatever the authors may say, belongs to the atmosphere of left-wing politics and of social protest. There is no national drama which serves as a central artistic phenomenon in the country's life. Much of it is the portrayal of the insecure and defeated elements in society, and, as has been suggested, success has rid some of the dramatists of this vision, and left them with nothing new to utter. To go further would be to enter regions of prophecy and to depart from history, and this is not part of the present endeavour. But obviously conditions are changing, and the possibilities of television drama have only recently come to the surface. There may too be a change in the national mood to something more positive and less defeatist. The young dramatists of today cannot remain young and, if the history of the theatre shows anything, it is that no single tradition, however cherished, will permanently continue.

INDEX